CHOMSKY: A GUIDE
FOR THE PERPLEXED

GUIDES FOR THE PERPLEXED AVAILABLE FROM CONTINUUM

Adorno: A Guide for the Perplexed, Alex Thomson
Deleuze: A Guide for the Perplexed, Claire Colebrook
Levinas: A Guide for the Perplexed, B. C. Hutchens
Sartre: A Guide for the Perplexed, Gary Cox
Wittgenstein: A Guide for the Perplexed, Mark Addis
Merleau-Ponty: A Guide for the Perplexed, Eric Matthews
Gadamer: A Guide for the Perplexed, Chris Lawn
Husserl: A Guide for the Perplexed, Matheson Russell
Quine: A Guide for the Perplexed, Gary Kemp
Existentialism: A Guide for the Perplexed, Stephen Earnshaw
Kierkegaard: A Guide for the Perplexed, Clare Carlisle
Rousseau: A Guide for the Perplexed, Matthew Simpson
Hobbes: A Guide for the Perplexed, Stephen J. Finn
Hegel: A Guide for the Perplexed, David James
Derrida: A Guide for the Perplexed, Claire Colebrook
Hume: A Guide for the Perplexed, Angela Coventry
Kant: A Guide for the Perplexed, T. K. Seung
Leibniz: A Guide for the Perplexed, Franklin Perkins
Marx: A Guide for the Perplexed, Martin McIvor
Nietzsche: A Guide for the Perplexed, R. Kevin Hill
Plato: A Guide for the Perplexed, Gerald A. Press
Spinoza: A Guide for the Perplexed, Charles Jarrett
Halliday: A Guide for the Perplexed, Jonathan J. Webster
Chomsky: A Guide for the Perplexed, John Collins

CHOMSKY: A GUIDE FOR THE PERPLEXED

JOHN COLLINS

continuum

Continuum International Publishing Group

The Tower Building
11 York Road
London SE1 7NX

80 Maiden Lane, Suite 704
New York
NY 10038

British Library Cataloguing-in-Publication Data
A catalogue record for this book is available from the British Library.

Library of Congress Cataloguing-in-Publication Data
Collins, John, 1969-
Chomsky: a guide for the perplexed/John Collins.
    p. cm.
  Includes bibliographical references.
  ISBN: 978-0-8264-8662-2 (Hardback)
  ISBN: 978-0-8264-8663-9 (Paperback)
1. Chomsky, Noam. I. Title.

P85.C47C65 2008
410.92—dc22

                     2008018912

Typeset by Newgen Imaging Systems Pvt Ltd, Chennai, India
Printed and bound in Great Britain by MPG Books, Cornwall

To
the Memory of

Jim Collins
1927–1997

CONTENTS

Preface   viii
Cited Works of Noam Chomsky   x

1 Problems with the Chomskys   1
2 Methodological Foundations   22
3 Transformations   59
4 The 'Cognitive Turn': Nativism and Universal Grammar   82
5 The Review of Skinner   112
6 Language: Inside or Outside the Mind?   131
7 Developments in Syntax   156
8 The Minimalist Program   191

Notes   218
References   222
Index   227

PREFACE

Noam Chomsky polarizes opinion. I make no excuses for the following chapters being in favour of Chomsky. I trust, however, that I have been guilty of no distortion or undue charity towards my subject. I have also endeavoured to give some major criticisms an airing, even if only to refute them. Some might find my approach doctrinaire. I offer three points of exculpation. First and trivially, in a book of this size, it is impossible to cover all of the topics Chomsky has discussed over the past fifty years or so; still less, then, can I be expected to offer an adjudication of the many debates Chomsky has entered with philosophers, linguists, psychologists and others. I do broach some key points of contention but only to cast light on Chomsky's own reasoning. Second, I find much of the criticism of Chomsky to be premised upon misunderstanding. It would be a worthy pursuit to correct all of the various errors of reasoning and misattributions, but, again, space precludes such a task. Third, my aim is not simply to defend Chomsky but to present his reasoning in what I regard as its best and most consistent light. Those in the know about the various debates will hopefully see what positions I am staking out on contentious issues and be able to excuse my not being as thorough as I would be were I writing a specialized volume or a journal article. Those not in the know will hopefully be immunized from the all too common misinterpretations that have fuelled so much of the debates.

What can be said of Chomsky's work with sober confidence is that it has changed the landscape of our understanding of mind and language. By that I mean, not only did he replace falsehoods with truths, but also in so doing reconfigured the ways in which we might fruitfully approach the phenomena. In a phrase, he invented a new science: linguistics as we now know it.

I have tried to make the book as accessible as I can without compromising the inherent complexity of the ideas. This was an especially difficult task with the linguistics chapters. Rather than attempt to cover the data or survey the many varied theories to account for them, I have attempted to spell out the main theoretical threads and appealed to various data only for their motivation.

Chomsky's writings have an impersonal air, and he assiduously shuns any oration. The book will have served its purpose if you go away wanting to read Chomsky or any other generative linguist, or if you feel that you should reread much, or if certain scales have fallen from your eyes. It is Chomsky's ideas that are important, not the fact that they happen to be his.

* * *

I thank Oxford University Press for permission to publish part of Chapter 5. For discussions on Chomsky and related issues, I thank Guy Longworth, Michael Devitt, Paul Pietroski, Barry Smith, Steven Gross, Robert Chametzky, Wolfram Hinzen, Peter Ludlow, Gareth Fitzgerald, Robert Matthews and Frankie Egan. I must also mention Dunja Jutronic and Nenad Misevic for organizing the wonderful Dubrovnik conferences. My special thanks go to Georges Rey. We disagree about much, and have been arguing for about three years now with no end in sight, but I have learnt a great deal from him and he is, to my mind, a model, both as a philosopher and human being.

I also thank Noam Chomsky for much email correspondence over the years. My intellectual debt to him should be obvious. I hate to bother him, so he has not read the following chapters except for passages here and there.

My thanks go to my colleagues at University of East Anglia (UEA), especially Peter and Nadine, for making the place so easy going, and all the students who have followed my *Logic* and *Language in Mind* units, especially Fi, Gareth and Jon, who have stayed on at UEA to do graduate work. I also thank UEA itself for a period of research leave in which I completed this work.

Lastly, I should like to thank a number of other friends, who have provided pleasant distraction during my writing of this book: Tim, Nicky (and Edie and Jim), Nina, Alberto, Sarah, Tom, Jen, Laura and Miles Davies.

CITED WORKS OF NOAM CHOMSKY

(MMH) *Morphophonemics of Modern Hebrew*. MA diss., University of Pennsylvania. New York: Garland Press (1951/79).

(LSLT) *The Logical Structure of Linguistic Theory*. Chicago: Chicago University Press (1955/56/75).

(SS) *Syntactic Structures*. The Hague: Mouton (1957).

(RSVB) 'Review of B. F. Skinner's *Verbal Behaviour*'. *Language*, 35, 26–58 (1959). References to the reprint in J. Fodor and J. Katz (eds), (1964), *The Structure of Language: Readings in the Philosophy of Language*. Englewood Cliffs: Prentice-Hall, pp. 547–78.

(SMR) 'Some methodological remarks on generative grammar'. *Word*, 17, 219–39 (1961).

(EML) 'Explanatory models in linguistics', in E. Nagel, P. Suppes and A. Tarski (eds), *Logic, Methodology and Philosophy of Science*. Stanford: Stanford University Press, pp. 528–50 (1962).

(FPG) 'Formal properties of grammars', in R. D. Luce, R. R. Bush and E. Galanter (eds), *Readings in Mathematical Psychology, Vol. II*. New York: John Wiley and Sons, pp. 323–417 (1963).

(CILT) *Current Issues in Linguistic Theory*. The Hauge: Mouton (1964).

(ATS) *Aspects of the Theory of Syntax*. Cambridge, MA: MIT Press (1965).

(CL) *Cartesian Linguistics: A Chapter in the History of Rationalist Thought*. New York: Harper and Row (1966).

(TTGG) *Topics in the Theory of Generative Grammar*. The Hague: Mouton (1966).

(PRSVB) 'Preface to "A Review of B. F. Skinner's *Verbal Behavior*"', in L. A. Jakobovits and M. S. Miron (eds), *Readings in the Psychology of Language*. Englewood Cliffs: Prentice-Hall, pp. 142–43 (1967).

(QEA) 'Quine's empirical assumptions'. *Synthese*, 19, 53–68 (1968).

(LM) *Language and Mind* (Extended Edition). New York: Harcourt Brace Jovanovich (1968/72).

(PKF) *Problems of Knowledge and Freedom: The Russell Lectures*. New York: Vintage (1971).

(SSGG) *Studies on Semantics in Generative Grammar*. The Hague: Mouton (1972).

(RL) *Reflections on Language*. London: Fontana (1975).
(OI) – Katz, J., 'On innateness: a reply to Cooper'. *Philosophical Review*, 84, 70–87 (1975).
(EFI) (1977) *Essays on Form and Interpretation*. Amsterdam: North-Holland (1977).
(FC) – Lasnik, H., 'Filters and control', *Linguistic Inquiry*, 8, 425–504 (1977).
(HLSS) 'Human language and other semiotic systems'. *Semiotica*, 25, 31–44 (1979).
(RR) *Rules and Representations*. New York: Columbia University Press (1980).
(LGB) *Lectures on Government and Binding*. Dordrecht: Foris (1981).
(RFF) 'On the representation of form and function'. *Linguistic Review*, 1, 3–40 (1981).
(GE) *The Generative Enterprise*. Dordrecht: Foris (1982).
(KoL) *Knowledge of Language: Its Nature, Origin, and Use*. Westport: Praeger (1986).
(OFFL) 'On formalization and formal linguistics'. *Natural Language and Linguistic Theory*, 8, 142–47 (1990).
(BPS) 'Bare phrase structure', in G. Webelhuth (ed.), *Government and Binding Theory and the Minimalist Program*. Oxford: Blackwell, pp. 481–439 (1995).
(MP) *The Minimalist Program*. Cambridge, MA: MIT Press (1995).
(PP) *Powers and Prospects: Reflections on Human Nature and the Social Order*. London: Pluto Press (1996).
(SOE) 'Some observations on economy in generative grammar', in, P. Barbosa, D. Fox, P. Hagstrom, M. McGuiness and D. Pesetsky (eds), *Is the Best Good Enough? Optimality and Competition in Syntax*. Cambridge, MA: MIT Press, pp. 115–127 (1998).
(NCMP) – Cela-Conde, C. J. and Marty, G., 'Noam Chomsky's Minimalist Program and the Philosophy of Mind. An Interview'. *Syntax*, 1, pp. 19–36 (1998).
(OINC) – Stemmer, B., 'An on-line interview with Noam Chomsky: on the nature of pragmatics and related issues'. *Brain and Language*, 68, pp. 393–401 (1999).
(NH) *New Horizons in the Study of Language and Mind*. Cambridge: Cambridge University Press (2000).
(AL) *The Architecture of Language*. New Delhi: Oxford University Press (2000).
(LBS) 'Linguistics and Brain Science', in A. Marantz, Y. Miyashita, and W. O'Neil (eds), *Image, Language, Brain*. Cambridge, MA: MIT Press, pp. 13–28 (2000).
(MI) 'Minimalist inquiries: the framework', in R. Martin, D. Michaels, and J. Uriagereka (eds), *Step by Step: Essays on Minimalist Syntax in Honour of Howard Lasnik*. Cambridge, MA: MIT Press, pp. 89–155 (2000).
(DbP) 'Derivation by Phase', in M. Kenstowicz (ed.), *Ken Hale: A Life in Language*, Cambridge, MA: MIT Press, pp. 1–52 (2001).
(ONL) *On Nature and Language*. Cambridge: Cambridge University Press (2002).

(FL) – Hauser, M, and Fitch, W. T., 'The faculty of language: what is it, who has it, and how did it evolve?'. *Science*, 298, 1569–79 (2002).

(RE) 'Reply to Egan', in L. M. Antony and N. Hornstein (eds), *Chomsky and His Critics*. Oxford: Blackwell, pp. 268–74 (2003).

(RtR) 'Reply to Rey', in L. M. Antony and N. Hornstein (eds), *Chomsky and His Critics*. Oxford: Blackwell, pp. 274–87 (2003).

(BEA) 'Beyond explanatory adequacy', in A. Belletti (ed.), *Structures and Beyond: The Cartography of Syntactic Structures, Vol. III*. Oxford: Oxford University Press, pp. 104–31 (2004).

(L&M) 'Language and mind: current thoughts on ancient problems', in L. Jenkins (ed.), *Variation and Universals in Biolinguistics*. Oxford: Elsevier, pp.379–406 (2004).

(TFLD) 'Three factors in language design'. *Linguistic Inquiry*, 36, 1–22 (2005).

(ELF) – Hauser, M. and Fitch, W. T., 'The evolution of the language faculty: clarifications and implications'. *Cognition*, 97, 179–210 (2005).

(PML) 'Preface', in N. Chomsky, *Language and Mind* (Third Edition). New York: Columbia University Press, pp. vii–xii (2006).

(UGB) 'Approaching UG from below', in U. Sauerland and H-M. Gärtner (eds), *Interfaces + Recursion = Language? Chomsky's Minimalism and the View from Syntax-Semantics*. Berlin: Mouton de Gruyter, pp. 1–29 (2007).

CHAPTER 1

PROBLEMS WITH THE CHOMSKYS

*I have learned that when you say anything controversial, you are
likely to be blamed not so much for what you have said as for what
people think that someone who has said what you said would also
say. Still, it's better than finding that you have made no one angry.*
Weinberg (2001, p. 231)

1 INTRODUCTION

Noam Chomsky initiated a new approach to the empirical investigation of the human mind and, in particular, linguistic competence.
Chomsky created a new science, we may say, although he traces its
origins back to the Cartesian tradition, what Chomsky refers to as
the 'first cognitive revolution' (*Cartesian Linguistics: A Chapter in the
History of Rationalist Thought* (CL) and *Powers and Prospects:
Reflections on Human Nature and the Social Order* (PP)). The essence
of this *generative* view is that the human mind/brain contains a
dedicated, species-specific component, a language faculty, whose
development in combination with other such cognitive components
constitutes language acquisition, and whose maintenance in such an
assemblage constitutes our mature competence. From this perspective, linguistics is a field concerned with the development and
structure of the language faculty and its interfaces. Thus, the most
general assumption of this science is that central features of language
are cognitive; our linguistic wherewithal is neither simply something
we *do*, nor is it a social, cultural or historical entity. This approach
does not suggest that it is uninteresting, still less incoherent, to ask all

manner of social or cultural questions about language. Answers to such questions, however, cannot be the whole truth; further, if our concern is with language in particular rather than, more generally, politics, or gender, or history etc., then non-cognitive questions are not the most fundamental ones that can be asked.

Largely, the following chapters will be a presentation and defence of a scientific program. This program, although initiated by Chomsky, is not his; for the past 50 years or so, Chomsky has been one contributor among many. One should assess the science in terms of its results, its likely future fecundity, its merits relative to alternative approaches, its coherence with related fields etc. The science cannot be refuted or corroborated merely by considering what Chomsky has to say. Still, the field of generative linguistics has developed largely under the influence of Chomsky's work or in opposition to it. Moreover, Chomsky is a major philosopher in his own right and, for good or ill, is the perceived spokesperson for the field. Our primary concern, then, will be with what Chomsky has contributed to science and philosophy, not at the level of detail which concerns the working linguist but at a more abstract, synoptic level. Chomsky is commendably keen to remove his 'personality' from linguistics. On the other hand, it is difficult to understand what is important about generative linguistics to other academic fields and our general understanding of ourselves without focusing on Chomsky, for it is he who has made the science so central to the past 50 years of thought on language and mind.

1.1 The three Chomskys

Chomsky's writings broadly divide into three categories. There are the technical or scientific books and papers on linguistics, which, prior to the mid-1960s, are more or less equally distributed across the sub-fields of mathematical linguistics (a field he practically invented), phonology and syntax. Since the mid-1960s, Chomsky has been seriously concerned only with syntax. (Chomsky [*The Generative Enterprise* (GE), p. 57] has explained that when he began to devote an increasing amount of his time speaking and writing against the US assault on South Vietnam he realized that he had increasingly less time for those areas of his research that he felt were less intellectually fruitful.) Chomsky's major publications stand as markers for the various shifts in theoretical framework generative linguistics has gone through. For those outside the field, and perhaps for many inside, these shifts have been confusing. Chomsky is keen to point out, however, that one should expect and welcome such instability in a young science – it shows that the right questions are being asked, ones that lead to new insights, which in turn alter the research agenda. Chomsky's reputation as a mind of the first rank, as the creator of the new science of generative linguistics that centrally contributed to the rise of cognitive science, rests upon this scientific work.

From the mid-1960s, Chomsky has also produced a steady stream of books and papers that we may call 'philosophical'. In the main, these works have presented the methodology of generative linguistics and set it in the context of contemporary work in related fields, such as philosophy and psychology, and the history of thought on language, mind and science. It is tempting to classify these works as 'popular'; perhaps we may say that they are books for researchers in related fields. It would be a mistake, however, to think that these works are unimportant. They have lent the field of generative linguistics a unity, a shared set of basic assumptions. Further, the works, along with Chomsky's famous review of B. F. Skinner's *Verbal Behavior*, have had a tremendous impact on philosophy. Consider, for instance, that in the early 1960s the very idea of innate cognitive competencies was widely viewed as a metaphysical extravagance, a conceptual howler to be diagnosed and dismissed in the common room before afternoon tea. Today, serious philosophy of mind is largely informed by cognitive science and much of it takes innateness for granted. Similarly, contemporary philosophy of language, with its preoccupations with 'knowledge of language', compositionality, logical form etc., is simply unimaginable without Chomsky. It would not be hyperbolic to say that Chomsky's work has shaped the philosophical landscape as much as that of any other thinker of the late twentieth century.

Although this division of work is broadly accurate, it is perhaps also misleading. *Syntactic Structures* (1957), Chomsky's first and perhaps most seminal book, is largely methodological. *Aspects of the Theory of Syntax* (1965) includes an opening chapter that is essentially a rationalist/scientific manifesto for the study of language. *Reflections on Language* (1975) entwines detailed philosophical argument with new developments in linguistics. *Knowledge of Language* (1986) introduces the novel notion of an *I-language* that has had an equal impact within linguistics and philosophy. Chomsky's philosophical understanding is not a separable component of his scientific work; it is, as it were, the light in which one can properly appreciate the scope and intent of the linguistic theories.

Finally, there is a third set of Chomsky works: the books, articles, interviews and talks on political matters that have poured forth since the mid-1960s. The following chapters will have nothing to say about the detail of these works, which is transparent. Chomsky thinks of these work as almost trivial; not trivial in the sense of being unimportant, but in the sense that anyone with the time and commitment could produce them, and we can all understand the works' content. No peculiar intelligence or intellectual training is required to understand, say, that 'our' current 'war on terrorism' is a re-packaging of the 1980s 'war on terrorism' fought against El Salvador and Nicaragua in which the isthmus was turned into a charnel house so that the countries might not follow a social democratic development free of US corporate hegemony. (Marxism for the people meant nothing more than health care and education for their children.) Similarly, no intellectual insight is required to understand that the US attacked the peasantry of South Vietnam in order to support a corrupt business/military elite that ran the country for its own benefit and that of its US corporate backers. That such truths are not treated as trivialities is a signal of the degradation of our political culture. In a culture animated by truth, honesty and decency, Chomsky would be regarded as one of the leading political thinkers of the past century, but then if there were such a culture, there would be no need for a Chomsky.

2   PROBLEMS OF INTERPRETATION

Chomsky's views have generated much philosophical controversy. For Chomsky, this controversy is misplaced. My aim in the remainder of this chapter is to highlight certain aspects of Chomsky's work that might explain the philosophical resistance to and misunderstanding of the generative enterprise.

2.1   Shifting frameworks

Generative linguistics has gone through various shifts of framework under which assumptions central to one framework are rejected in the next one. So presented, it is easy to see the development of the field as fickle, as if the reasoning goes, 'Well, that doesn't work, so let us try this completely different idea'. Such shifts in framework have led some critics to imagine that there is a lag between the philosophical complaints rejected and Chomsky's eventual realization that the critics were right all along (e.g. Searle, 2002; Seuren, 2004). It has been said to me by someone far from unsympathetic to Chomsky that 'He has a tin ear for philosophy – it always takes him some time to appreciate the point'. If, *pro tem*, we put to one side the question of the veracity of this remark, these shifts in framework have given rise to a number of fundamental misunderstandings. Before we detail these, it will be useful to have a sketch of the development of generative linguistics. The following table delineates the main frameworks (if the terms do not mean much to you now, that is OK).

Period	Framework	Main texts
1955–59	Early transformational grammar	*The Logical Structure of Linguistic Theory* (1955–56) *Syntactic Structures* (1957) 'Review of Skinner' (1959)
1962–66	The Standard Theory	*Aspects of the Theory of Syntax* (1965) *Cartesian Linguistics* (1966)
1968–72	Extended Standard Theory	'Remarks on Nomianlization' (1970) *Studies on Semantics in Generative Grammar* (1972)
1973–80	Revised Extended Standard Theory/Conditions	'Conditions on Transformations' (1973) *Reflections on Language* (1975) *Essays on Form and Interpretation* (1977)
1980–90	Government and binding/ principles and parameters	*Lectures on Government and Binding* (1981) *Knowledge of Language* (1986)
1991–99	The Minimalist Program	'A Minimalist Program for Linguistic Theory' (1992) *The Minimalist Program* (1995)
2000–	Phase Derivation/Level Free	'Minimalist Inquiries' (2000) 'Derivation by Phase' (2001) 'Beyond Explanatory Adequacy' (2001)

Some words of caution are in order.

(i) The idea that each of these frameworks marks a paradigm shift (to use Kuhn's much abused term) from the preceding one is absurd. The labels are merely useful ways of differentiating between periods of research. That is not to say that there have not been radical shifts in perspective and assumptions; each period does mark the introduction of new ideas and/or the rejection of some hitherto central assumption. Yet much is shared, and often times, assumptions that are explicitly rejected in one framework were never genuinely central to the preceding one. Further, in certain respects, the latest minimalist research harks back to the earliest work. In short, the history is complex; it is not a series of jumps into the unknown *a la* the standard caricature of Kuhn's picture of science.

(ii) Although I have only listed Chomsky's work, it would be a gross distortion of the history to think that Chomsky is the only one driving the research forward. Katz and Postal's *An Integrated Theory of Linguistic Descriptions* (1964) was central to the so-called 'Standard Theory'. Similarly, Jackendoff's *Semantic Interpretation in Generative Grammar* (1972) was central to the demise of the Standard Theory. The development of the 'Government and Binding' approach was a joint affair, with many Romance linguists playing a leading role. In more recent times, so-called 'level free' theories of syntax have been pursued by many linguists, with Chomsky not the first to do so (e.g. Epstein et al., 1998; Uriagereka, 1998, 1999). In short, generative linguistics is not the personal philosophy of Chomsky, with linguists generally being mere acolytes. It is a field of research with many divergent views and leading contributors. Equally, however, Chomsky does have a unique place in the field. Not only is he its creator and perhaps its leading contributor, he also articulates the methodology, defends the field against opposition, is a leading philosopher in his own right and is the point of reference for the field to the outside world. If, during the course of the following, it seems that Chomsky is the only person who has had any good idea about language, bear these remarks in mind.

(iii) Just as Chomsky is not the only generative linguist, so generative linguistics is not the only research agenda in syntax, still less does it constitute linguistics as a discipline. One occasionally finds polemicists claiming that Chomsky is some kind of intellectual autocrat who presides over linguistics *in toto* with dauntless dissenters here and there (Lappin et al., 2000a, b, 2001; Seuren, 2004). Such claims are self-serving nonsense. Linguistics is a highly variegated field, including sub-fields such as syntax, semantics, phonetics, discourse analysis, computational parsing, neurolinguistics, psycholinguistics, historical linguistics, translation studies etc. In a certain respect, all of these fields perhaps owe something to Chomsky in the sense that his work put linguistics on the map. More directly, in their present constitution, areas such as computational parsing and psycholinguistics are difficult to imagine in the absence of Chomsky's early work. All that said, since the mid-1960s, Chomsky has made no contribution to any of these fields apart from syntax. Within syntax itself, there are various alternative approaches that to a greater or lesser extent depart from the generative tradition.

It is perhaps a credit to Chomsky that his standing outside of linguistics is such that many unthinkingly identify the discipline with him. The identification is, nonetheless, silly. Still, for simple convenience, I shall hereon, context permitting, refer to generative linguistics as 'linguistics'.

With such matters stated, we may now turn to the more serious confusions to which the various shifts of framework have given rise.

2.1.1 *Ignorance*

I mean this label to be simply descriptive. Many who cite Chomsky, whether in praise or criticism, especially in philosophy, but also more generally, are broadly ignorant of his linguistic work and that of any other serious linguist. Being charitable, the framework shifts are largely to blame. There is no central text, no *Critique of Pure Reason*, or *Philosophical Investigations*, if you will. There are a series of texts, and it is difficult to understand one without understanding those that preceded it. Thus, unless one is prepared to spend the time and effort seriously to study linguistics, an inevitable ignorance will prevail. I said that the shifts of framework are largely to blame for this, but they do not excuse it. No one is obliged to write on Chomsky.

For Chomsky, his philosophical works often serve to set the linguistics into various wider contexts. Unfortunately, negative conclusions about the linguistic theories are often drawn solely from the philosophical works. There is no alternative to studying the linguistics, at least if one wants to show that Chomsky is mistaken.

2.1.2   False fundamentals

As explained at the beginning of this chapter, generative linguistics takes as its object that aspect of the mind/brain that supports linguistic competence – the language faculty. The various shits in framework have largely been concerned with the *architecture* of the language faculty: the faculty's component parts, their organization and the character of the faculty's outputs. As remarked above, some see these developments as almost arbitrary; such a view encourages the ignorance just described. Numerous times I have been asked questions such as, 'What is one supposed to say now about the passive?', or, 'Are there any grammatical rules left?'. Some appear to have the view that there is not much point in struggling to understand a new theory, when a newer one will be along soon. This leads to erroneous views about what is fundamental to the generative view. Without the background that can only be provided by a full discussion, examples of this phenomenon might mislead more than enlighten. I shall, then, only give one example here; the logic of the situation is what is presently important, not the particular claims involved.

Chomsky often refers to the object of study as 'knowledge of language', with this phrase being more or less synonymous with 'competence', the 'language faculty' and 'I-language'. Viewed from the present, it is fairly clear that not much at all hangs on these different terms of art; they are all different ways of marking the fact that the object of study is the cognitive structures that stand in an explanatory relation to our 'grammatical' judgments and general linguistic performance. It is, though, naturally tempting to think of linguists' use of 'knowledge of language' as implying that the speaker/hearer knows a *theory* of her language, has propositional knowledge of some *thing*. In his work of the 1950s and 1960s, Chomsky *did* speak of the language faculty as being theory-like, with the language-acquiring child testing and selecting hypotheses from an innate store (see Chapter 6). Indeed, the faculty was viewed as if it were a theory put inside the head, as it were: it contained general principles and rules by which one could derive a set of structures that 'described' sentences of the language in question. Subsequently, the philosophical discussion of linguistics continues to be dominated by questions about 'knowledge' and the epistemology of 'rule following' (e.g. Barber, 2003; Devitt, 2006). These issues, however, are at best peripheral and are mostly based upon confusion.

If we consider the accounts of the language faculty from *Lectures on Government and Binding* (1981) onwards, it is perfectly clear that the faculty is not a theoretical structure inside the speaker/hearer's head. It is also explicitly argued that acquiring a language is not remotely comparable to confirming a theory. Indeed, by recent accounts, there is no such thing as a language that could be an external object of theorization for the child. These developments have continued apace, so much so that if the most recent accounts had been the first to be proposed, then no one in their right minds would have understood 'knowledge of language' in the sense so many did. One can only conclude that much of the 30-year-old philosophical debate about Chomsky's views on 'knowledge of language' has nothing seriously to do with linguistics (Collins, 2004).

The crucial point here is not that philosophers and others have not kept pace with developments in linguistics; rather, they have been misled by terms of art in the context of one framework into imagining that the whole generative approach is premised upon dubious epistemological assumptions. For example, the confirmation model of language acquisition was *never* presented as if it were an accurate or even sensible model. It was simply used as a stand in for whatever mechanisms were actual. As the latter developments were to show, the model was inessential and could be happily ditched. Likewise, descriptions of the language faculty being a theory were always metaphorical, their purpose being to highlight that the child brought rich resources (unobservables, as it were) to the learning situation that were not derivable from the data. The point here was that the child's linguistic understanding, just like a theory, is not merely a set of generalizations over data. Again, as developments were to show, this essential point can be retained while our understanding of the faculty is transformed so that it does not resemble a theory at all.

This particular example of a 'false fundamental' will loom large in what is to follow, although, as we shall see, it is but one example among many.

2.1.3   The false impressions

Syntactic Structures is Chomsky's first book and is perhaps the most influential book of the twentieth century within disciplines concerned with language. Many are surprised, though, when they first see it. Excluding a preface and two appendixes, it is less than a hundred pages long. Further, upon reading it, one finds the arguments quite schematic and incomplete. The whole work feels fragmentary; its reputation leads one to expect something decidedly more substantial. There is a reason for this. Chomsky neither intended nor expected the book to be a foundational document. It was a series of lecture notes Chomsky had complied for a class he was teaching at MIT (mainly to electrical engineers). A much larger and more substantial book – *The Logical Structure of Linguistic Theory* – had failed to secure a publisher (it was eventually published in 1975). Mouton (a Dutch publisher) expressed an interest in publishing a short work of Chomsky's, a request that resulted in *Syntactic Structures*: a brief compendium of material from the larger book and a précis of some of the main results of Chomsky's work in mathematical linguistics. In fact, the book was so widely read principally because of a very favourable review (Lees, 1957) in the leading linguistics journal of the time – *Language* – that appeared just after the book came out.

Of course, this curious history of *Syntactic Structures* does not mean that its content is misleading – the content is not misleading, if understood in the right context. Still less am I suggesting that the work was in some way botched – it deserves all its praise. The work, however, quickly became foundational and was read independently of the required context. The work begins with a number of chapters on Chomsky's mathematical findings that concern what came to be called the *weak generative capacity* of a grammar. Chomsky's real concern, however, has always been with *strong generative capacity*; the first notion is significant in light of the second. *Syntactic Structures* thus gives the impression that the former notion is the crucial one. The difference between these two notions will be explained fully later; for the moment, we may think of the weaker notion as referring to the set of symbol strings a grammar can generate; the stronger notion refers to the set of phrase structures a grammar can generate. Thus, if we take grammars to be relative to languages, the weaker notion enshrines the idea that the language is a set of strings in some sense independent of the grammar, for a set of strings can be specifiable in many ways independently of the particular grammar. On the other hand, the stronger notion carries no such implication, for phrase structures are not specifiable independently of the grammar that generates them. In a very real sense, Chomsky's concern has always been for grammars not languages, at least if languages are understood to be 'objects' independent of the particular cognitive structures of speaker/hearers. The opening of *Syntactic Structures* obscured this issue, and it continues to encourage the epistemological concerns alluded to earlier, as if a language is an independent thing of which the speaker/hearer has knowledge. Much of Chomsky's recent work has sought to rectify these errors and confusions.

We have, then, a number of historical factors, generated by the shifts in framework, that have caused much confusion and are likely to trip up the unwary reader. We shall now turn to some much more general problems of interpretation.

2.2 Science and philosophy

Chomsky is a scientist and leading philosopher in equal measure; for Chomsky, these are not distinct interests but a unified attempt to understand the phenomena of mind and language. This attitude has caused much misunderstanding, at least among contemporary philosophers.

Chomsky's attitude is now uncommon; before the turn of the nineteenth century it was the norm. Descartes, Leibniz, Spinoza, Berkeley, Hume and Kant are now all known as philosophers, but they were equally knowledgeable about science and mathematics, and many made serious contributions to those disciplines (the cases of Descartes and Leibniz do not require comment). Berkeley made a stunning critique of Newton's nascent calculus and Kant's early works were all scientific, including a proposal for a non-Euclidean geometry in 1755!. To the same degree, many of the leading scientists and mathematicians of the period were equally at home with philosophy, for example, Galileo, Newton, Euler, Lambert etc. In general, the distinction between philosophy and the natural sciences simply did not exist. Modern philosophy up to Kant was an effort to understand the world as it appears to us and our place in it on the *basis* of the scientific revolution of the previous century and a half. That is, philosophers did not attempt to *justify* science, as if they were in a place to stand in judgement over it; rather, philosophy proceeded from the results of science. The situation changed in the nineteenth century, partly due to the increasing complexity and specialization of the sciences. The rise of analytical philosophy in the twentieth century was in part a revolt against the then dominant idealism, and it was largely informed by developments in logic, mathematics and physics that were often viewed as confirmation of an empiricist philosophy or at least a refutation of the Rationalist/Kantian/Idealist tradition (e.g. Reichenbach, 1951). Unfortunately, this commendable scientific orientation led to an empiricist/behaviourist approach to issues of language and mind that precluded any serious investigation of the phenomena (e.g. Quine, 1960; 'Quine's empirical assumptions' (QEA) and *Reflections on Language* (RL)). More recently, while empiricism has been on the wane, it has not been replaced by a similarly scientifically informed philosophy. All too often philosophers have made *ex cathedra* judgements based on conceptual reflection about the possibility of a science of language and mind. This attitude is informed by the view that science must conform to a certain crude schema of causal connection realized between instances of categories sanctioned by our commonsense world view. Such a conception of science renders language and mind outside of theoretical understanding. Yet *physics* long rejected any such schema; one has to go back to the pre-Newtonian understanding to find it. When the operative conception of science is one that doesn't hold in *any* domain, it is little wonder that there is scepticism about the prospects of a science of the particular domains of language and mind. It is in such a context that Chomsky's work is all too often received.

Chomsky's enlightenment conception of philosophy gives rise to a number of misunderstandings. I shall only highlight three such errors here.

Often within philosophical circles, a priori arguments are expected; that is, the theses on offer are meant to be supported independent of appeal to the 'facts', and the extent to which such an appeal is necessary is the extent to which the theses are thought to be philosophically uninteresting. The irony here, of course, is that any philosophy of language or mind *must* make some empirical assumptions about the phenomena. The problem Chomsky poses for philosophy, then, is simply that he highlights that the relevant assumptions are empirical and are mostly false. Let us look at a few cases.

Dummett (1993, p. 187) writes '[generative linguistics] is a completely unphilosophical way of looking at the matter. Philosophy is not concerned with looking at what *enables* us to speak as we do, but what it is for our utterances to have the meanings that they have, and nothing that happens in the brain can explain that'. This is a very revealing passage and far from untypical of Dummett (see his 1989). First, Dummett is confused on the aims and results of generative linguistics. Linguistic theory does not attempt to offer a theory of the enabling conditions of speech (although it will contribute to such theories). Dummett is simply conflating competence with performance (see Chapters 4 and 5). Second, Dummett stipulates what is and is not of philosophical interest. Parochialism apart, presumably Dummett does think that there are some facts in the area to be discovered; hence, his *ex cathedra* claims amount to nothing more than the assertion that the facts are irrelevant. How does Dummett know they are irrelevant given that no one knows what the facts actually are? I cannot conceive of any serious inquiry that would bar the relevance of unknown factors. Third, again Dummett stipulates that a particular line of inquiry cannot explain a complex phenomenon ('meaning'). How does Dummett know this? Clearly human biology has *something* to do with the matter, given that no other species is linguistically competent. We don't know until we know.

The irony here is that Dummett (1978, p. 362) is perfectly happy to assert, without argument or evidence, the empirical claim that language acquisition is a matter of 'training' (cf., McDowell's (1978/98, p. 296) equally bald talk of 'the training that results in competence with a language'). Following Dummett's logic, the facts of the matter are relevant so long as the facts support one's philosophical prejudices; if the facts are not obliging, then they are philosophically uninteresting. As we shall see, the 'training' assumption is false, but my point here is just about the logic employed.

Davidson (1997) is happy to concede that linguistic nativism is supported by 'impressive empirical evidence' (ibid., p. 20), but then he proceeds to develop an a priori error-correction model of language acquisition that is flatly inconsistent with the 'impressive empirical evidence'. Perhaps one is supposed to conclude that evidence is not 'philosophically significant'. Worse still, Brandom (1994, pp. 365– 6) acknowledges Chomsky's point that our linguistic competence is creative over an unbounded range but then he declines the 'heroic postulation' of innate structure to account for this species property. Instead, Brandom offers a substitutional model of sentence structure involving 'training' that has been known to be empirically inadequate since Chomsky's early work (*The Logical Structure of Linguistic Theory* (LSLT)). The truth is indeed more 'heroic' than inherited philosophical dogma. I should emphasize that such sentiments are the norm rather than the exception in much post-Wittgenstein philosophy and that the cited authors are some of the most influential philosophers of today. This characteristic immunity to empirical research appears to be motivated by two factors (here we may charitably exclude other likely factors).

First, one finds explicit complaints that the generative proposals fail to account for or otherwise accommodate some feature of linguistic competence that is putatively a priori sanctioned by our colloquial concepts. Thus, for example, Strawson (1970), Searle (1972), Bennett (1976) and Dummett (1989) have complained that Chomsky's approach fails to find space for 'communication', and this is an essential failing, for communication is what language is *for*. Similarly, Wright (1989) complains that Chomsky's approach fails to find space for our 'self-knowledge' of language, and, again, this is an essential failing, for it is a priori constitutive of being linguistically competent that one possesses such knowledge.

The problem with this line of thinking is not so much that communication and self-knowledge should necessarily fall outside of the scope of linguistic theory but that precious little has been said by philosophers to think that such phenomena *should* fall within its scope. A priori stipulations do not suffice. There is no rational reason to expect any theory to cover every pre-theoretically salient aspect of a phenomenon. We do not even expect such coverage from physics; it is perverse to expect it from linguistics. Further, it is wholly unclear if there is any theoretically tractable phenomenon of communication or self-knowledge.

Consider communication. Practically any organism can be said to communicate; thus, communication is not simply a linguistic phenomenon. Language can be used for communication but so can a smile or a wave of the hand. If the notion of communication is to act as a constraint on linguistic theory, then we need a precise understanding of what is covered by the notion and why it determines the structure of language as opposed to being an interaction effect involving language and other capacities. Only then would it make sense to so much as suggest that linguistic theory fails to accommodate communication. However, this is far from an easy task and, to my knowledge, no one has attempted to pursue it.

Similar remarks hold for 'self-knowledge'. Normal speaker/hearers do have self-knowledge of what they mean by their words, but it is far from clear that (i) this is a theoretically tractable phenomenon or (ii) something for which linguistic theory has responsibility. As with communication, to say that self-knowledge might not be theoretically tractable is not to impugn any particular theory; rather, it is to suggest that there is no unified phenomenon beneath our intuitive category; upon investigation, the notion would fragment. Likewise, to decline responsibility for a phenomenon is not necessarily to limit one's theory in any significant respect. Any species of self-knowledge appears to be a massive interaction effect involving, minimally, self-consciousness in general. The idea that linguistic theory is obliged to explain such an open-ended obscure notion is slightly absurd. We should like, of course, for linguistic theory to be compatible with any good ideas anyone has about our mental life, but our inchoate conceptions of self-knowledge are hardly in a position to constraint linguistic hypotheses.

The second respect in which philosophers often view Chomsky through an a priori lens is less explicit than the first, although in some respects more insidious. We may refer to it as the 'back of a beer mat phenomenon'. Over the years, Chomsky and linguists generally have developed theories of increasing complexity and sophistication that have been corroborated by many diverse sources of data. A serious challenge to this work must come to terms with the fact that generative linguistics is a rich and successful empirical research program. What one finds from too many philosophers, however, is the presentation of at best doubtfully coherent ad hoc proposals whose mere freedom from obvious contradiction (the empirical findings are never discussed, of course) is supposed to undermine some central prop of generative linguistics. This attitude was exemplified in the three cases presented immediately above. Such a level of thought can only be rationally explained on the assumption that such thinkers imagine that they are challenging a priori claims. If such claims were in dispute, it would suffice to outline an alternative on the 'back of a beer mat' to show that the claims were unsafe. It bears noting that this attitude is not the preserve of those who suffer from a phobia of empirical inquiry. Cowie (1999), Prinz (2002), Millikan (2005) and Devitt (2006) are recent examples of empirically minded philosophers who quite explicitly imagine that the object is to show that some or other alternative to the standard generative picture is not logically false. Some brand of empiricism or externalism might indeed not be *logically* false, but Chomsky has never proposed that it is and no theory in linguistics presupposes that it is (see Collins, 2003, 2006).

Any time a response to Chomsky takes the form of 'OK, but it *could* be that the child has data from some other source', or 'OK, but the speaker/hearer *could* extract general patterns from the data', there is a presumption in play that the issue is a priori, for the alternatives are simply inchoate responses free of supporting argument or data. In such cases, the appropriate response is 'Yes, it *could* be like that, but in fact it isn't, or at least there is no good reason to think that it is like that'. This response is not dogmatic; it simply asks for an alternative account that is not known to be false, that would suggest that current linguistics is mistaken. In the absence of some alternative model, the 'debate' would be merely a priori and of no significance, for Chomsky is happy to admit that empiricism is not logically false.

The second major area where Chomsky's enlightenment philosophy produces problems of interpretation is the issue of *naturalism*. In general, we think of 'naturalism' as meaning 'empirical, non-a priori'. Science is naturalistic insofar as it seeks to explain features of the natural world as they in fact are, not as they putatively *must* be, nor as we unreflectively take them to be. In recent years, Chomsky (*New Horizons in the Study of Language and Mind* (NH)) has distinguished two kinds of naturalism: *methodological* and *metaphysical*. As the adjective indicates, the former kind of naturalism is solely methodological, that is, it carries no substantive commitments as to what the natural world contains nor how it is organized; rather, it constitutes a set of working assumptions as to how we ought to investigate phenomena. Perhaps the most central issue for Chomsky is that a methodological naturalism is *monistic*; that is, all phenomena should initially be approached in the same way. This is not to say that ultimately the way in which we pursue biology or linguistics, say, will correspond in any interesting way with the methods of physics. Still less is it to say that there is only one kind of 'stuff'. The thought is only that particular kinds of phenomena do not a priori demand different modes of investigation or restriction on what would count as relevant data. For example, in the hard sciences there is no a priori restriction on what is relevant to the corroboration of hypotheses. In practice, of course, many avenues of investigation are not pursued, but this is on the basis of judgements as to their fecundity, not via a priori stipulation. Throughout the twentieth century, restrictive assumptions were often made as to what kind of data are relevant to language and mind (the most common assumption here is the thought that only publicly available phenomena are somehow relevant to our understanding of linguistic cognition; see Wittgenstein, 1953; Quine, 1960; Davidson, 1984; Dummett, 1989). Chomsky (NH) refers to this tendency as *methodological dualism* (in the earlier *Rules and Representations* (RR), Chomsky used the phrase 'bifurcation thesis'). The attitude is dualistic in the sense that it presupposes that the methods appropriate for the investigation of the natural world cease to apply when one is dealing with phenomena whose locus is above the human neck. Again, it is not that Chomsky dogmatically insists that there is nothing peculiar about human mental life that requires a distinct methodology; his claim is only that any methodological peculiarity has to be arrived at, not stipulated: phenomena do not tell us how they should be investigated. Besides, as we shall see, Chomsky does think that aspects of human mentality do fall outside of our known methods of investigation, but this does not signal methodological dualism. Chomsky's moral is that there are limits to our theorization.

A related aspect of methodological naturalism is the prioritizing of *integration* over *reduction*. This means that we should seek to integrate our various theories over related domains. For example, it would clearly be desirable to have a unified theory of human mental capacities that includes its physical, chemical, biological, neurophysiological and cognitive aspects. Integration here would mean that, to some interesting degree, we would be able to see that we were dealing with a single class of phenomena, with explanation and data in one field being explicable in another one. What does not follow is that we would be able to *reduce* one theory to another, show that only one species of explanation – the physical, say – is required. Chomsky's claim is not that reduction is impossible, only that it is exceedingly rare – much rarer than the philosophical discussions would suggest – and is not the goal of science. Perhaps the major flaw with an uncritical reductionist doctrine is that it presupposes that the reducing theory is more stable or corroborated than the reduced one. However, there is no reason to think that, in general, higher level sciences are less confirmed than lower level ones. So, even if one thought that ultimately everything *is* physical, it simply does not follow that it would be rational to pursue a higher level science as if it reduced to physics, for one's current theories in physics might be completely in error. A concrete example of Chomsky's point here is the relation between chemistry and physics (see NH, pp. 111–12). Up to the early 1920s, much of chemical theory (e.g. valence theory) was treated as if it were a mere calculating device, for the then current physics could not accommodate it. Yet it was only after the *physics* changed with the advent of quantum mechanics that it was seen that the chemistry had been broadly right all along and was explicable in physical terms – it was the physics that was in error. The moral is clear: we might be in exactly the same situation with linguistics vis-à-vis the brain sciences. Integration looks for multilevel and multidirectional explanation; reduction seeks only unidirectional explanation.

Chomsky, then, commends *methodological* naturalism. *Metaphysical* naturalism is not, for Chomsky, a species of naturalism at all. It is a metaphysical position that has no bearing on how science is or should be pursued. Metaphysical naturalism essentially consists of the thought that one can a priori decide on the kind of conceptual resources that any science will employ; typically, such resources are restricted to some unqualified notion of causality or an even more obscure notion of *materialism*. It bears emphasis that materialism is assumed by friends and foes of naturalism. For example, a philosopher who wishes to hive off a class of problems – consciousness, meaning, knowledge, morality, etc. – for essentially non-scientific investigation can appeal to metaphysical naturalism and claim that, as it might be, meaning is not causally underwritten (e.g. McDowell, 1994; Putnam, 2000). Equally, one who thinks that a 'science' in such areas is possible may instigate a 'naturalisation program' under which our colloquial notions are reanalysed or somehow rationally reconstructed in causal terms (e.g. Dretske, 1981; Millikan, 1984; Fodor, 1987). One finds philosophical debate on these issues being characterized as clashes of materialist explanation versus description or understanding. For Chomsky, both approaches are fundamentally confused for the same reason: there is no a priori determination of the kind of resources available to a science, and certainly not one in the shape of Cartesian billiard balls, a position rejected as far back as Newton (McDowell's (1994) plea for a 're-enchantment of nature' is predicated on a rejection of a scientific model over three hundred years out of date). In Chomsky's (LM; NH) judgement, materialism is an anachronism that is simply unintelligible in the context of modern science. Equally, *physicalism* is in no better repair.

Physicalism is the doctrine one often finds emerging after materialism is pressed somewhat. The doctrine is basically the idea that physicists are the arbiters of what there is. However, who are the physicists? Surely physicists of the past are not intended, nor the physicists of today, unless the philosophers have worked out a unified field theory without telling anyone. Physicalism, therefore, amounts to not much more than an appeal to 'correct physics', but if physics is heading in the right direction, then physicalism is absurd as a guide for reflection, unless one expects string theory, say, to cast light on whether there are such things as beliefs or moral facts. No one has a clue how to address the question of whether our colloquial entities are compatible with the baffling exotica of modern physics.

Given the nature of the philosophical debate, it is all too easy to move from Chomsky's methodological naturalism to the quite contrary doctrine of metaphysical naturalism (materialism, physicalism). To repeat, this fallacious move is made by friends and foes alike.

A final aspect of Chomsky's enlightenment attitude that is liable to trip up the unwary is a consequence of his methodological naturalism, but it deserves separate mention. It perhaps goes without saying that the hard sciences do not work by our commonsense categories of discrimination and explanation. This is obvious from the mere fact that much of what the theories concern have no correlation within our common ontological scheme: enzymes, superconductivity, quarks, massless photons, etc. More fundamentally, there is no constraint on the sciences of these low-level entities and properties that they answer to our common categories. To take a banal example, we recognize swimming when we see it: an organism propelling itself through water. However, there it is not a pursuit of biology to offer a theory of swimming (cf., the discussion of communication above). There just is no biological phenomenon of swimming beyond our common notion that covers a heterogeneity of activities. Likewise, we know a physical object when we see one, but there is no theory of physics that tells us what a physical object is: a putative physical object is whatever is included in a physical theory. These claims about the physical sciences are perhaps trivial, but by methodological naturalism they should be extended to the realm of phenomena above the neck. The mainly unarticulated fear of many appears to be that this would entail that there are no persons or beliefs or experiences or minds. However, this is absurd. We do not take physics to have shown us that tables and chairs do not exist; we simply recognize that systematic investigation of the natural world is not constrained by our given categories; it invariably involves the creation of novel categories that serve to streamline explanation and cut out the vagaries and 'noise' of our intuitive understanding. It is not so much that science *must* depart from commonsense; rather, that is just what successful science of the past three hundred years has done, and there is no reason to think that the categories we begin with are apt to offer any insight into how the world is organized, including that fragment of the world that constitutes the area above our necks.

Without an appreciation of this aspect of Chomsky's method-ological naturalism, many of his main theses might seem completely bizarre. For instance, Chomsky takes linguistics to be the study of *I-languages*, where each speaker/hearer has her own particular I-language on a theme fixed by the physical structure realized in the development of the human brain. 'But surely a person's language is not a state of her brain.' Of course it is not, if one is speaking of the commonsensical notion of a language according to which people in the United States and the United Kingdom speak English or the notion under which one is supposed to pronounce Latin /c/ hard rather than soft. For Chomsky, no such notion of a language is of theoretical interest; under it falls a welter of political, normative and cultural factors of which no unified theory is possible. Chomsky's concern is for the properties of the human mind/brain that make available to us our ability to match sound with meaning over an infinite range. This aspect of our general linguistic wherewithal might be recorded in commonsense, but it is irrelevant if it is, just as it is obviously irrelevant to biology whether our commonsensical concep-tion of life includes bacteria and coral. As remarked above, the objects of theoretical concern are not determined by the categories of commonsense but by the shape of our successful theories, that which is tractable to systematic inquiry. There can be no complaint against a position that insists that language is a social phenomenon, a shared 'object', as it were. However, the insistence is wholly uninter-esting, for it simply reflects the features of our common concept. Equally, however, complaints against linguistics based on the com-mon notion of language are fundamentally confused, not merely uninteresting. There is a philosophical cottage industry attempting to show that there is a coherent notion of a public language or at least a language that is independent of speaker/hearers' brain states. It might be of some curious interest were such efforts to prove successful, but their relevance to linguistics is wholly obscure, for no one has made any serious suggestion how such a public notion might fruitfully enter into our understanding of the empirical questions of the structure and development of linguistic competence. A metaphysics of our commonsense concept of a language challenges no thesis of linguistics.

The claims and counter-claims sketched out above will form the argumentative backdrop of the following chapters. My principal purpose is to layout the development of Chomsky's linguistics and how the various frameworks interact with broader philosophical issues. The aim, then, is constructive, not merely destructive of the misplaced challenges, but unmet challenges tend to fester.

CHAPTER 2

METHODOLOGICAL FOUNDATIONS

[A] representation of nature that foretold that even in the most minor investigation of the most common experience we would stumble on a heterogeneity in its laws that would make the unification of its particular laws under universal empirical ones impossible for our understanding would thoroughly displease us.

Kant (1790/2000, 5:188)

1 INTRODUCTION

Syntactic Structures (1957) is typically cited as the beginning of the so-called 'Chomskyan revolution', and it is probably the first port of call for those embarking on a study of the work of Chomsky or generative linguistics more generally. This is hardly surprising. *Syntactic Structures* (hereafter, SS) is Chomsky's first published book (it received a lengthy and highly favourable review in the leading linguistics journal of the day (see Lees, 1957) that might have saved the book from anonymity); it features a brilliant analysis of the English auxiliary system that remains a paradigm of the generative approach, and it contains seminal methodological discussions of the goals and scope of linguistic theory, especially as regards the 'autonomy of syntax'. Notwithstanding all of this, SS is liable to mislead; indeed, it is perhaps fair to say that SS is responsible for much of the confusion to which I alluded in the previous chapter.

First, SS may be usefully viewed as an introductory 'highlights package' of Chomsky's previous work on the computational capacity of grammars and syntactic theory more specifically (in fact, SS was commissioned to serve such an end). The latter work comprises

The Logical Structure of Linguistic Theory (LSLT), a considerably larger text than the svelte hundred or so pages of SS. Inevitably, SS is a truncated, if not elliptical, rendering of Chomsky's views at that time. The relatively formal aspects of SS are, for sure, elegantly presented and are not given to undue misunderstanding, but the crucial methodological remarks are all too brief.

Second, although SS deserves its status as a classic, linguistic theory has progressed at some pace ever since. Crucial in this regard is the 'cognitive construal' of linguistics, that is, the understanding that linguistic theory is a branch of cognitive science, ultimately human biology. Needless to say, it is this philosophical or meta-theoretical perspective that is most closely associated with the name 'Chomsky' and has made linguistics a central concern of philosophers, psychologists and others. SS, however, contains no explicit discussion of these cognitive concerns, still less arguments against empiricism/ behaviourism and ones for nativism. The cognitive construal of linguistic theory was to become explicit in the late 1950s/ early 1960s. Chomsky was to explain some years later in a preface to the eventually published LSLT (1955–56/75) that cognitive issues formed an essential (unstated) background to his thinking in the 1950s. We shall look at this matter below; *pro tem*, we may simply note that, for Chomsky, human cognitive capacity has always been the proper object of linguistic theory; that the seminal SS neglects cognitive issues has essentially contributed to the thought that linguistic theory is one thing, human cognition is another. This attitude has two incarnations. On the one hand, one might, as it were, accept the syntax of SS and LSLT and/or later work, but question the cognitive construal of the theory, or even dismiss it as mere psychology. Whatever the merits of such attitudes in themselves (one might, of course, have no positive or negative interest in syntax apart from its formal elaboration), they do not reflect the position of Chomsky in *any* period of his work. On the other hand, the thought that syntax and cognition come apart has led to a dominant philosophical view of Chomsky's position that, I shall argue, is fundamentally in error.

Third and related, the format of SS gives a false impression of the architecture of linguistic theory as envisaged by Chomsky. A discussion of the computational limitations of certain conceptions of grammar precedes Chomsky's positive articulation of the generative conception, making it seem as if such computational issues and their presuppositions are the basis for what follows. This is simply not the case. For sure, the computational issues are of substantial interest. The fact remains, however, that, quite apart from their formal failure, the grammars under discussion transparently fail to satisfy the kind of explanatory purposes Chomsky has in mind. In other words, the formal demonstrations are strictly surplus to requirements for Chomsky's principal aims. Furthermore, *all* of the computational results bear on the *weak generative capacity* of grammars, that is, a grammar's ability to classify symbol strings drawn from an alphabet as belonging to the language for which the grammar serves. For Chomsky, such a capacity in itself has never been of theoretical interest; to take it as central to linguistic theory, as encouraged by the presentation of SS, is effectively to take a language to be a set of symbol strings. Much of Chomsky's philosophical work over the past couple of decades has been devoted to arguing against such a conception of language (what Chomsky calls an 'E-language' conception). But for the misleading arrangement of SS, Chomsky might well have been saved much of his recent efforts.

This chapter's first concern then is to present the major methodological concepts of Chomsky's early work, most of which retain the greatest relevance to contemporary theory. Second, the critical points adumbrated above will be fully explained.

2 LINGUISTICS BC

It was suggested in the previous chapter that many of the philosophical ripostes to generative linguistics misfire because they fail to incorporate Chomsky's fundamental methodological precept that linguistics is a science and not an a priori discipline that may be constrained by our current pre-theoretical conceptions of what language is or is for. Now, this claim should not be read as implying that before Chomsky there was no science of linguistics, or that linguistics BC was a mere pseudo-science, or otherwise worthless. As we shall see, Chomsky has been the first to highlight that many of his key ideas are (independently arrived at) recapitulations of ideas that go back centuries. Indeed, with an undercurrent of irony, Chomsky (PP) refers to the intellectual 'revolution' he (among others) initiated as the 'second cognitive revolution', a remembering of lost insights, as it were.

The genuine break with the past that Chomsky did bring about pertains to the scope and substance of linguistics as then prevailed. In essence, Chomsky proposed a new scientific way in which linguistics might be pursued, accompanied by the thought that linguistics as then practiced was methodologically suspect. With the help of hindsight, we may see Chomsky as proposing that linguistics, *qua* a discipline concerned with a natural phenomenon (language), should be conducted along the same methodological lines as the hard sciences: physics, chemistry and areas of biology. This is not to suggest, of course, that linguistics is soon likely to enjoy the success of physics; rather, the more modest thought is that there is a rational unity to science and, further, that the linguistics of the day, to its detriment, was pursued in a way that radically departed from that found in the developed sciences. As indicated in the previous chapter, in more recent work, Chomsky has coined the term *methodological dualism* for the thought that human (inclusive of the social) phenomena somehow demand a methodology of inquiry that no one thinks appropriate for the hard sciences, and which is, anyhow, unjustifiable.

The substance of Chomsky's work in linguistics, from the earliest to the latest, may be seen, then, to flow from a methodological proposal: linguistics should be pursued as a science like any other. To flesh out just what a science is would take us too far into the philosophy of science; besides, in a certain respect, the greatest service Chomsky has provided for philosophy is to do philosophy of science via the construction of a new science. In this light, the best way to proceed is to present the science and pay attention to the philosophy as we go. All that said, some broad remarks are required for orientation, which will also serve in support of my thesis that the development of Chomsky's work displays a remarkable consistency.

Chomsky invariably describes the linguistics that prevailed among his immediate predecessors as being merely 'taxonomic' or 'descriptive'. Of course, descriptive accuracy and taxonomic fidelity are to be prized in any science. Yet, and this is the crucial point, such virtues do not exhaust the value of a science; far from it, science does not seek to describe and classify phenomena so much as it seeks to explain them. In broadest terms, this is the flaw Chomsky discerned in the linguistics of the 1950s.

Linguists BC were, for sure, as diverse in their particular beliefs as any actual group of thinkers in any given period. It would, for instance, be absurd to claim that Bloomfield, Sapir and Harris were spokesmen for the same dogmas. Still, certain presuppositions were shared to a significant degree not only among linguists but also among philosophers and psychologists concerned with language.

2.1 The 'corpus' and 'discovery procedures'

American linguistics of the first part of the twentieth century was shaped by the study of native-American languages. There are two aspects to this. First, the languages themselves had to be identified and their various features discerned. This involved field work where the linguist would record and study the speech of users of the language in question. There was, it should be said, a certain political or even moral motive to this work, for the native-American languages were dying. Second, the native languages appeared to differ radically from all hitherto studied languages and certainly from the familiar Indo-European languages for which there existed a rich tradition of analysis (see Baker, 2001, for a modern treatment of native-American languages).

The object of a linguist's inquiry, then, was a *corpus*, that is, a set of recorded utterances from a population of speakers. In effect, a corpus is a sample from a language and, as such, can be judged on grounds of statistical accuracy, that is, whether it includes all of the major features of the language under study. However, a corpus is not questioned in broader terms. For instance, it is not asked why a corpus should contain certain kinds of constructions as opposed to others, or whether constructions not found in any given corpus might still properly be said to belong to the language. Such questions invite an explanatory inquiry that is not restricted to the material at hand. With a corpus in hand, the job of the linguist is to enact a *discovery procedure* that results in an analysis of the sample. The kind of analysis envisaged was hierarchical in the following sense. Sets of sounds (identified acoustically) are mapped onto phonemes (roughly, elementary units of speech); sets of phonemes are mapped onto morphological items (word stems, affixes and various other markers); sets of morphological items are mapped onto words; words are mapped onto grammatical or syntactic categories (noun, verb etc.); finally, sets of grammatical categories are mapped onto sentences/ phrases. The mappings involved here are conditioned by substitutional criteria. For instance, two putative words (sets of morphological items) belong to the same grammatical category if they are intersubstitutable under preservation of phrase or sentence identity, that is, changing one word for another in the context of a sentence does not change the sentence into a non-sentence. (What constitutes a sentence was left somewhat obscure, but appeals to meaning or significance were often made.) Likewise, two putative phonemes are the same morphological item, if they are intersubstitutable under the formation of words. Completed, the analysis constitutes a grammar for the language for which the corpus acts as a sample.

Evidently, such a methodology is merely descriptive or taxonomic; its goal is to classify the language material provided by the corpus into a hierarchy of categories, where each category is defined extensionally in terms of the items which fall under it. Ultimately, the definitions bottom out onto acoustic properties. The business of the linguist was to organize the language material in a systematic way; theory did not stretch beyond what data the corpus provided. Needless to say, this methodology signalled a goal or aspiration of the linguist rather than actual achievement.

2.2 Indefinite variety

It was remarked just above that native-American languages were found to differ radically from Indo-European languages. This discovery contributed to the thought that languages could freely differ along all dimensions (phonology, morphology etc.). Otherwise put, the opinion was that there are no universals in language; languages differ as do the speakers' cultures, histories and environmental settings.

Quite apart from the empirical fact that native-American languages do display peculiarities, the thesis of indefinite variation naturally followed from the methodology described above. If one's theoretical apparatus is restricted to the structural classification of language material, then there is simply no scope for the hypothesizing of language universals beyond what might happen to be found in the intersection of the set of corpora investigated. Furthermore, at best, the methodology would result in merely structural constants that simply reflect the relations of hierarchy imposed upon the corpus. For example, it might be found that verbs and tense markers occur in every language investigated, but since there is no notion of a verb or tense marker independent of the mappings provided by a given analysis, such would-be universals would merely mark the fact that the same mappings work for different languages: sets of words S_1 and S_2, drawn from languages L_1 and L_2 respectively, map onto grammatical category C. Here, C would merely be the set $\{S_1, S_2\}$. In other words, the universal would not be playing a constraining or explanatory role in the analysis; it would be a mere accident of the analysis.

2.3 Immediate constituent analysis

While the methodology presented above could be stretched to grammatical categories and sentential syntax in the way indicated, the focus of linguistic attention was very much on phonology and morphology. The thought appeared to be that syntax could wait, as it were; for if the mapping from phonology to morphology to words could be achieved, then the analysis of phrase and sentence would naturally drop out. That said, grammatical analysis was conducted in the form of *immediate constituent analysis* (ICA). As the name suggests, such analysis breaks a sentence down into a set of embedded sub-categories. For example,

(1)   a.   Bill loves Mary
      b. $[_S [_{NP} [_N Bill]][_{VP} [_V loves] [_{NP} [_N Mary]]]]$

Here, each pair of brackets marks out a constituent, with the subscript label indicating the constituent type. Thus, the string of words as a whole is a sentence (S). S is divided into two major constituents: a noun phrase (NP) and a verb phrase (VP). In turn, these constituents consist, respectively, of a noun (N) and a verb (V) and a further NP that, like the previous one, consists of a noun. The analysis is complete once we reach constituents (e.g. N and V) that consist of nothing other than words. (We shall return to this kind of analysis at length below.)

Immediate constituent analysis is perfectly consistent with the discovery procedure methodology elaborated above. Once we have reached the level of words, then ICA allows us to view sets of words as phrases and sentences to the extent to which such sets might be partitioned into immediate constituents. In this light, the sentence (1)a may be seen as an incarnation of the structure $[_S [_{NP} [_N]] [_{VP} [_V] [_{NP} [_N]]]]$, as depicted in (1)b. In short, ICA provides a grammatical taxonomy over sets of words, just as, say, morphology provides a taxonomy over sets of phonemes. *Qua* taxonomy, ICA does not promise to answer *any* questions about the structure of a given language or similarities between languages apart from those of the form, *What category does X belong to?* For sure, given a completed ICA for, say, a corpus of English, we might, somehow, extrapolate what relation holds between (1)a and, say, *Who does Bill love?* or *Mary is loved by Bill*, but the structure of the ICA would not enshrine the relations itself.

2.4 Intuition and behaviourism

The methodology and presuppositions so far presented fall squarely within a broader behaviourist conception of the human sciences. Behaviourism is not a uniform doctrine, but more of a set of methodological precepts that are variously shared among psychologists, philosophers, linguists and others. We shall turn to the behaviourism of B. F. Skinner and the philosophers in due course; *pro tem*, a few broad remarks will suffice.

It will be noted from above that the object of study for the linguist as so far understood is essentially the behaviour of speakers as recorded in a corpus. Otherwise put, the speaker is treated not as the generator of the language but simply as the locus of the speech episodes recorded. This is so in two respects. First, as indicated, the object of study is the speaker's behaviour, not the speaker's understanding of the language. Second, the linguist seeks no evidence from the speaker beyond the utterances made; in particular, the speaker's judgement on her language is disregarded. In this light, language is a form of behaviour.

Behaviourism more broadly was born of the thought that scientific appeal to mental states, or complex internal states more generally, was a form of outmoded mysticism. Such states appear to differ from one individual to another; further, they are accessible to the individual alone via introspection. Such states do not appear to be the things for which we could have a science. A science of the human, therefore, should be restricted to the observable and measurable, viz., behaviour. A behavioural episode is thus treated as a *response* to *stimulus*, and laws are available for behaviour to the extent to which regularities hold between responses and stimuli.

It would be a distortion to brand all American linguists BC as behaviourists. Some, such as Bloomfield and Hockett explicitly commended a behaviourist methodology; Harris and others were simply indifferent to such broad methodological considerations. The important point is that the dominant methodology in linguistics was perfectly flush with behaviourism, whether or not anyone was particularly interested in labelling it so. One might, for example, eschew any consideration of the cognitive resources of the speaker, not because one thought that such resources did not exist, but because one deemed them irrelevant to the taxonomic business at hand. Further, behaviourist presuppositions come into greatest relief in the context of language acquisition, and such considerations were rarely raised. If raised, then the methodology of the synchronic study of language would mandate a similar diachronic account. That is, if language is merely a form of behaviour answering to a certain taxonomy, which may differ to the same degree as other cultural forms, then its acquisition would appear to be similar to that of a habit, a mode of behaviour shaped and reinforced by its occurrence within a speaker's family and peer group. In short, if one's conception and analysis of language as such does not involve any appeal to the notion of a speaker's cognitive structure, then there is no reason to expect acquisition of language to be explicable in such terms.

In sum, by 'linguistics BC' I mean the constellation of presuppositions just sketched: language is a form of (speech) behaviour that is open to indefinite variation, and whose study is exhausted by various taxonomic analyses that don't seek to explain the properties of the corpora targeted nor how the speaker acquires her language. Before we move onto Chomsky's challenge to this conception of linguistics, it bears noting that 'linguistics BC' is not intended to suggest that everything changed with the advent of Chomsky's work, nor even, as earlier indicated, that *all* of previous thought on language was animated by the above presuppositions. That is simply not the case. Many linguists still view their discipline as essentially descriptive or otherwise formal without being behaviourists of any stripe; they are simply unconcerned with cognitive issues. However, a good number of linguists and psychologists explicitly reject what is often labelled 'Chomskyan linguistics' and commend a form of heated-over behaviourism. Further, the majority of contemporary philosophers concerned with language have a behaviourist-like conception, at least to the extent to which they understand language to be an aspect of human behaviour (see Chapter 1). Linguistics BC, then, is still to be fought, and in this regard the lessons of Chomsky's early work retain the greatest relevance.

3 LINGUISTICS: A SCIENCE LIKE ANY OTHER

In the preface to SS, Chomsky gives two reasons for the likely fecundity of a 'formalized general theory of linguistic structure'. First and negatively, '[b]y pushing a precise but inadequate formulation to an unacceptable conclusion, we can often expose the exact source of this inadequacy and, consequently, gain a deeper understanding of the linguistic data' (SS, p. 5). Second and positively, 'a formalized theory may automatically provide solutions for many problems other than those for which it was designed' (SS, p. 5). In contrast, 'obscure and intuition-bound notions' fail in both respects. They can't lead to absurd conclusions, nor to new insights, simply because their lack of rigour precludes any clear deductive chain of reasoning. Such notions can, for sure, be easily rendered absurd in the absence of ad hoc reformulation; equally, they can be massaged to fit new phenomena. However, in neither case is any insight gained. Although perhaps not obvious at first glance, Chomsky is here offering a plea that linguistics be pursued like any other science.

3.1 The nature of linguistic theory

It is standard to divide the study of language into at least four areas: phonology, syntax, semantics and pragmatics. Phonology is concerned with articulation of sound. Syntax is concerned with the form of language and seeks, ultimately, to explicate notions of grammatical and ungrammatical as applied to particular languages. Semantics covers questions of meaning. Pragmatics, somewhat more loosely, covers questions of how speakers use language. To sanction this four-way division is not to presume that there are sharp boundaries between the respective areas of investigation that any adequate overall theory must respect; rather, the division simply marks out phenomena that, *prima facie*, can be independently approached. It is the business of theory rather than stipulation to decide just how form, meaning and use fit together. When Chomsky speaks of a 'general theory of linguistic structure' he has in mind a theory of syntax. As we shall see, Chomsky indeed thinks that problems in syntax can be fruitfully tackled independently of issues arising in semantics or pragmatics. This is a controversial thesis we shall assess later; for the moment, let it be granted.

For Chomsky, inquiry into syntax is in turn divided into *general linguistic theory* (GLT) and particular *grammars*. Let us first consider the second notion. 'A grammar for a particular language,' Chomsky suggests, 'can be considered, in what seems to me a perfectly good sense, to be a complete scientific theory of a particular subject matter' (LSLT, p. 77). So, a grammar will consist of general 'laws' framed in terms of 'hypothetical constructs' from which we may derive statements that cover familiar and novel phenomena. Thus, the grammar will be predictive and explanatory over the particular language. As with any theory, our data will be finite. In the present case, we have available to us some finite sample of linguistic material, and from this we seek to construct a grammar that will project to (be predictive over) the language as a whole. What the theory/grammar seeks to explain is our general capacity to be competent with language over an infinite range and the various structural characteristics of this competence. On the first desideratum, Chomsky (LSLT, p. 61; cf., SS, p. 15) writes,

> A speaker of a language has observed a certain limited set of utterances in his language. On the basis of this finite linguistic experience he can produce an indefinite number of new utterances which are immediately acceptable to other members of his speech community. He can also distinguish a certain set of 'grammatical' utterances, among utterances that he has never heard and might never produce. He thus projects his past linguistic experience to include certain new strings while excluding others.

Note, the datum here is not that we understand an *infinity* of sentences. Given the vagaries of the notion of 'understanding' and metaphysical suspicions over the infinite, such a claim would needlessly attract irrelevant objections. The datum, rather, is that our competent use of language is 'indefinitely new' or 'continuously novel'; far from finding ourselves stumped at novel sentences, the vast majority of sentences we produce and consume are entirely novel to us (such as the very sentences you are now reading). If our competence were somehow finitely bounded, then our apparent ability to project 'acceptable' or 'grammatical' across an indefinite range would be a kind of fortunate accident, as if there were a finite upper bound but one sufficiently great to be unnoticed. Such a speculation is irrelevant and, anyhow, false.

The idea of a finite bound on the sentences with which we might be competent is irrelevant because the problem of projection would remain exactly as before given that the distance between our initial sample and full competence must be so great as to support continuous novelty. That is to say, our competence must still involve a projection from a sample, and placing a bound on the projection leaves the nature of the projection unexplained.

Apart from such an explanatory lack, the thought that there is a finite upper bound is false, for there is no longest sentence. In other words, if the bound were set at finite n, then we wouldn't be competent with a sentence featuring $n+1$ clauses or noun phrases. However, consider the generation in (2):

(2)   a. The boy behind the girl is blonde.
       b. The boy behind the girl behind the boy is blonde.
       c. The boy behind the girl behind the boy behind the girl is blonde.

This sequence can be extended indefinitely, but an understanding of its first member appears to suffice for an understanding of all following members. Clearly, the thought that this sequence terminates at some finite point would, without further ado, be an arbitrary stipulation. *Prima facie*, placing a finite upper bound on the sentences with which we may be competent is as absurd as placing a finite bound on the natural numbers we might understand.

The general point here can be put as follows: if a grammar is to explain our competence with continuously novel sentences, then it must generate structural information for the (infinite) language as a whole. Understood as a theory, a grammar is a *finite* system that generates an infinity of predictions. For example, an adequate grammar for English must be able to generate the structure for (2)a in such a way that it is automatically able to generate structures for the other members of the sequence. This would amount to the grammar predicting that an understanding of (2)a suffices for an understanding of the sequence as a whole.

There are various ways in which this first demand of infinite generativity can be satisfied in an unenlightening way, the most trivial of which is simply a list of the 'grammatical' sentences, on the assumption that we can somehow determine the content of 'grammatical'. Infinite generativity in itself, therefore, fails to cast any light on a speaker's 'large store of knowledge about his language and a mass of feelings and understandings we might call "intuitions about linguistic form"' (LSLT, p. 62). The point here is that we want a grammar to generate the grammatical sentences in a way that explains the character of our competence with the sentences, that is, the 'intuitions about linguistic form'. For example, we understand that certain pairs of sentences relate to each other as declarative to interrogative (e.g. *Bill can swim* and *Can Bill swim?*; *Bill loves Jane* and *Whom does Bill love?*). Likewise, we understand that certain sentence pairs relate to each as active to passive (e.g. *Bill loves Mary* and *Mary is loved by Bill*). There are many more such structural relations. Many sentences are also structurally ambiguous, such as Chomsky's famous case of *They are flying planes* (*they* can refer to planes in the air or to, say, children in control of model aircraft). Even if we have never explicitly pondered such cases, we appear to understand the ambiguity perfectly, for we can effortlessly use tokens of the same sentence type to describe quite distinct events.

Similarly, the sentences in (3) appear to have the same form:

(3) a. Bill is easy to please.
     b. Bill is eager to please.

Again, even if we have never pondered such sentences, we understand that there is a structural difference between them. For instance, we know that (3)a has the paraphrase

(4) It is easy to please Bill.

This shows that (3)a roughly means that Bill's being pleased is easy to bring about. One the other hand, (5) is not a paraphrase of (3)b:

(5) It is eager to please Bill.

The thought that Bill's being pleased is eager to bring about is simply nonsensical. Note also that *it* in (4) and (5) is playing quite different roles. In (4), *it* plays a purely functional role much like in *It is raining*. *It* in (4) cannot be construed as referentially picking out, say, a dog. For sure, we can say, *It easily pleases Bill*, with *it* referring to some non-person, but we know that (4) simply can't be used to express that thought. The opposite situation prevails with (5). There *it* can only be used referentially and, unlike (4), conspicuously fails to provide a paraphrase. We seem to know all of this even though very few of us have bothered to think about it explicitly. If we had to think consciously about the structural difference between the adjectives *eager* and *easy* every time we used the words, language use would be something quite different from what it is. Notwithstanding the interminable analogies with chess and other games, using language, at least in the present respect, is nothing like a game.

A second empirical condition on a grammar, then, is that it contributes to an explanation of the kind of implicit knowledge that makes us so effortlessly competent with such relative complexities. It might be noted that the kind of facts of understanding adumbrated above are all obvious enough once brought to one's attention. This doesn't alter the explanatory demand on a grammar. That apples fall to the ground was an obvious fact to Newton, but he still wanted it explained. Likewise, it is one thing to note that, say, a sentence is three ways ambiguous; it is quite another thing to see how precisely three readings of the sentence, as opposed to two or four, follow from a theory that assigns a structure to each sentence of the language and by so doing explains a host of similar facts across the language as a whole. That something is obvious does not mean that it is understood or does not require explanation.

We could construct a grammar to generate all the grammatical sentences of a language without constraining it to speak to the kinds of intuitive connections spelt out above. It is difficult, however, to see the virtues of such a policy. The resulting account would appear to be a jumble of ad hoc components each designed for some distinct task. Demanding that our various structural intuitions be explained via the same theory that meets the generativity condition promises a more principled explanation as the two empirically necessary conditions would constrain each other.

On Chomsky's conception, then, grammars work like theories for their respective languages: they are predictive of the sentences (grammatical strings) of the particular language and concomitantly explain a host of structural features. The grammar is not a mere taxonomy that partitions the language; indeed, like a scientific theory, a grammar is free to contain 'hypothetical constructs' that improve its explanatory power, and there is no constraint that such constructs be reflected in a taxonomy of the language. For example, the partition of *Bill can swim* and *Can Bill swim?* into the set of declarative and interrogative sentences respectively cannot be faulted on taxonomic grounds, but so much leaves entirely unexplained the relation between the two types of sentence. The point here becomes transparent in the light of *general linguistic theory* (GLT).

It might be thought that, if we can produce an adequate grammar for any given language, then a *general* theory for language would be redundant, a mere recapitulation. Such a thought is simply a reflex of the dogma that languages are indefinitely varied. Our discussion so far about the abstract nature of grammars is itself a part of GLT, albeit quite unformalized. The crucial point is that the very notion of a grammar or a successful theory for a language is 'not antecedently clear . . . a field of investigation cannot be clearly delimited in advance of the theory dealing with this subject matter; in fact, it is one of the functions of a theory to give such a precise delimitation' (LSLT, p. 61). For example, biology can be said to be concerned with *life*, but contemporary biology is not the least bit constrained by any pre-theoretical notions of life; it is biological theory itself that sets its boundaries of investigation via reflection of the nature of the particular theories that fall under 'biology', itself an a posteriori question. Likewise, physics can be said to be concerned with *matter* and *forces*, but no one but the completely addled would suggest that our pre-theoretical understanding of such notions is up to constraining physical theories – likewise for linguistics. The notion of a grammar, or of language itself for that matter, is not antecedently clear enough to constrain the development of theory. In a sense, then, a denial of GLT is simply a denial of thought about the grammars constructed. Thus, some notion of a GLT, however inchoate, follows from our requiring a *theory* of a language as opposed to a mere intuitive catalogue of its features. However, we can say more.

As grammars are like theories, so GLT is like a 'philosophy of science . . . [of] a set of rather special scientific theories' (LSLT, p. 119). General linguistic theory defines in general terms the mechanisms and concepts that enter into particular grammars, and, crucially, it offers criteria for the selection of a grammar among a competing set relative to a given language. Again, this is not to suggest that the linguist first determines the nature of GLT and then cranks out grammars. The development of GLT goes hand in hand with the development of particular grammars: as we improve a particular grammar for a language, so we can revise GLT, and such a revision based on grammar G_1 might lead us to revise G_2 for some quite distinct language (cf., LSLT, p. 79; SS, p. 50). Note that this perfectly rational way of proceeding – revising one theory on the model of another theory that has proved successful – is simply unavailable in the absence of GLT to mediate.

We have, then, a model of grammars as theories of languages and a GLT (a 'philosophy') which provides the resources for the construction and evaluation of grammars. Before we move on, something must be said about grammar evaluation.

As with any other theory, a grammar is assessed by confrontation with data. Chomsky (1LSLT, p. 80; SS, pp. 49–50) proposes that a grammar must meet 'external conditions of adequacy'. This means that a grammar for a language should (i) generate structures that are acceptable to a speaker of the language and (ii) explain the kind of structural characteristics mentioned above. In effect, then, the principal data source for a grammar is the 'intuitions of linguistic form' of the speakers of the language, including the linguist herself. Such intuitions are precisely of the kind hopefully elicited by the examples provided above. Chomsky (LSLT, pp. 101–3) hoped for 'more convincing and acceptable' behavioural criteria, while recognizing that such criteria appear to rest on antecedent intuitions as to what is intuitively acceptable. Chomsky was soon to overcome his reticence (e.g. 'Explanatory models in linguistics' (EML) and *Current Issues in Linguistic Theory* (CILT)). One works simply with the data that are available, without ruling any data source out. Further, it is unclear how the attempt to make the intuitive data firmer via behavioural criteria advances our understanding. If we disregard behaviourist scruples, there appears to be nothing misleading in intuitive judgments, and, as in any other science, one is always free to disregard data if one suspects that they are tainted. We shall see later that this kind of discussion over the nature of data is somewhat jejune in light of present theory, for, in a very real sense, the object of theory is not a language as such but speakers' linguistic capacity. A speaker's intuitive judgement, therefore, is as direct a data source as one could wish for.

Paired with the external adequacy conditions is an 'internal' adequacy condition (LSLT, pp. 80–1; SS, p. 50). The external conditions relate a given grammar to the facts (data); the internal condition relates a given grammar to GLT. This notion is something more than the innocent idea that a given grammar may be evaluated in relation to one's ongoing general conception of a grammar as determined by the set of grammars under construction. General linguistic theory, Chomsky (LSLT, chapter 4) hopes, may provide a *simplicity* metric by which one could choose the *simplest* grammar among a set that all meet external conditions of adequacy. Simplicity, of course, is a general virtue of theories and is notoriously nebulous. Chomsky's idea was that for grammars in particular, if not every theory, one could rigorously evaluate simplicity in terms of shortness or compactness; that is, it turns out that the simplest grammar among a set of grammars will be the shortest one. An example of this idea in action will be given below.

As should be clear, the kind of grammar evaluation Chomsky had in mind significantly departed from the discovery procedure method. In principle, there are (at least) three methods by which one could evaluate a grammar relative to GLT (LSLT, pp. 79–80; SS, pp. 50–3). First, one could seek to determine the correct grammar for a language direct from a corpus. This is the 'discovery' method. A weaker requirement would be that the correct grammar between a pair is selected on the basis of the corpus. This is a 'decidability' method and would give a 'Yes'/'No' pair for any submitted pair of grammars. Finally, there is a still weaker method, which allows one to decide that G_1 is better than G_2 on the basis of the corpus. This is the 'simplicity' approach. Assuming that grammars are like theories, we can assess these three methods at a fairly abstract level. The discovery method amounts to the idea that data directly determine the correct theory. Clearly, no science proceeds in that way. Indeed, the idea that we could practically determine that we had the correct theory would bring scientific dispute to an end. Commitment to such a method betrays a view of linguistic theory as a mere descriptive exercise. The second method is weaker but still far stronger than anything found in the sciences (outside of mathematics). So-called 'crucial experiments' *might* tell us that certain theories are false (a 'No'), but no one expects such experiments or any other data to be such as to deliver a definitive 'Yes'/'No' answer for *any* pair of theories. Finally, even the simplicity method is stronger than anything found in the natural sciences. Still, its judgement is only comparative, not categorical. Furthermore, it reflects the virtues of simplicity and economy that animate the sciences. The difference is that in the special case of linguistics we might have available a way of making rigorous these inchoate notions.

We shall see later that notions of simplicity and economy still play a most significant role in linguistic theory (Chapter 8). The terms of the debate, however, have changed greatly. The present point, then, is not that a simplicity metric of the kind Chomsky envisaged in the 1950s is achievable or even still relevant. Rather, we can see that from the beginning Chomsky is approaching linguistics as a science like any other. The challenge to the linguistics of the day was not that its results happened to be incorrect, but that its whole approach was mistaken, including its methodology: the questions it asked and the animating philosophy. For sure, at the time it did not seem as if Chomsky was being so radical. In part, this was no doubt because LSLT remained unpublished and SS and other publications were less explicit and more given to misinterpretation. Still, all that was to follow may be properly seen as an unfurling of the initial insight that language, seen as a natural phenomenon like any other, should be approached scientifically, free from the unrealistic and explanatorily penurious methods of structuralism, empiricism and behaviourism.

3.2   The autonomy of syntax

The study of language, as already mentioned, is typically divided into syntax (or grammar, inclusive of phonology and morphology), semantics (meaning) and pragmatics (use). Chomsky is often credited with an 'autonomy thesis', that is, that grammar is independent of semantics and/or matters of language use (statistical or otherwise). The 'thesis' has proved to be very controversial and is still the centre of much debate. In fact, however, Chomsky has never held an 'autonomy thesis' of the form too often attributed to him. Chomsky (LSLT, p. 97) writes,

> At this stage of our understanding of linguistic structure there seems to be little point in issuing manifestoes *for or against* the dependence of the theory of linguistic structure on meaning. We can only try to construct such a theory and investigate its adequacy . . . At *present*, it seems to me proper to say that whereas we know of many grammatical notions that have no semantic basis, we know of none for which a significant and general semantic analysis is forthcoming. This justifies the *tentative* assertion that the theory of linguistic form does not have semantic foundations. (My emphasis)

A number of points bear emphasis here. First, the 'thesis' is not a positive claim about how grammatical theory should or must be pursued; rather, a negative suggestion is made: there is as yet no good reason to think that semantic notions will be foundational for grammatical theory. Chomsky does not affect to offer a proof: 'It is, of course, impossible to prove that semantic notions are of no use in grammar, just as it is impossible to prove the irrelevance of any other given set of notions' (SS, p. 100). Chomsky's real target is the presumption that semantic notions are somehow essential to grammatical theory. In the absence of a theory of either grammar or semantics, the presumption is mere dogma (LSLT, pp. 94–5).

Second, Chomsky's 'thesis' in no way suggests that the study of meaning ('an essential task for linguistics' (LSLT, p. 97)) is uninteresting or to be forever forlorn. Indeed, grammatical theory may be reasonably expected to shed light on or 'support' the study of meaning insofar as it accounts for the structures which are put to use in our meaningful linguistic behaviour and there is some correlation, albeit imprecise, between structural relations and semantic ones (SS, pp. 101–03).

Ultimately, in the absence of a good reason to think syntax depends on meaning, the 'autonomy of syntax' is an academic matter. What certainly does not show such a dependence is the linguist's appeal to intuitions. We saw above, for example, that the adjectives *eager* and *easy* differ in their effects on the structures into which they enter. Is this intuition a semantic one? To think it obviously is semantic betrays far too broad a conception of the semantic. After all, the intuitions are best elicited by comparison with other structures, not by an analysis of what *eager* and *easy* mean. In such a light, mere reflection on the respective concepts seems quite pointless. Alternatively, a good way to see the difference is to reflect that *being easy* is a property of events (people, say, cannot be easy in the relevant sense), so *being easy* is a property of Bill's being pleased, not of Bill alone, while *being eager* is a property of people and other animate things, and so *eager* is a predicate of *Bill* alone. Pre-theoretically, it is unclear whether this is a semantic matter or a syntactic one. Further, even if we were to insist that our intuition marks the difference as primarily semantic, there is no a priori bar to an adequate grammar being able to reflect such a difference structurally (this seems to be case), and so a pre-theoretical aspect of our semantic notion would be subsumed under grammatical theory (cf., LSLT, p. 97; SS, p. 102). There is nothing the least peculiar about pre-theoretical categories being narrowed, broadened or fragmented under the weight of theoretical advance; it is the norm.

The 'autonomy thesis', then, is but a methodological guide that can be properly evaluated only in light of attempts to construct grammatical theories. That said, Chomsky does think that there are relatively clear cases that show that grammaticality is not a semantic notion.

Here we come to perhaps Chomsky's most famous example. As the example is often cited without a proper explanation of the use to which Chomsky puts it, it is worthwhile to spend a little time on it.

We are assuming that a grammar should generate an infinity of structures for a given language, with the grammar being evaluated as a 'good' theory for the language to the extent to which its structures are explanatory of the 'intuitions of linguistic form' of speakers of the language. If, then, the generation were guided by semantic notions, we should naturally expect our intuitions of linguistic form to be flush with our intuitions of semantic coherence or significance. If not, it would be wholly unclear what it would mean for a grammar to be based upon semantic notions, for the object of a grammar is just our understanding of grammatical form. Now consider the following sentence:

(6)   Colourless green ideas sleep furiously.

(I use the American English spelling.) About (6), Chomsky (LSLT, p. 94; cf., SS, p. 15) writes, '[it] is thoroughly meaningless and nonsignificant, but it seems to me that as a speaker of English, I would regard this as a "grammatical" sentence'. Thus, a grammar for English should assign a structure to (6) that explains this intuition in the face of the fact that (6) appears to be gibberish. If all of this is so, then 'grammatical' just does not equate to a semantic notion. Let us consider some objections and queries.

First off, it might be thought that (6) is in fact ungrammatical. Again, without a developed notion of what grammatical amounts to, such a claim would be empty or a mere stretching of 'semantic' over 'linguistic form' that stands in need of justification. To see this, compare (6) with (7):

(7)   a. Colourless green ideas sleeps furiously.
       b. Furiously sleep ideas green colourless.

Both of these sentences are unacceptable in a way (6) is not. (7)a contains an agreement error, with the verb stem *sleep* being inflected as if it were in agreement with a singular subject, but the head of the subject NP is plural. (7)b, on the other hand, is just word salad. Indeed, it will be noted that the pronunciation of (7)b has a flat intonation contour, as if one were merely listing a string of words. On the other hand, the pronunciation of (6) has a natural rising intonation contour. We may also note that (6) smoothly admits to various grammatical operations that (7)b precludes. For example,

(8) a. Colourless green ideas do sleep furiously. [emphasis]
b. Colourless green ideas don't sleep furiously. [negation]
c. Do colourless green ideas sleep furiously? [interrogative]
d. It is colourless green ideas that sleep furiously. [cleft]
e. What sleeps furiously are colourless green ideas.
[pseudocleft]

Furthermore, we can freely change the tense, aspect and modality of (6) with no change in its relative acceptability. All of this suggests that we are dealing with a perfectly well-formed structure, albeit gibberish.

A different response might be that (6) is in fact meaningful, and so its apparent grammaticality does not show that being grammatical is not a semantic property. Well, this response depends on what one means by 'meaningful'. The apparent meaninglessness of (6) arises, in part, from its contravention of sub-category restrictions, that is, only animate things can sleep, but ideas are abstract, and only concrete things can be green, but, again, ideas are abstract. Further, it is contradictory to describe a thing as both green and colourless, and it is wholly opaque how anything can sleep in a furious manner. Still, one response might be that only meaningful sentences can possess truth values; (6) is false; therefore, (6) is meaningful. This is a perfectly valid argument, but the operative notion of meaning is so weak as to make no difference to the point at hand, for it appears that truth predication is supported by so little as grammatical form. For example, (9)a is as acceptable as (6) and (9)b is as unacceptable as (7)b.

(9) a. It is false that colourless green ideas sleep furiously [because ideas don't sleep].
b. It is false that furiously sleep ideas green colourless.

Unless we are told how truth predication depends upon more than grammatical form, the response appears to be just another example of stretching 'semantic' to cover 'linguistic form'.

A different response along the same general lines is to argue that, context willing, (6) can be used to express meaningful claims.

For example, (6) might be used poetically to describe a seed in the ground, with the 'green ideas' being its potential sprouting into a plant etc. This tactic is not to the point. It is the case that (6), along with other nonsense, can be used in some non-literal way. However, to take the mere possibility of some figural use of a sentence as criterial of meaning and so, *per* the suggestion, grammaticality, is just to distort the phenomenon. We require some setting up of context to 'understand' (6) and, on that basis, we essentially impose an interpretation upon the sentence, much as a poet elicits a certain metaphorical interpretation from her readers. However, we require no such context or imposition when dealing with a structure of the same apparent grammatical form as (6):

(10)   Friendly young dogs seem harmless.

It is true enough that (7)b appears unfit for any use whatsoever, metaphorical or otherwise, but this in itself provides no reason to think that the ultimate difference between (6)/(10) and (7)b is essentially semantic. We should be as ready to conclude that mere grammaticality suffices for non-literal use, much as it suffices for truth predication. The fact is that we have robust intuitions as to the grammaticality of (6) and (10) (witness (8)) and the ungrammaticality of (7)b *independent of any context*. We should like this difference to be explained, and the separation of 'grammatical' from 'meaningful' promises to do that, for, *ex hypothesi*, grammaticality is not a context dependent notion. On the other hand, the proposal at hand amounts to a decree to ignore the data in the name of a loose notion of meaning depending on a still looser notion of context. (Chomsky (LSLT, chapter 4) sought to place the sentences we are considering on a scale of grammaticalness based on degrees of category deviation; see 'Some methodological remarks on generative grammar' (SMR), pp. 384–5, for a study of the option discussed and Chapter 7 for more detail.)

A somewhat different response to the 'autonomy thesis' is to take grammaticality to be, in some sense, a matter of our use of language, both on the production and consumption side. On this view, examples such as (6) are not grammatical, because they are simply not 'the kinds of things people say', and if we were to witness a sincere utterance of (6), we would not know how to respond; we would have a 'bizarreness reaction' (see LSLT, pp. 144–46; SS, pp. 15–7; *Topics in the Theory of Generative Grammar* (TTGG), pp. 34–6). However, such thoughts might best be finessed; the underlying idea betrays a behaviourist aversion to explanation. It is certainly true that sentences such as (6) – nonsense – tend not to be sincerely uttered ((6), accidentally, is now a quite common sentence), and if they were to be, we would indeed not know how to respond. However, so much is simply data; we should like to know why this is the case. That apart, it is quite absurd to think that (6) and its like can be identified as ungrammatical, meaningless or otherwise unacceptable on the basis of mere observation of what people say and how they respond to each other. Since any English speaker has at her disposal an infinity of sentences and language use is continuously novel, the prior probability of an utterance of any given English sentence is asymptotic to zero. That the probability of a sincere use of (6) is close to zero is thus of no interest whatsoever. We might try to reduce the class of available sentences in some fashion (by, for example, excluding all sentences over a million words long), but the class will still be so large as to keep the probabilities close to zero. Quite apart from any question of probability, the fact that a sentence is not used fails to distinguish it in any syntactic or semantic sense. Neither (6) nor (7)b, let us grant, fall within a speaker's typical repertoire, but our intuitions about them remain strikingly distinct. Likewise, people tend not to utter obvious truths ('My sister is female', 'A train is faster than a bicycle') or obvious falsehoods ('2 + 2 = 5', 'London is the capital of France'), or sentences that are otherwise odd ('Whom the fuck do you think you are talking to?', 'A ticket to Jupiter is £4, Sir'). Unless, absurdly, we are to classify all such sentences as ungrammatical, then we have no reason to think that (6) is ungrammatical *qua* unused.

The only way, it seems, to improve the tactic is to seek to identify (6) with some class or kind of sentence, and then to claim that members of such a class are not used. Pretty clearly, however, this is a self-defeating path: it will not be facts of usage that mark members of the class as deviant but the membership condition on the class itself.

Similar points hold for the thought that (6) is ungrammatical, because we would take a sincere utterance of it to be bizarre. We do and would find many utterances to be quite bizarre without doubting their grammaticality. Likewise, a sincere utterance of word salad such as (7)b would undoubtedly be met with consternation, but our intuitions about it remain different from those which (6) attracts. In short, the mere presence of a 'bizarre factor' tells us nothing definite about the given structure. We could go on to assess variations on this theme, but enough has been said, I hope, to cast the gravest doubt on the very idea of accounting for grammaticality intuitions via the facts of language use.

In conclusion, it is worth noting again that Chomsky's 'autonomy thesis' is a methodological admonishment that, in the nature of the case, can't be proved true. Further, Chomsky does not seek to argue for 'autonomy' via any a priori stipulation about the content of 'grammatical' or 'meaningful'. His arguments are wholly methodological and empirical. The ultimate vindication of 'autonomy', therefore, can only be found in a successful grammatical theory that does not appeal to semantic notions for its foundation (cf., *Essays on Form and Interpretation* (EFI), pp. 52–5). A word of caution, however, is required. As intimated several times above, 'autonomy' in no sense implies that semantics is a worthless pursuit; rather, the tentative suggestion is that grammatical theory might be a sound way to advance semantics either by providing the structures that constrain the interpretation of sentences or, more radically, by swallowing up what might pre-theoretically be thought of as semantic phenomena. As we shall see later, both of these suggestions have borne considerable fruit.

4 EXPLANATION IN LINGUISTICS

So far we have dealt with methodological issues about how linguistics ought to be pursued. For the remainder of this chapter we shall look at how Chomsky's early work put flesh on the bones of the methodology. We shall also explain and defend the claims made at the top of this chapter as to the misleading character of SS.

4.1 'Language'

At no place in LSLT does Chomsky stipulate what a particular language *is* nor what language is in general. He does not define language as a form of behaviour, nor as an abstract object, nor as a set of social conventions, nor as any other kind of 'thing' at all. If linguistics is to be a science, this is just what one would expect. It is absurd, for example, to expect physics to tell us what 'matter' and 'forces' are independent of particular elaborated physical theories. Just so for biology and chemistry. As previously mentioned, no developed science has a fixed a priori domain of inquiry that may be stipulated prior to actual inquiry; rather, the genuine object of a science is arrived at via the construction of successful theories. Furthermore, under scientific investigation, our *folk*, pre-theoretical categories invariably give way to created categories that are suited to the data and explanatory demands of the particular inquiry. Chomsky approaches linguistics in this spirit. He offers no definitions of language, grammar or meaning in a way that is intended to constrain inquiry; the notions remain in play, but only to point to the range of phenomena at issue. Once we have at hand theories of some substance that enjoy empirical support, we may propose that they should guide our theoretical conceptions of 'language', 'grammar' etc. How such conceptions stand to our commonsensical notions is a legitimate area of inquiry, but such inquiry does not decide whether our theories that support such conceptions are correct or incorrect. Put simply, linguistics is concerned with our linguistic intuitions as data and not with our intuitions about what language is.

Chomsky, then, presents GLT, as reflected in particular grammars, as being about our 'large store of knowledge about . . . language and a mass of feelings and understandings that we might call "intuitions about linguistic form"' (LSLT, p. 62), or, more simply, our 'intuitive sense of grammaticalness' (LSLT, p. 95). In other words, linguistic theory has as its primary data source our 'knowledge' which enters into (but by no means exhausts) our consumption and production of linguistic material. As it stands, this is somewhat opaque; for the moment I want to leave problems and queries in limbo. All that needs to be emphasized now is that Chomsky sets up linguistic theory as being concerned with an aspect of native speakers' *cognitive* capacity with language, or the 'knowledge' they bring to language, rather than with language or grammar *tout court*. This is nothing more than a reflection of the fact that the data for a grammar are speakers' intuitive judgements, and it is quite unclear what it would be to have data 'direct' from the language, with the speakers bypassed, as it were. A somewhat different conception of the domain of linguistic theory *appears* to animate SS. We shall see that the impression is misleading.

4.2 The concept of language in *Syntactic Structures*

SS begins in earnest with the following statement:

> I will consider a *language* to be a set (finite or infinite) of sentences, each finite in length and constructed out of a finite set

of elements. All natural languages in their spoken or written form are languages in this sense, since each natural language has a finite number of phonemes (or letters in its alphabet) and each sentence is representable as a finite sequence of these phonemes (or letters), though there are infinitely many sentences. Similarly, the set of 'sentences' of some formalized system of mathematics can be considered a language. The fundamental aim in the linguistic analysis of a language L is to separate the *grammatical* sequences which are the sentences of L from the *ungrammatical* sequences which are not sentences of L and to study the structure of the grammatical sequences. (SS, p. 13)

Here we seem to have Chomsky defining '*language*' as the domain of linguistic theory in advance of inquiry; that is, the object of theory is a set of symbol sequences, and its aim is to separate the grammatical from the ungrammatical ones, that is, to identify the actual language from any other set of sequences drawn from the same alphabet. This conception can be most clearly understood, as Chomsky suggests, via a consideration of formal languages in mathematics.

One of the most simplest formal languages that has been studied is that of the propositional (sentential/functional) calculus (PC). The language consists of a stock of variables (P, Q, R, . . .) and *logical constants* (for our purposes, we may restrict these to '¬' (negation) and '&' (conjunction)). The purpose of the language is to codify relations of logical validity that depend on no more than the truth or falsity of whole formulae. Let a *symbol sequence* be any finite concatenation of these symbols. Clearly, the members of the set of such sequences are mostly symbol salad. We want to define, then, *well-formed formula of PC* (wff or 'sentence') such that all and only wffs can receive a truth-value under an interpretation. The standard way of doing this is as follows:

(PC wff-df)
 (i) P, Q, R, . . . are wffs.
 (ii) If X is a wff, then $\neg X$ is a wff.
 (iii) If X, Y is a wff, then $X \& Y$ is a wff.
 (iv) These are all the wffs.

Here 'X' and 'Y' are meta-variables that range over any symbol sequence. We see from (i) and (ii), then, that '¬P', '¬Q' etc. are wffs.

From (iii), we see that 'P & Q', '¬P & Q', etc. are also wffs. We can also see that, say, '¬P &' is not a wff, for by (iii) an occurrence of '&' must be flanked by wffs. Likewise, we see that '¬P¬' is not a wff, for '¬' can only occur to the left of a wff. It should also be noticed that there are an infinity of wffs. For example, taking 'P' to be value of 'X' in (ii), we have '¬P' as a wff. In turn, taking this wff to be the value of 'X' in (ii) gives us the wff '¬¬P'. And so on. Any such wff will be finite, but there is no finite upper bound on the number of wffs that can be so generated. We can, therefore, take (PC wff-df) to be a definition of the (infinite) set of wffs of the language of PC.

In mathematical jargon, (PC wff-df) is a *recursive* definition. Such definitions consist of a *base* and a *recursive part*. In the present case, the base is (i), which specifies the primitive wffs, and the recursive part is (ii) and (iii) that specify new wffs of the same type as the wffs to which they apply. Recursion can be figuratively viewed as a 'loop', where the wffs generated can be fed back into the given rule to generate further wffs.

In one sense, a recursive definition does not tell us anything new. For example, anyone numerate will know, for any given numeral (a name of a number), whether it refers to a positive integer or not. However, one may still ask, 'Is there an *explicit* way to specify all and only the positive integers?'. The notion of *explicitness* is crucial. It is one thing to know, for any given numeral, whether it refers to a positive integer or not, but it is quite another thing to specify how all and only positive integers are generated. A specification of this would be explicit in the sense that it would provide a rule that does not depend on intuition or the like by which one could decide, for any given numeral, whether it referred to a natural number. This, it turns out, is easily done. Consider

(PI-df)
  (i)   1 is a positive integer.
  (ii) If x is a positive integer, then s(x) is a positive integer.
  (iii) These are all the positive integers.

Where 's(x)' means 'the successor of x', we see that all positive integers (save for the *base* 1) are generated as values of the successor function taking previously generated integers as its argument range. The resulting set – {1,2,3,4, . . . } – contains no surprises; still, the definition encapsulates the infinite set in a way which enables us to see how the set is generated.

So, in general, even such simple recursive definitions as we have looked at are not trivial. They give us explicit procedures of generation that at no place rely on intuition to decide whether a given element is a wff/integer or not. Further, both are finite statements that (explicitly) characterize an infinite set. Suffice it to say that the study of recursion is now an established branch of mathematics and has led to *surprising* results, such as Gödel's incompleteness results and Church's theorem (that first-order logic is undecidable). More centrally for our purposes, via the Church/Turing thesis, computation is just recursion defined over a finite set of primitive functions (the precise functions differ between systems, but they are known to be equivalent). To all intents and purposes, if one wants explicitly to define an infinite set, recursion is required.

It appears, then, that Chomsky's expressed aim in SS is to find a recursive definition of 'grammatical sentence of L', for any given natural language L, where the resulting set will be L. The appearances, however, are misleading.

First off, defining the set of wffs for a formal language such as PC is a fairly straightforward exercise, for what is to count as a wff is a matter of decision or stipulation. The decision, of course, can't be willy-nilly; the notation must be consistent and clear and, hopefully, elegant. However, within such parameters, a formal language can follow any design so long as its purpose is achieved. In the simple case of PC, the purpose of the language is to encode antecedently understood relations of validity that only depend on the truth of whole sentences. Defining 'grammatical sentence of English', say, is quite a different exercise. The notion of 'grammatical' is not antecedently clear; hence it is that a grammar is like a *theory* of a language. Understood as a natural phenomenon, the nature of a language is to be discovered; our construction of the grammar is not guided by a clear conception of what a language is *for*. After all, it is far from obvious that languages are *for* anything at all. Consider, for example, the following cases:

(11) a. The boat the sailor the dog bit built sank.
      b. The horse raced past the barn fell.
      c. No head injury is too trivial to ignore.
      d. Many more people have been to Paris than I have.

The first two appear to be gibberish; the last two appear to be fine. Yet in their different ways, each of these constructions is problematic. It turns out that a and b are perfectly grammatical, c is grammatical but does not have the 'meaning' it appears to have, and d is nonsensical, even though it appears perfectly suited to express a coherent proposition. I shall leave the explanation of these cases hanging; the current point is that we do not find such phenomena in formal languages. A formal language is essentially a notation that ought not to contain surprises; if it does, then we count that against the language and design a more perspicuous notation. In sum, a grammar should be understood as a theory of real phenomena; a definition of a formal language is essentially a stipulation of a system of notation.

Plainly, Chomsky was never confused on this issue. There is, however, a profounder objection to taking the study of a formal language to be analogous to the construction of a grammar.

With a definition of wff for a formal language, we can only be interested in what is usually referred to as *weak generative capacity*: the capacity of a definition/grammar to generate the symbol sequences that are wffs/sentences. That is to say, our interest in the definition of wff for a formal language is wholly exhausted by the definition generating just those symbol strings that are wffs. A given definition might *overshoot*, generating *all* the wffs and more symbol strings besides; it might *undershoot*, generating *only* wffs, but not every wff. Either way, the definition would be inadequate. The definition should generate all and only wffs; otherwise, it is inadequate.

A natural language, on the other hand, is an extant phenomenon that cannot be stipulated into existence by a definition. We thus want a grammar to be *explanatory* of any relevant properties of the language. This gives rise to an interest in *strong generative capacity*: the capacity of a grammar to generate *structural descriptions* for the language in question. A structural description is an analysis of a sentence in terms of phonology, morphology and syntax. For the moment, we can take a structural description to be restricted to an analysis along the lines of ICA, that is , the symbol string is partitioned into phrases under which fall sub-phrases that eventually terminate in category labels for the lexical items that make up the sentence.

Now, these two capacities are clearly not equivalent. Weak generative capacity imposes no restriction on a grammar other than that it generates all and only the relevant strings. Consider, then, the following grammar for a fragment of English.

(G)   Σ: S
      F: S → VP NP
      VP → NP V
      NP → N
      V → {likes, loves, . . . }
      N → {Bill, Mary, . . . }

Here we take 'S' ('Sentence') to be a primitive symbol of the grammar, and '$x \to y$' to mean 'Rewrite x as y', or, conversely, 'y is an x'. The grammar generates all and only the sentences we want; it cannot be faulted on grounds of weak generative capacity. Note, however, that in generating (e.g.) the sentence *Bill likes Mary*, it treats *Bill likes* and *Mary* to be the main constituents. It is well understood that the main constituent break here is between *Bill* and *likes Mary*; that is, in general, we take a transitive verb and its object to function as a unit in relation to the subject of the verb. There are numerous ways of seeing this. For instance, pro-forms, such as pronouns, *did, so* etc. are substitutable for main constituents. Thus, we can have *He likes Mary* and *Sam likes Mary and Bill does (as well)*. So, *Bill* and *likes Mary* appear to be constituents. On the other hand, no substitutions are possible for the sub-string *Bill likes*. We don't find *He Mary* or *Does Mary* (the latter, of course, can be an elliptical question) but here *Mary* would be the subject of the elided verb (e.g. *Bill swims, but does Mary?*) and not the object. It appears, therefore, that while G does serve to generate all the sentences we want, it does so by misrepresenting the structure of the sentences. Hence, the grammar fails the most minimal explanatory desideratum. An adequate grammar should assign a structure to our sentence that will, among other things, explain our intuitions about constituent breaks.

We appear to have landed ourselves in a puzzle. On the one hand, in SS Chomsky introduces grammatical theory as being concerned with *language* – a set of symbol strings – and the task is the construction of a grammar that will generate the strings of the language, that is, a grammar should have adequate weak generative capacity, which is the familiar task of 'syntactic theory' as regards formal languages. On the other hand, we have seen that, just as in any other science, linguistic theory cannot stipulate its domain. In particular, to define a language as a set of symbol strings excludes the most interesting questions that linguistic theory is set up to answer, that is, questions pertaining to our understanding of linguistic structure. Further, the explanatory desiderata linguistic theory and particular grammars that are set up to satisfy are simply not applicable to the theory of formal languages. Otherwise put, the only condition applicable to a grammar or definition of a formal language is that it is adequate as regards weak generative capacity, but such adequacy is so weak that it is even consistent with the grammar misrepresenting the most obvious structural features of a language. In short, weak generative capacity is not an explanatory condition on a grammar.

This puzzle arises through the encapsulated nature of SS. In LSLT, a language is not defined as a set of symbol strings and weak generative capacity is not so much as mentioned. Furthermore, Chomsky has made it clear on a number of occasions that he has never had an interest in weak generative capacity as a constraint on grammars (LSLT, p. 5/53, n. 75; CILT, 53, n. 4; *Aspects of the Theory of Syntax* (ATS), pp. 60–2; RR, pp. 123–7; *The Minimalist Program* (MP), p. 162, n. 1; 'Minimalist inquiries: the framework' (MI), p. 141, n. 21). To conflate the weak capacity with the desired strong capacity would be a 'gross error' ('Formal properties of grammars' (FPG), p. 326). Chomsky's identification of language with a symbol string set in SS is best thought of as simply an analogy. That is, there is a *minimal* demand on a grammar that is shared with a definition of wff for a given formal language. Thus, to treat natural language *as if* it were a formal language is a good way of bringing this demand into relief. The demand at issue is that a grammar be a finite recursive 'device' that can generate an infinity of structures. Thus, the very least we want from a grammar is just the kind of thing we get from the familiar syntactic definitions in logic and mathematics.

Consider, then, some putative grammar G of English. If it can be shown that G is not even *weakly* adequate, that is, it fails to generate structures of English, then G can be immediately dismissed without a consideration of its explanatory resources. In other words, the notion of weak generative capacity can play a useful negative role, but it has no positive import. Likewise, to take a language to be a set of symbol strings is just a reflex of the application of the notion of weak generative capacity. This is just the procedure Chomsky follows, which is signalled in the preface to SS as quoted above: a formal model is pushed so far as to reveal the inadequacy of the underlying conception.

In more recent work, dating back to ATS (Chapter 4), Chomsky has explicitly eschewed the idea that the class of all and only 'well-formed strings' or 'grammatical sentences' has a substantive role to play in linguistic theory, for if language is the object of empirical inquiry, then we cannot decide prior to inquiry just what aspect of our competence will fall under the core generative component of a grammar as opposed to wider processes of thought, including semantics. Analogously, the core grammar might generate 'sentences' that are unusable. In short, the set of structures generated by a grammar will just be whatever the set is; we cannot stipulate it before hand as we can in the study of a formal language (for discussion, see EFI, chapter 2; RR, chapter 4; *Lectures on Government and Binding* (LGB), chapter 1).

4.2 The critical role of weak generative capacity

A minimal requirement of a grammar, then, is that it generate an infinity of structures. Since we ignore the trivial case where the grammar is infinite, the requirement means that our goal is a recursive device. The simplest recursive device is a 'finite state machine' (the notion of a 'machine' here is wholly abstract). For our purposes, the most salient property of such machines is that each state of the machine is determined by its previous state (apart from a designated initial state). Thus, if we think of each word of a given sentence as corresponding to a state of a machine, then the machine will generate the sentence insofar as each word of the sentence is determined by the previous word. This appears to work for the simplest cases of agreement. For example,

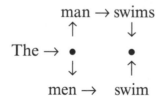

Figure 1 A state diagram for a finite state machine.

With addition of single 'loops' into such a diagram, the machine can generate sentences with, say, an adjective (e.g. *young*, *old* etc.) modifying *man/men* or an adverb (e.g. *happily*, *powerfully* etc.) modifying *swims/swim*.

Evidently, with the addition of loops, such machines are quite powerful. They are, however, restricted to the generation of strings that are *serially dependent*, that is, each word must depend on the previous one. In general, the machine goes into state S_n as a function of state S_{n-1}. In effect, then, the only structure such machines can produce is linear order. Intuitively, such a model might seem to be on the right lines, for *if* sentences are just linearly ordered strings of words, and our linguistic wherewithal is exhausted by our ability to produce and understand linearly ordered utterances, then a finite state machine *should* be an adequate model. However, Chomsky *proved* that the model is inadequate, and so there would appear to be more to language than our production and consumption of linear strings.

To see how Chomsky's argument works, consider two artificial languages:

L_1 = {ab, aabb, aaabbb, ... }, that is, all and only strings consisting of *n* occurrences of a followed by *n* occurrences of b.

L_2 = {aa, bb, abba, baab, bbbb, aabbaa, abbbba, ... }, that is, all and only strings consisting of string *X* followed by *X* in reverse (its mirror image).

The question is, what kind of recursive device can generate the languages? Chomsky *proved* that finite state machines do not generate either L_1 or L_2. This result would be of no interest to linguistics were it not that natural languages such as English exhibit the kind of structure that L_1 or L_2 exhibit in the raw, as it were. A finite state machine, therefore, cannot serve as a grammar for English, for it fails even on weak generative capacity. Here is Chomsky's informal reasoning.

If a finite state machine were to generate L_1 it would have to 'write out' a string of 'a's and then a string of 'b's, as if each 'a' or 'b' depended on the previous symbol. However, such a procedure fails, for which symbol – 'a' or 'b' – occurs in a given ordinal position of a string does not in general depend on the previous symbol but on a corresponding symbol of the first half of the string. Of course, if we just considered a given string, say, 'aaabbb', then there is no reason to think it is structured one way or another. However, the string is a part of a 'language' that follows a strict pattern of dependence, and to figure out the structure its 'sentences' possess we must look to how the language as a whole is generated. The simplest (finite) grammar for L_1 is GL_1:

(GL₁) Σ: Z
       F1: $Z \rightarrow$ ab
       F2: $Z \rightarrow$ aZb

As will be noted, the grammar does not generate strings left to right; rather, the grammar works by *embedding* strings one into another. For example, here is the derivation of aaabbb:

(DL₁) (i) ab   F1
       (ii) aabb   F2
       (iii) aaabbb F3

(Each rule F applies to the previous line to generate the next string.) Letting 'Z' mean 'phrase', we see that 'aaabbb' is derived by two embeddings of simpler sentences (phrases). In effect, then, aaabbb has the following structure:

(12) [₂ a [₂ a [₂ ab] b] b]

Here, the sixth symbol 'b' depends on the first symbol 'a'; the fifth symbol 'b' depends on the second symbol 'a' and so on. In other words, the structure of the sentence is not linear, but hierarchical, and so it falls outside of the scope of a finite state machine.

The language L_2 is generated in much the same way:

(GL2) Σ: Z
       F1: $Z \rightarrow$ aa
       F2: $Z \rightarrow$ bb
       F3: $Z \rightarrow$ aZa
       F4: $Z \rightarrow$ bZb

An example derivation:

(D*) (i) bb   F2
     (ii) abba   F3
     (iii) aabbaa F3

Again, we find hierarchical structure generated by multiple embeddings, where a given symbol does not depend on the previous one. A central feature of the grammars GL_1 and GL_2 is highlighted by Chomsky (SS, p. 31):

> It is important to observe that in describing th[ese] language[s] we have introduced a symbol Z which is not contained in the sentences of th[e] language[s]. This is the essential fact about phrase structure which gives it its 'abstract' character.

Chomsky's point is this. A finite state machine understood as a grammar treats each sentence as a sequence of symbols that has no organization other than the *order* in which the machine receives the symbols as input. It was for this reason, among others, that finite state machines were seriously proposed as models for how humans process language, for linguistic material can only be received in a linear order (one cannot literally hear the words of a sentence simultaneously). However, it doesn't follow that the structure of the language is determined by the exigencies of how it is received by us. Indeed, the cases of L_1 and L_2 suggest otherwise. In their cases, an adequate grammar must generalize over strings such that any generated string can serve as input to the grammar and thus be identifiable as a constituent or phrase of the terminal string (output). Put otherwise, GL_1 and GL_2 analyse a string as not merely being made up of the symbols of the language; the analysis gives a string a structure that cannot be reduced to a linear order. Thus, such grammars are 'abstract' in two related senses. First, they appeal to a variable item (Z) that is not identifiable with any given symbol sequence. Second, such grammars are abstracted from the (linearly ordered) material consumed or produced by users of language.

A methodological point bears emphasis here. Chomsky is not proposing that a language is an abstract entity, as if he has made a philosophical discovery. What is stated to be abstract is the grammar or description of the language. The notion of language is left unanalysed; the proxy of symbol strings indicates no more than that the present discussion is restricted to weak generative capacity. Chomsky's crucial point is that linguistics should be concerned with the abstract structure that might cast theoretical light on the data. This insight is lost if one refuses to look beyond what is visible or concrete in the linguistic material we consume and produce.

As mentioned above, while Chomsky's result is interesting enough from a formal point view, it is of no significance to linguistics in general and, in particular, Chomsky's methodological imperative 'to go abstract' is unsupported, unless natural languages exhibit structures corresponding to the kind of embeddings witnessed in L_1 and L_2. This they do.

In fact, as Chomsky (SS, p. 22, n. 3) notes, even simple languages such as PC are not generatable by finite state machines. This is essentially due to the hierarchical structure of PC, where formulae can be embedded into formulae of the same type to produce the kind of paired bracketing found in PC. For example, if we have '(A → B)' as a formula, we also have '((A → B) → (A → B))' (the latter is a consequence of the former). Translated into English,

(13) If, if A, then B, then, if A, then B.

The embedding of 'if . . ., then . . .' gives rise to a dependency of the second 'then' on the first 'if', and the first 'then on the second 'if'. Iterated embeddings would produce a series of nested dependence relations corresponding to the type of bracketing found in (12). Obviously, replacing the variables of (13) with suitable declarative sentences of English would result in a perfectly grammatical sentence of English. Just so for any further 'if . . . then . . .'. For sure, such sentences are not 'the type of things we utter', but, as hopefully already established, such a criterion is vacuous for what is to count as being of theoretical interest. Perhaps more graphically, we find the same kind of structure in sentences such as (14):

(14) a. Sailors sailors sailors fight fight fight.
      b. The boat the sailor the dog bit built sank.

((14)b is (12)a repeated for convenience.) (14)a looks like a 'mirror' sentence, but the far more important point is that both sentences have the structure of (12)a. Take (14)a. The first occurrence of *fight* is paired (in agreement) with the third *sailors*. This pair forms a relative clause embedded within the clause beginning with the second *sailors*, which is paired with the second occurrence of *fight*; in turn, this pairing is a relative clause modifying the first 'sailors', which is paired with the third occurrence of 'fight'. Thus,

(15) Sailors [(that) sailors [(that) sailors fight] fight] fight.

So, on the basis of the most minimal demand we can place on a grammar – that it caters for each sentence of the language – we can rule out finite state machines as the grammatical recursive devices for natural languages. We must look to a grammar that is (at least) as powerful as the kind to which GL_1 and GL_2 belong, viz., the class of *phrase structure grammars*. As we shall see, however, even these grammars are inadequate.

CHAPTER 3

TRANSFORMATIONS

[S]implicity is part of what I mean by beauty, but it is a simplicity of ideas, not simplicity of the mechanical sort that can be measured by counting equations or symbols.

Weinberg *(1993, p. 134)*

1 INTRODUCTION

In the previous chapter, we saw that the notion of weak generative capacity was of interest to Chomsky merely as a means to rule out certain simple grammatical models. Insofar as weak generative capacity is restricted to string generation, it is of no inherent interest. Still, employment of the notion shows us that we minimally require a phrase structure grammar (PSG). We also saw that what was crucial for Chomsky is that a grammar does some explanatory work. In this chapter we shall see how this demand led to the idea of a transformational grammar.

2 PHRASE STRUCTURE

For our purposes, a PSG is simply a rule system whose vocabulary includes variable category symbols, that is, symbols that may be rewritten as such symbols or items of the language itself. Such a grammar is essentially abstract in the sense that it includes symbols that do not feature in the language. Here is a toy example.

(PSG)
(i) S → NP+VP

(ii) NP → DET+N
(iii) VP → V+NP
(iv) DET → the
(v) N→ boy, girl
(vi) V→ loves

Given a natural interpretation of the symbols, (i) tells us that a noun phrase (NP) followed by a verb phrase (VP) *is a* sentence (S); (ii) tells us that a determiner (DET) followed by a noun (N) *is a* NP and so on. Each rule provides a categorical specification for the kind of structure generated by the rule. Obviously, this categorical information is not definitional. The grammar is designed to account for a particular language; it is the job of general linguistic theory to give a general account of the resources available to any given grammar. The information (PSG) contains can be encapsulated in the two structural descriptions (or phrase markers) it generates:

(1)   a. $[_S [_{NP} [_{DET}$ The$] [_N$ boy$]] [_{VP} [_V$ loves$] [_{NP} [_{DET}$ the$] [_N$ girl$]]]]$

      b. $[_S [_{NP} [_{DET}$ The$] [_N$ girl$]] [_{VP} [_V$ loves$] [_{NP} [_{DET}$ the$] [_N$ boy$]]]]$

There are a range of technical issues pertaining to the derivations phrase structure grammars admit and how best to formalize them in order to eliminate redundancy. For our purposes, such technicalities may be elided.

Is a PSG adequate as a theory of the structure of a natural language? The minimal way of construing this question is to ask whether such a grammar for a given language L can generate each string of L. Paul Postal (1964) argued that PSGs cannot even meet this minimal demand for certain native-American languages (e.g. Mohawk). A far more important consideration for Chomsky, however, was a PSG's explanatory worth rather than its mere weak generative capacity. That is, even though a PSG might fail for one or another language as regards weak generative capacity, *if* a PSG is weakly adequate for L, the question remains whether it explains all the relevant phenomena of L? This question comes in two parts:

(i) Can a PSG express the generalizations that hold over L?
(ii) Can a PSG express the 'felt relations' that hold within and between sentences of L?

Chomsky's answer to both of these questions is 'No'.

2.1 The auxiliary system of English

A focus of both LSLT and SS is the morphology of English auxiliaries. Auxiliaries are verb-like elements that occur along with verbs and carry tense and agreement morphology. The following sentences provide an example of the system.

(2)   a. Bill sings
     b. Bill may sing
     c. Bill has sung
     d. Bill is singing
     e. Bill may have sung
     f. Bill may be singing
     g. Bill has been singing
     h. Bill may have been singing

Now, these eight forms do not in themselves pose a problem for PSG; for instance, we could postulate the following rules, where 'T' is tense (past and present), 'M' is modality (*can, may, will* and the past forms), 'HAVE' is perfect (again, including its various forms), and 'BE' is the copula (again, including its various forms):

(3)   a. AUX → T
     b. AUX → T M
     c. AUX → T HAVE
     d. AUX → T BE
     e. AUX → T M HAVE
     f. AUX → T M BE
     g. AUX → T HAVE BE
     h. AUX → T M HAVE BE

Now, for any range of phenomena whatsoever, we want a theory to explain it, not merely be consistent with it. This means that we want the theory to express a generalization that covers the individual phenomena. In the present case, while each of the rules suffices to derive the corresponding forms exemplified in (2), various generalizations are missed. So, while a PSG supplemented with the rules in (3) might be powerful enough to generate all strings we want, it remains inadequate, for striking generalizations are missed. A first generalization pertains to the precedence relation that auxiliaries have to one other in a sentence.

(AUX PRED) T precedes any other AUX; M precedes any other AUX apart from T; HAVE precedes any other AUX apart from T and M; BE precedes any other AUX apart from T, M and HAVE. (T < M < HAVE < BE.)

From (AUX PRED), we can predict just the forms given in (2). For example, consider (4):

(4) a. *Bill may be have sung
     b. *Bill has might be singing

In (4)a, BE occurs before HAVE, which contravenes the third and fourth clauses of the generalization. In (4)b, HAVE occurs before M, which contravenes the second and third clauses of the generalization. From (AUX PRED), we thus correctly predict that the strings in (4) are not sentences of English, while all those in (2) are, just so for an indefinite number of other cases. Clearly, our grammar shouldn't miss this generalization. Chomsky proposed the following rule to capture it.

(AUX) AUX → T (M)(HAVE)(BE)

This rule is an encapsulation of the information given in (3)a–h. The brackets mark the flanked material as optional in a sentence, and the precedence of the brackets marks the order in which the flanked items can occur.

The new rule (AUX) complicates without departing from a PSG approach. If we look closer at the examples in (2), however, we find another generalization that proves much harder to capture.

(AUX MORPH) HAVE and BE affect the morphology of the following verb-like item.

As is witnessed in (2), if HAVE occurs in a sentence, then the next auxiliary or verb has perfect morphology (we can mark this as -*en*), and if BE occurs in a sentence, then the next auxiliary or verb has progressive morphology (-*ing*). Slightly modifying (AUX), we now have

(AUX M) AUX → T (M)(HAVE-*en*)(BE-*ing*)

(5) Bill may have be(en) sleep(ing)

This rule captures the fact that HAVE and BE introduce particular morphological forms. Unfortunately, the rule doesn't capture the (AUX MORPH) generalization. The generalization tells us that there are *cross-serial dependencies* as exhibited in (5). Phrase structure grammars, as we saw in Chapter 2, are very good at capturing nested dependencies, but they cannot capture crossing dependencies. In essence, nesting is simply a flanking operation, and so we can specify a variable such that any value of that variable can be flanked to produce another value that can in turn be flanked. In general, with crossing dependence, no such approach is available, for the dependencies are neither uniform nor independent of each other. If we attempted to derive (5) via (AUX MORPH), the best we could produce would be

(6)   Bill T may have-en be-ing sleep,

for we have no PSG rule that allows us to generate the dependent forms *been* and *sleeping*.

2.2   Felt relations

If we are to construe a grammar for *L* as being theory-like, then we clearly want it to capture generalizations like those that characterize the English auxiliary system. It is not enough for a grammar merely to produce a structural description for each sentence. From Chomsky's perspective, then, PSGs are inadequate. Casting our net wider, we find that there are many structural relations that appear to be unexpressed by PSGs. Following Chomsky (LSLT, chapter 9, SS, chapters 5, 8), I shall refer to these relations as 'felt relations'. The thought here is that we intuitively recognize such relations in how we interpret the sentences that exhibit them.

2.2.1   *PSG structures are invariant over structural differences of interpretation*
There are innumerable cases where we have two or more sentences that share the same PSG structure but whose elements stand in different structural relations to one another. Consider (7):

(7)   a. This picture was painted by a real artist
      b. This picture was painted by a new technique

The two sentences share the same structure from a PSG perspective, but they differ markedly in how we interpret the elements in relation to one another. In (7)a, *a real artist* is the agent of *paint*; (7)b does not admit such an interpretation – *a new technique* informs us *how* the picture was painted, not *who* painted it.

    (8)   a. A real artist painted this picture
            b. *A new technique painted this picture

Consider (9):

    (9)   a. Bill is easy to please
            b. Bill is eager to please

Again, the PSG structures are the same, but the sentences differ in respect of who is being pleased. In (9)a, Bill is being pleased; in (9)b, someone or other is being pleased. The difference is clear when we paraphrase the pair:

    (10)   a. It is easy to please Bill
            b. It is eager to please Bill

Note that (10)b is only well-formed if *it* is read as referring to a dog, say; if *it* is pleonastic, as in (10)a, then the structure is incoherent.

Prima facie, such structural relations should be captured by a grammar, but they can't be captured by a PSG.

2.2.2 *Ambiguity*

Many sentences with the same PSG structure admit a number of structural interpretations. Consider the following cases:

    (11)   a. The shooting of the soldiers scared the tourists
            b. Bill found the boy studying in the library
            c. Bill knows how good meat tastes

These are examples that Chomsky offered in the 1950s. Many forms of ambiguity solely depend on the properties of words, but many others do not. Again, insofar as ambiguity depends on structure, we should expect a grammar to account for it. However, a PSG appears to deliver just one structure per sentence.

University of Chester, Seaborne Library

Title: The articulate mammal : an introduction to psycholinguistics / Jean Aitchison, with a foreword by th
ID: 36108736
Due: 05-05-12

Title: The psychology of language : from data to theory / Trevor A. Harley.
ID: 36027098
Due: 05-05-12

Title: The language instinct: the new science of language and mind / Steven Pinker
ID: 36074556
Due: 05-05-12

Title: The "language instinct" debate / Geoffrey Sampson with a foreword by Paul M. Postal.
ID: 36076242
Due: 05-05-12

Title: Chomsky : a guide for the perplexed / John Collins
ID: 36074830
Due: 05-05-12

Total items: 5
14/04/2012 14:46

Thank you for using Self Check

2.2.3 Sentence types and relations

Familiarly, there are many different types of sentence – active, passive, declarative, interrogative, imperative – with each broad class admitting many structurally distinct instances. We should like to know what the relations are between these types. For example, we clearly feel that there is an intimate relation between a declarative and an interrogative. Consider the following cases:

(12) a. Bill sings
      b. Does Bill sing?
      c. Is it Bill who sings?
      d. Bill, is it, who sings?
      e. Bill sings, does he?
      f. Is it singing that Bill does?
      g. Bill SINGS? (capitals mark heavy stress)

Sentences (12)b–g are all different ways of questioning (12)a, but we intuitively feel that some are more distant from the declarative than others. Our intuitions on such cases are very robust and are not straightforwardly a matter of meaning; after all, questions are not statements and even active/passive pairs often differ in their possible interpretations. Again, a PSG elides such relations. It is not that we could not 'work out' the relation between various forms of interrogatives and their corresponding declaratives; the point, rather, is that we want a grammar, theory-like, explicitly to capture such relations.

2.2.4 Primitiveness

Chomsky suggests that we feel that certain forms are more primitive or basic than others. In particular, active monoclausal declaratives appear to be the basic structures from which other more complex structures are built. There is something surely correct about this thought; for example, our understanding of a question appears to depend on our understanding of potential declarative answers to it, whereas no such dependence holds in the other direction. That said, the intuition is not as clear a phenomenon as the cases detailed above. Whatever the standing of the intuition, a uniform PSG for a language fails to capture it, for it will treat all sentences equally. Again, it is not that a PSG is inconsistent with the intuition; rather, it simply doesn't explicitly encode it.

The general problem that all these cases reflect is that a PSG for a given language fails both to relate sentences one to another and to reveal unapparent structural relations that hold between a sentence's words. Just intuitively, then, it would appear that a form of grammar is required that relates sentences to each other in ways that go beyond the structure they appear to possess. In other words, the two kinds of failure are linked. A PSG cannot relate sentences to each other in a revealing way, because it is restricted to recording their surface constituency. Chomsky's great innovation was to develop a form grammar that would meet these explanatory demands as well as capture the kind of generalizations that characterize the English auxiliary system.

3 TRANSFORMATIONS: A MODEL OF A GRAMMAR

Chomsky (LSLT and SS) borrowed the expression 'transformation' from the work of Zelig Harris, who Chomsky had been working with from the late 1940s. Chomsky's notion, however, is quite distinct. For Harris, a transformation was an equivalence relation that held between strings of a language. For example, active sentences are equivalent to (transformations of) passives, because for any given active string, we can find a corresponding passive that contains the same morphemes save for those dependent on form. Chomsky's notion departs from this conception in a number of ways.

First, Harris's transformations were aids to taxonomy, that is, transformations were the means to the end of classifying the various constructions of a language. Harris was perfectly explicit in his regard; he had no explanatory ambitions and wholly shunned the idea of a general linguistic theory. On the other hand, Chomsky's goal was explanatory. A grammar was to be a theory that explained the various structural phenomena of a language, such as detailed in the previous section. In a sense, we might say that Harris's transformations, insofar as they held of a language, were simply data; Chomsky's transformations had the job of explaining the data.

Second, Chomsky's notion of a transformation was a derivational rule and not an equivalence relation. This crucial difference will be explained shortly; *pro tem*, a transformation in this sense is a computation over structures, not a mere recording of the structures.

Third, Chomsky's transformations apply to phrase markers or structural descriptions of sentences, not strings. Again, this means that transformations are not taxonomic tools; they promise to relate sentences one to another in terms of their underlying structure, not their surface morphological pattern within a language.

3.1 The design of a transformational grammar

Chomsky's LSLT sets out in mathematical detail a transformational analysis of a part of English. For our purposes, we may simply highlight the principal architectural features. Ignoring the contribution of phonology, a transformational grammar (TG) consists of two parts, the *base* component and the *transformational* component. The base consists of a (context-free) PSG that is restricted to providing structural descriptions (phrase markers) for monoclausal active declaratives. In a sense, therefore, the idea is that a PSG is adequate for at least a part of the language. This is not quite correct because of the problematic AUX rule; we shall return to this point below.

The transformational component consists of a set of rules that map the base phrase markers onto other phrase markers, which in turn can be mapped to further phrase markers by the rules. In essence, the rules perform three kinds of operations: deletion, substitution and adjunction (adding new material). Each rule is defined by two conditions: a *structural analysis* (SA), which defines the kind of structure to which the rule has application, and a *structural change* (SC), which defines how the rule alters the structure as defined in the analysis. The rules come in two broad categories. *Singular* rules apply to a single phrase marker and they can be *optional* or *obligatory*. An optional rule is one that does not apply in every derivation of a phrase marker for a sentence of the language. For example, let Tp be a transformational rule that transforms an active into a passive. Clearly, the rule only optionally applies because not every English sentence is a passive, but the rule remains a necessary part of the grammar insofar as there are passive constructions. An obligatory rule is one that applies in every derivation (an example will be provided shortly). The other kind of rule is *generalized*. A generalized rule (always optional) applies to two or more phrase markers, for example, a rule that coordinates two phrase markers by the inclusion of 'and'.

From the above sketch, we can define the *kernel* of a language as the sentences whose phrase markers are generated by the base and the application of obligatory transformations to such phrase markers.

The kernel will thus consist of every monoclausal active declarative. It is crucial to note that the transformational rules apply to the base phrase markers and not to the kernel sentences.

3.2 A transformational solution to the AUX problem

We saw above that the auxiliary system of English looks to be anomalous from the perspective of a PSG. In particular, if a PSG is to capture the auxiliary precedence generalization, then we require the inclusion of the AUX rule, but then we have no account of the cross-serial dependence of the morphology of HAVE and BE. Transformations offer a solution to this quandary.

Following Chomsky's relatively informal presentation in SS, let us introduce two obligatory singular transformations:

T15: *The Number Transformation*
SA: X – T – Y
SC: T $\rightarrow$ -*s* in the context NP$_{sing}$
$\emptyset$ in other contexts
past in any context
T20: *The Auxiliary Transformation* ('Affix Hopping')
SA: X – Af – v –Y (where '*Af*' is T affix or -*en* or -*ing*; and '*v*' is a verb-like thing, either M, V, HAVE, or BE)
SC: $X_1 - X_2 - X_3 - X_4 \rightarrow X_1 - X_3 - X_2 \# - X_4$ (where '#' marks a word boundary, that is, '$X_3 - X_2$' form a single word)

('X' and 'Y' specify any other material, potentially zero.) Both transformations are very simple in their effects. The SA of T15 specifies the context of a (base) phrase marker with tense T as obligatorily provided by AUX as part of the base. The structural change T15 brings about is simply the insertion of a morpheme as the terminal node of T within the phrase marker ('$\emptyset$' marks the zero-morpheme). Here is a simple example:

(13) a. [$_S$ [$_{NPsing}$ Bill] [$_{VP}$ [$_V$ [$_{AUX}$ T] [$_V$ walk]]]]

   b. [$_S$ [$_{NPsing}$ Bill] [$_{VP}$ [$_V$ [$_{AUX}$ [$_T$ -*s*]] [$_V$ walk]]]]

(13)a satisfies the SA of T15, and so T15 has application. Applied, (13)b results, which merely amounts to the inclusion of the morpheme -*s*. Now note that (13)b satisfies the SA of T20: -*s* is an *Af* and *walk* is a *v*. The application of T20 results in

(14)   [$_S$ [$_{NPsing}$ Bill] [$_{VP}$ [$_V$ [$_{AUX}$ T] [$_V$ [$_V$ walk] [-s #]]]].

T20 allows for the stranded affix to hop over the verb *walk* such that '[$_V$ [$_V$ walk] [-s #]]' becomes a word. We can thus see how a cycle of applications of T20 solves the cross-serial problem of AUX: T20 allows for a series of hops, whereby, in turn, each stranded affix is attached to the next verb-like thing. This gives us the (simplified) phrase marker (15):

(15)   Bill [$_{AUX}$ [$_T$] [$_M$ may-∅#] [$_{HAVE}$ have] [$_{BE}$ be-en#]] swim-ing#,

where (i) the zero-morpheme of T is introduced by T15; (ii) via T20, the morpheme hops onto the modal; (iii) again via T20, -*en* hops onto *be*; and (iv) via a third application of T20, -*ing* hops onto *swim*.

It is worth noting that T15 is a rewrite rule, and not really a transformation. The difference, however, is that the SC of T15 is context sensitive; for this reason, Chomsky placed it in the transformational component, restricting the base to context-free rules. T20, on the other hand, is genuinely distinct from the PSG rules. A PSG rule just allows for the rewriting of symbols, and a PSG derivation is complete once all variable symbols are rewritten such that a (terminal) line of the derivation contains only symbols of the language itself. A consequence is that there is no PSG route around the AUX problem, for the elements of AUX don't require rewriting – they need to *move*. T20 serves this end. A transformation targets a completed structure and, in the present case, moves elements within it. Conceptually, this is very striking. If the job of a grammar were merely to describe the well-formed structures of a language in some compendious manner, then transformations would appear to be a redundant extravagance. Chomsky, however, has always seen a grammar's purpose as being explanatory. From this optic, there can be no essential complaint against transformations. The language itself, as it were, appears as the data that the grammar explains via the derivation of structures that describe each sentence. Moreover, since transformations apply to phrase structure and the structure of every sentence will be in part transformational (given obligatoriness), each sentence will not have a single structure but a base and a transformational structure. For example, the sentence *Bill walks* will be associated with three structures: (13)a–b and (14). The linkage of these three structures is a *T-marker*.

$$(\text{TM}) \ \text{Base} \rightarrow S_1$$
$$\uparrow$$
$$T15 \rightarrow S_2$$
$$\uparrow$$
$$T20 \rightarrow S_3$$

The T-marker for *Bill may have been swimming* will constitute the linkage of five structures: the base structure, the result of an application of T15 and three results of T20. We can thus see each sentence as associated with a computational procedure that produces the final morphological form. Again, from a descriptive perspective, this approach is widely extravagant. From an explanatory perspective, precisely such structure is required to capture the generalizations that hold for the language. In this sense, the grammar *explains* the given form by explicitly stating a range of generalizations from which each given form that is subsumable under the generalizations can be transformationally derived. We can now see how the new transformational technology explains the range of data that fall outside the scope of PSG. Again, note that the issue here is not whether a PSG can provide structures for the relevant sentences; the crucial point is that new resources are required to explain the phenomena.

3.3 Transformational explanations

The first range of phenomena considered consisted of sentences that look to have the same structure even though the interpretation of the sentences suggests that the elements stand in distinct structural relations. Consider the following case ((7)a,b above):

(16)   a. This picture was painted by a real artist
       b. This picture was painted by a new technique

(16)a is a passive construction, with *a real artist* being the agent of *paint*. In (16)b the prepositional argument – *a new technique* – is not the agent of *paint*. Thus, we want to explain how it is that two structures look the same yet have structurally distinct interpretations.

First let us introduce the passive transformation:

T12: *Passive* (optional)
SA: NP – AUX – V – NP
SC: $X_1 - X_2 - X_3 - X_4 \rightarrow X_4 - X_2 + be + en - X_3 - by + X_1$

Now consider the two base structures:

(17) a. $[_S [_{NP}$ A real artist$][_{VP} [_{AUX}$ past$] [_V$ paint$][_{NP}$ the picture$]]]$
    b. $[_S [_{NP}$ It$][_{VP} [_{AUX}$ past$] [_V$ paint$][_{NP}$ the picture$]]]$

(The *it* of (17)b is a dummy expression that will have no morphological reading.) Applying T15 to (17)a, and then T12 to the result, produces (16)a, where 'AUX + *be* + *en*' is morphologically rendered as *was*. The account of (16)b is only slightly trickier. Following the same procedure on (17)b, we arrive at the passive structure

(18) The picture was painted by it.

Applying a deletion or elliptical transformation, we simply drop the prepositional phrase, *by it*. This gives us a perfectly acceptable agent deleted passive. However, now we can apply a further transformation that adds a manner adverbial – *by a new technique*. These two further transformations yield (16)b.

Thus, while from the PSG optic (16)a and b are structurally equivalent, from the transformational perspective of their respective T-markers, the structures are very different. The T-markers, which record the derivational history of the structures, thus explain how it is that two structures that look exactly alike can have quite distinct structural interpretations. Similar reasoning applies to many other kinds of example.

The second range of phenomena considered above was ambiguous structures. There are, of course, many kinds of ambiguity. Chomsky's claim was not that every kind can be explained by transformations. His point was merely that where ambiguity is clearly structural, a grammar should be able to explain it. The problem for PSGs is that they appear constitutively incapable of doing so.

Consider the following, repeated from above:

(19)   The shooting of the soldiers scared the tourists

The ambiguity of (19) depends on how we read the NP *the soldiers* in relation to the verb *shoot*: are the soldiers shooting or are they being shot? The details of the solution Chomsky (LSLT, pp. 467–70) offered in this case are somewhat complicated. A sketch will suffice for our purposes.

Let us hypothesize that the base doesn't contain any structure of the form 'NP – V + *ing* – of – NP', but that it does contain structures of the form 'NP – V – N' and 'NP – V', corresponding to the transitive and intransitive readings of the verb *shoot*. Now let there be a transformation, $T_{ing\text{-}of}$, that converts any V into '*ing* – V + of'. Let there be two further transformations, T_{sub} and T_{ob}. T_{sub} applies to any verb form, transitive or intransitive, and produces, '*ing* – V – of – NP_{sub}'. T_{ob} applies only to transitive verb forms and produces '*ing* – V – of – NP_{ob}'. Thus, we can see how (19) is ambiguous at the transformational level: the one string can be derived via two distinct transformations to give the two respective readings, where the soldiers are either shooting or being shot. In other words, the ambiguity of (19) is explained by its association with two distinct T-markers. Equally, we can see how substituting *the barking of the dogs* for the subject NP in (19) is not ambiguous, for there is no base structure where *the dogs* is the object of *bark*, and so T_{ob} can't apply, that is, there is only one derivation, via T_{sub}, that can produce the string; the string has just one T-marker, not two.

The third class of phenomena we considered above is the range of sentence types there are. Intuitively, they bear structural relations to each other: a passive is related to an active, a question is related to a declarative etc. Again, the problem for a PSG approach is not that it cannot furnish a phrase marker for each instance of a sentence type, but that it fails to make explicit the relations that hold between them. We have perhaps already seen enough as to how a TG satisfies this desideratum. For example, the passive transformation relates an active to a passive in that the base form, after obligatory transformations, is the phrase marker for an active. The passive transformation targets the phrase marker and produces a marker for a passive.

Consequently, the T-marker for a passive explicitly records the relation between the active and the passive as intuitively felt at the surface. This relation holds generally. A further relation worth pausing over is that between declarative and interrogative.

Consider polar interrogatives (ones that may be coherently answered with a 'Yes' or a 'No'):

(20) a. Bill is swimming
      b. Is Bill swimming?
      c. Bill should swim
      d. Should Bill swim?
      e. Bill might have been swimming
      f. Might Bill have been swimming?

The generalization that holds here is easy to see: a polar interrogative relates to a declarative by the movement of AUX (in particular, the element that carries tense, witness e–f) over the subject NP. A transformation easily captures this relation:

T18: Tq Transformation (optional)
SA: NP – T – V . . . (T + M – . . .)(T + HAVE – . . .)(T + BE – . . .)
SC: $X_1 - X_2 - X_3 \rightarrow X_2 - X_1 - X_3$

T18 simply moves the tense carrying AUX element, as defined in the SA, over the subject. The T-markers for b., d. and f. will record this movement and so explicitly relate the pairs of phrase markers as declarative-interrogative. However, now consider the following type of case:

(21) a. Bill swims
      b. Does Bill swim?

Here it looks as if nothing has moved, but this is still a polar interrogative. On closer examination, however, we can observe that there is a difference in verb form: in a, *swim* is inflected, in b, it is not. We already have nearly all the resources to explain this apparent anomaly.

(21) a is formed from the base structure (22) a and the application of obligatory T20 (discussed above) that drops the affix T –*s* onto the verb:

(22) a. Bill – -*s* – swim
      b. Bill – T – swim +-*s*#

Alternatively, optional T18 can apply to (22)a., which moves the affix over the subject. However, this results in a deviant structure:

(23) -*s* – Bill – T – swim

Hence, we need another transformation:

T21: *do* Transformation ('do support')(obligatory)
SA: # – *Af*
SC: $X_1 - X_2 \rightarrow X_1 - do + X_2$

T21 obligatorily applies where there is a stranded affix, as in (23). All the rule does is support the affix with a dummy verb *do* (in the present case, X_1 is null). If T21 seems somewhat *ad hoc*, note that it can apply in other cases, such as negation. Let there be an optional negation transformation that adds -*n't* to T.

(24) a. Bill – -*s* – swim
      b. Bill – -*s* + n't – swim

Note that here the negation transformation applies before T20 (affix hopping), and T20 thus cannot apply to the phrase marker of (24)a., for it fails to have the right SA, that is, -*n't* intervenes between the *Af* and *v*. Thus, T21 obligatorily applies and produces the phrase marker for

(25) Bill doesn't swim

Here we have a nice simple example of how transformations work together such that the T-markers for the respective strings explicitly exhibit their derivational histories and so encode the systematic relations that are only intuitively felt upon reflection on the strings alone. Similar explanations are straightforwardly available for much more complex examples, such as passive negative questions – *Wasn't the car washed?* Here, the number transformation obligatorily applies to the base structure; the negation transformation introduces –*n't*; the passive transformation swaps subject and object over, with the subject now being the argument of *by*; agent deletion then applies, eliminating the prepositional phrase, and, finally, the question transformation applies, moving the tense carrying element over the passive subject.

The final phenomenon we considered was the intuition that certain structures are more primitive than others. The status of this intuition is certainly less solid than the more empirically grounded phenomena we have just been discussing. If, for instance, a grammar could account for the kinds of phenomena we have so far analysed and any other relevant data as well, but failed to classify structures as more or less primitive, we should hardly think it a failure. That said, the intuition is not groundless; it enshrines what appears to be an *asymmetric dependence* between our understandings of structure types. For example, our understanding of a polar interrogative seems to depend upon our understanding of the associated declarative, but not *vice versa*. To understand a question is to understand what would be a coherent answer to it, which in this case is simply the corresponding declarative or its negation. However, it is very odd to think that an understanding of a declarative depends upon our understanding a querying of it. Similarly, an active structure appears more basic than a passive, an affirmative than a negation, a simple sentence than a conjunction that features it, a simple declarative than the corresponding cleft constructions etc. Of course, any competent speaker is proficient with all these types; the issue is about dependence, not whether all the structures exist in the world's languages, still less whether one could imagine the roles reversed. This last elucidation is crucial. The present issue is not a conceptual concern about any *possible* language but a straightforward empirical intuition about our understanding of our language. With enough imagination, we could probably understand the roles to be reversed, but we can nigh-on imagine anything. Our concern is with the empirical facts of language and not the logical scope of our concept of language. It might well be that Martian is different, but that is of no immediate interest.

One way of grounding the intuition of asymmetric dependence is to reflect that the less basic forms involve the *addition* of various morphological items: *do*, affixes, prepositional phrases, *wh*-adjuncts etc. (the morphological technology differs across languages, but the same general relation appears to hold). Thus, it seems that we can just *see* that the more basic form is contained in the complex form in a way that simply doesn't hold in reverse. It should be obvious by now how the transformational approach constitutively cleaves to this dependence and so explains the general intuition. On the model so far presented, monoclausal active declarative strings are generated by the base after all obligatory transformations have been applied that can apply. Thus, as *per* intuition, these are the most basic sentences. Questions, negations, passives etc. are generated via non-obligatory transformations, with the strings here generated being the less basic sentences that depend on the base structures for their understanding. A given T-marker for sentence *S*, therefore, will record what structures are more basic than *S*, insofar as the marker encodes structures for strings more basic than *S*. This explanatory capacity of the transformational component is strictly a bonus. Transformations are explanatory in many other ways and they are not designed only to generate the 'less basic strings'. Indeed, there is nothing the least bit illegitimate with the inclusion, say, of the passive structure in the base from which the active would be derived. In fact, however, the derivation would be much more complex, as the passive transformation must apply after other transformations, such as number and affix hopping. We would thus require these transformations also to be in the base, which would complicate derivations elsewhere. Speculatively, then, we might say that the more economical the TG we devise, the more we capture the natural intuition that certain structures are more basic than others. This is some bonus and points ahead, albeit obliquely, to some of the most recent thinking on language design.

4 ARCHITECTURAL ISSUES

As explained in the previous chapter, Chomsky's new conception of grammar did not initially meet with success. LSLT remained unpublished and the svelte SS was easily misunderstood as a continuation of, rather than a break from, the then prevailing theories. Lees's highly favourable and insightful review of SS helped to 'spread the word', and by the early 1960s generative grammar was a distinctive approach in the field that was gaining much ground, especially among young linguists. The new ideas, however, were not to enjoy their full impact on wider thought about language and mind until Chomsky explicitly construed generative grammar to be a contribution to psychology. We shall turn to these developments in Chapter 4. Before we leave behind LSLT and SS a number of issues require clarification that will serve us later. The following remarks are divided for ease of reference.

4.1 Recursion

A minimal requirement on a grammar is that it be recursive, for recursion is the only known mechanism, randomness apart, which can generate infinite variety from finite resources. Every natural language appears to make infinite use of finite means, so any adequate grammar must be recursive. On Chomsky's early conception of a generative grammar, the transformational component is where recursion happens; the PSG base is non-recursive. The base thus generates finitely many monoclausal active declarative structures. Generalized transformations, in concert with singular transformations, iteratively combine these structures to generate increasingly complex structures.

There was nothing essential about this partition of responsibility. None of the later models exhibits it. The model of *Aspects* (1965) does without generalized transformations in favour of a recursive base, but singular transformations are retained. In more recent models up to the present, there is not a base/transformation distinction at all; there is a single operation that puts structures together, which, curiously, is a hark back to generalized transformations, although here there are no SA constraints provided by the base (see Chapter 8). The general moral is that recursion needs to be in the picture, but that bare desideratum does not dictate just how it should be accommodated.

4.2 Simplicity and economy

From his earliest work on, Chomsky has been keen to stress how considerations of simplicity and economy act as a desiderata on our choice of grammar. As Chomsky (*Morphophonemics of Modern Hebrew* (MMH), p. 1, n. 1) notes, 'such considerations are in general not trivial or "merely esthetic" . . . the motives behind the demand for economy are in many ways the same as those behind the demand that there be a system at all'. In other words, insofar as theoretical inquiry seeks an underlying systematicity behind observed phenomena, it will be guided by the demand to find economy and simplicity in the underlying system. Of course, this is a methodological presumption; language or the universe in general might be a mess. Yet, as Kant long ago observed, it appears to be regulative of any inquiry that there be an elegant economy to be discovered, for otherwise, there would be no motive to inquiry in the first place rather than rest content with a mere catalogue of the phenomena. These considerations will loom large once we turn to recent developments in generative grammar.

The 'simplicity' Chomsky appealed to in his work was 'shortness of derivation' and 'compactness of definition/rule' (MMH, p. 6; LSLT, chapter 4). These ideas serve to select between two or more grammars that adequately assign phrase markers to the sentences of a given language. We saw an example of this with the AUX rule. A grammar for English could feature eight rules for auxiliary morphology. Guided by simplicity, however, we saw how to reduce the eight rules to one. In so doing we capture the precedence generalization. In this light we can give some substance to Chomsky's thought that simplicity is not 'merely esthetic [*sic*]'.

Although it is particular grammars that we want to be simple, simplicity itself, understood as described above, is a condition imposed by general linguistic theory. That is, the general theory should define the basic resources available to any grammar with the greatest simplicity; particular grammars simply inherit the simplicity. It is by way of a discovery that we find that particular grammars, constrained by general linguistic theory, are not just adequate but also explanatorily revelatory of given languages.

4.3 The lexicon

So far we have been concerned with syntax – the rules that structure words into phrases, clauses and sentences. But what of the words themselves? Chomsky adopts the traditional model from Bloomfield that treats words – the lexicon – as idiosyncrasies, that is, what is propriety to a word is what is not generalizable in terms of some productive rule. Hence, various transformations – number, passive, auxiliary etc. – introduce morphemes that are broadly predictable. How a given word is pronounced when in combination with other words in a sentence is the business of a morphonemic component that takes as its input the terminal phrase markers of the T-markers. In other words, morphonemics does not care about derivational history, which is just as one would expect.

Two features of the relation of the lexicon to the grammar bear emphasis. First, as might have been noted, the lexicon is part of the base component, with lexical items being introduced into derivations via rewrite rules just like non-terminal symbols, such as 'NP' or 'V'. In one respect this is curious, for we naturally think of the lexicon as being separate from our capacity to generate sentences. Our lexical competence, for instance, is somewhat in flux, as we gain new words and perhaps forget about old words we rarely use, but our syntactic competence appears stable, at least after maturity is reached. Second and correlatively, words or morphemes enter the derivation dynamically, that is, there is no initial assemblage of the morphemes that are to comprise a sentence, with the transformational component merely shifting them around. This minimally follows from the first point inasmuch as words are part of the computational operation of the base. Further, transformations introduce morphemes and words, for example, generalized transformations introduce adverbs such as *so* and co-ordinate words such as *and* and *or*; the number transformation introduces tense morphemes, and the passive transformation introduces passive morphemes and the preposition *by*. These two properties of the early model, however, are separable.

It is indeed odd for the lexicon to be part of the grammar for the reason given and it was quickly separated and has remained evermore distinct from the grammar. However, it does not follow that the computation – the rules or whatever it is that generates structures – needs to assemble all of its items in one initial selection. The computation might select from an independent lexicon in stages, combining the words into the emerging structure as required; indeed, there are empirical reasons to think that such a multiple selection procedure is the right model. In this sense, the early transformational theories were perhaps correct, both in their appeal to generalized transformations and not making a one-off lexical selection.

4.4 The place of meaning

At its most simple, a language is a pairing of meanings or messages with signs (sounds or hand gestures). As we saw in Chapter 2, Chomsky left meaning very much in abeyance. This was not because, of course, meaning was thought to be irrelevant to language or syntax more particularly. The reason was that the notion of meaning was too undeveloped to impose constraints on syntactic theory and, moreover, it appeared that grammaticalness and syntactic transformations were not determined by properties associated with 'meaning'. Given this, it was perfectly rational for Chomsky to query why a grammar – a theory of sentence structure – should be built on the conception of meaning as opposed to assuming that it must be. Chomsky's 'autonomy thesis', as discussed in Chapter 2, has been needlessly misunderstood; it was simply a methodological precept that was supported by solid argument. A striking consequence, however, of this relative disregard for meaning was that the grammars proposed had no level of structure that coded for a sentence's meaning. The final phrase marker of the T-marker coded for morphonemic interpretation, but that level could not serve for meaning. Recall the pair: *The picture was painted by a real artist/a new technique.* A clear difference in meaning between these two sentences is the agent interpretation of *a real artist* and the instrument interpretation of *a new technique.* The phrase marker that codes for morphonemic interpretation doesn't reflect this difference. Equally, ambiguous sentences, such as *The shooting of the soldiers scared the tourists,* have but one structure that codes for morphonemic interpretation, which just means that the dual interpretation of the sentence is not reflected at that level. Nor can the base be the level at which meaning is encoded, for, again, the base does not provide two structures for the sentence; besides, if the base were where meaning is determined, then questions, conjunctions, passives etc., wouldn't be meaningful at all.

The only level left in the field, as it were, is the transformational component, that is, the T-marker. Yet a T-marker is not one structure but a linkage of any number of structures, with the meaning-relevant structure distributed across the links. In short, there is not a single structural locus for meaning.

Again, as with other aspects of the early model, we shall see that after moving away from this distributed model, it appears to have been on the right lines, at least if the most recent developments are correct (Chapter 8). It is important to note that even though Chomsky has always upheld 'autonomy' as a methodological guide, the place of meaning has always played a crucial role in shaping the general look of the grammar – apart from the earliest model. The distributed model, where the T-marker codes for meaning, perhaps reflects a disregard for meaning, not essentially, but merely *pro tem.* I say this, for at no place does Chomsky explicitly defend the distributed T-markers as the locus of structural interpretation. The thought seems to be that if the T-marker is the only place where, say, ambiguities can be resolved, then it simply must be the locus for semantic interpretation. The distributional model of the latest theories is motivated by computational considerations, not developed semantic considerations, although the general architecture of the model is fashioned by demands that derive from semantic interpretation. Autonomy still holds sway as merely a methodological precept. These issues will be discussed at much greater length as we proceed.

4.5 Empirical explanation

Finally, it is worth emphasizing that no aspect of the above model is intended to be a priori true. A particular grammar is an explanatory theory of the phenomena that hold for a particular language, and general linguistic theory is the meta-scientific account of the resources that are available to any given grammar. This enshrines the idea that all languages are cut from the same cloth, as it were. As we shall see, more or less nothing remains intact of the original model (at least as originally stated), but the data remain as they were and the explanations offered, as indicated, contain much that remains fecund. The crucial point is that Chomsky developed linguistics as a genuine branch of theoretical inquiry and not a mere taxonomy or a descriptive catalogue of peculiarities that enjoy no underlying systematicity. In this light, it is perfectly natural to expect most of the initial ideas to be false or at least ill stated. The real advance was the identification of unexplained phenomena that a grammar should explain and the development of powerful new tools that at least offered the resources to tackle the phenomena.

CHAPTER 4

THE 'COGNITIVE TURN': NATIVISM AND UNIVERSAL GRAMMAR

[W]hat reason would not be able to know of itself and has to learn from nature, it has to seek in the latter (though not merely ascribe to it) in accordance with what reason itself puts into nature.
Kant (1781/87/1998, Bxiv)

1 INTRODUCTION

Chomsky's name is synonymous with the claim that linguistic competence is a largely innate cognitive capacity as opposed to a behavioural repertoire or a communicative wherewithal. The work of the 1950s so far reviewed perhaps only obliquely hints at such a position; indeed, while the new generative approach to linguistics had certainly made its impact by the early 1960s, few ripples had been created in psychology and philosophy. This was to change with Chomsky's explicit construal of the generative program as a contribution to psychology.

2 THE PARTICULAR AND THE UNIVERSAL

As things stand, a grammar is to be understood as a theory of a particular language, where the T-markers the theory generates serve as explanations of a range of linguistic phenomena: syntactic, semantic, morphological and phonemic. General linguistic theory is a kind of philosophy of the grammars; it includes definitions of the resources available to each grammar and an evaluation metric by which given grammars that satisfy empirical desiderata might be judged and selected in terms of their relative simplicity. In Chomsky's terms, then, a given grammar G for language L has two justificatory conditions to meet. An 'external' justification of G relates to its empirical coverage of L, that is, do the T-markers of G explain and predict the kind of phenomena surveyed Chapter 3? For example, we want a grammar to predict that normal speakers of L will find certain sentences ambiguous; it will do so if, say, the relevant T-marker contains two or more structures that reflect the two or more readings of the given sentence. Such richness of structure will in turn explain how it is that the speaker can read the one sentence in two or more divergent ways. Minimally, G should entail a T-marker for every sentence of L. G must also meet an 'internal' justification condition that relates G to general linguistic theory, that is, G is internally justified to the extent to which it is an instance of the general schema that holds for all grammars and, relative to the empirical data, is the most simple grammar available. In sum, the external justification relates G to the observable (external) facts and internal justification relates a grammar to the general resources we expect each grammar to utilize.

Prima facie, the internal justification might seem redundant. After all, if G is predictive and explanatory of all relevant phenomena of L, what more could one ask of it? Why should each grammar fit the same mould? Chomsky (SS, p. 14) avers, 'it is . . . a reasonable requirement, since we are interested not only in particular languages, but also in the general nature of language'. Of course, Chomsky is not here supposing that we already know what the general nature of language is; his thought is essentially methodological. For any given language L, a range of possible grammars could be externally adequate. Internal justification offers a constraint on the range in the sense that any adequate grammar of L must be such that it is of the same kind as grammars G_1, G_2 etc. for languages L_1, L_2 etc. It might be that language is essentially heterogeneous, but it would be absurd to assume that constructing grammars for L_1 and L_2 are wholly independent enterprises. If one inquiry can usefully constrain the other, then it would be obtuse to eschew the discipline. Otherwise put, far from assuming that all languages are cut from the same cloth, Chomsky is suggesting that it is a matter for empirical inquiry. We construct individual grammars and test them against one another in terms of their shared resources. The extent to which the grammars all conform to the same general conditions and are externally adequate is the extent to which we are discovering something about language as such. Inquiry into particular languages thus goes hand in hand with the general inquiry into language, each constraining the other. The justification just given is methodological. That is, the assumption that adequate grammars should share the same resources allows us to better constrain the choice of individual grammars for particular languages. Is there, though, any reason to think that language does have universal features? First off, every language appears to exhibit the kind of phenomena witnessed in the previous chapter. For example, there is no known language that does not admit ambiguous sentences. If, therefore, transformations are the easiest way of accounting for structural ambiguity in English, then it is perfectly natural to assume prior to inquiry that transformations would also explain ambiguity in Italian, German, Swahili etc. Of course, one would have to construct the grammar. The present point is simply that if one explanation works for an instance of a phenomenon, then, ceteris paribus, we should expect it to work for all other instances of the same phenomena. Just investigating one language may thus shed real light on what is universal to language.

A second consideration is much more general. Normal speakers display what Chomsky refers to as *creativity* with their language:

> Any grammar of a language will *project* the finite and somewhat accidental corpus of observed utterances to a set (presumably infinite) of grammatical utterances. In this respect, a grammar mirrors the behaviour of the speaker who, on the basis of a finite and accidental experience with language, can produce or understand an indefinite number of new sentences. Indeed, any explication of the notion 'grammatical in L' . . . can be thought of as offering an explanation for this fundamental aspect of linguistic behaviour (SS, p. 14)

In other words, normal speakers' linguistic production is indefinitely novel, going far beyond the 'accidental' set of structures they have heard. Equally, they can understand the indefinite novelty of their co-conversationalists (there are other crucial aspects to creativity that will be discussed in the following chapter). Of course, some are more creative with language than others, but none of us, save for the impaired, are restricted to parroting what we have heard; we all effortlessly express new thoughts in new situations. If the idea is still somewhat opaque, consider the case of reading a newspaper, even the lowliest one. The sentences are new to us each day, idioms, clichés and the like apart, but we can understand them fine. Further, this creativity is clearly a universal phenomenon. There are no normal speakers who are restricted in their linguistic output to imitation, or who can't understand their fellow speakers when they go beyond, say, the sentences they themselves have previously produced.

As Chomsky suggests in the above quotation, each grammar for a language explains this capacity in the sense that each grammar generates infinitely many T-markers and so furnishes each speaker with an unbounded range of structures that may contribute to her linguistic production and consumption. However, this capacity is universal. Thus, whatever feature a particular grammar has such that it can explain the creative capacity of users of L will be shared by all other grammars. This feature, of course, is simply recursivity.

A third consideration is explicitly psychological and was not broached in Chomsky's early work (its first appearance in print was perhaps in EML (1962) followed up by CILT (1964), although it also occurs in the first chapter of ATS that was written in the late 1950s.) Each human being, barring pathological cases or later trauma, develops a language much the same as her peers by the age of five. Rocks, birds and chimpanzees, as well as everything else in the known universe, do not. In no sense, however, is an English child 'wired up' to acquire English, or a Japanese child 'wired up' to acquire Japanese etc. That is, uniquely, each child can acquire any language with equal ease. Encapsulating this fact, we may say that humans have a universal language acquisition capacity. For instance, whatever it was about George that enabled him to acquire English would also have enabled him to acquire German. Just so, whatever it was that enabled Hans to acquire German would have enabled him to acquire Japanese etc. Trivially, then, there is some property P of the human cognitive design that allows each of us to acquire any given language. If all of this is so, then it would appear that inquiry into what each language shares is a substantial pursuit, for we must all share something given that we can acquire any language, notwithstanding the many apparent differences between any two languages.

3 UNIVERSAL GRAMMAR AND LEVELS OF ADEQUACY

The cognitive turn, then, essentially arises via a consideration of how language is acquired. The internal justification of general linguistic theory becomes a condition of 'explanatory adequacy', where a grammar is adequate only if it is explicable as arising from what all humans share qua an organism that can acquire any human language. Following Chomsky (ATS, chapter 1), we will call whatever this shared property as *Universal Grammar* (UG). Chomsky (EML, CILT) also refers to UG as a Language Acquisition Device (LAD). This is simply a label for whatever it is about the human mind/brain that maps from exposure to language to a grammar. However, it is perfectly natural to construe general linguistic theory *as* UG, what all humans share. After all, every human acquires a language and so somehow represents the grammar for their language *qua* creative users of the language. Since, further, general linguistic theory describes the common resources of the grammars and there must be something common to all humans as acquirers of language, it looks as if general linguistic theory was all along an account of a universal human cognitive feature, that is, UG. In line with this cognitive construal of the old methodological notions, 'external' justification becomes a desideratum for 'descriptive adequacy', that is, a grammar should map a structural description to each sentence such that the set of descriptions explains our intuitions as to the structure within and between sentences. In general then, given a grammar G and language L, we may take G to be descriptively adequate of L if it explains the various systematic features of our knowledge or understanding of L via an assignment of structural descriptions to L sentences. G itself cannot be explanatorily adequate, but G is not adequate unless we are able to show that it is an acquirable grammar from UG and data to which the child is likely to be exposed. Explanatory adequacy relates UG to particular grammars; the condition distinguishes between, as it were, possible languages from 'arbitrary symbol systems' (ATS, chapter 1). In sum, linguistic theory becomes an account of human *knowledge of language*. Particular descriptively adequate grammars constitute theories of what speakers know when they know a language, and UG is what speakers know in virtue of them being able to acquire any given language, that is, to represent a given grammar for their language. It should be noted that Chomsky (LSLT, p. 62) has always been happy to treat language as an object of knowledge and so a psychological phenomenon. What is new with the work of the early 1960s is the explicit construal of linguistic theory as having psychological states of knowledge as their object.

There is much here that has given rise to confusion and much controversy. The remainder of this chapter will put flesh on these bones; later chapters will deal with the various controversies. Before all of that, however, three issues deserve some brief discussion: traditional grammar, the ambiguity of Chomsky's terms of art and the question of how much of a turn was the 'turn'.

3.1 Traditional grammar

Chomsky's conception of a grammar marks a fundamental break with the traditional conception. We normally think of a grammar as providing instruction in the 'proper' use of a language. A grammar for English, for example, should tell us that *none* is singular, that *whom* is an accusative form and should be used in place of *who* where the object of a verb is questioned, that marked infinitives should not be split etc. In this sense, such a grammar is *normative*, that is, it tells us how speakers *ought* to use the language or how, indeed, good or careful speakers do use the language. Such a grammar does not affect to tell us what we all already know without error. The grammar takes up the slack, as it were, between our effortless command across most of the language (what we know such that we can so much as follow the grammar's instructions) and some normative ideal. The taxonomic approach to grammar or syntax clearly does not follow this course, for it attempts to catalogue the constructions we do use. Similarly, the various behaviourist approaches to language pay no heed to the various concepts and categories of the traditional grammarian. Chomsky's break with traditional grammar was of a different kind.

For Chomsky, the job of a grammar is essentially explanatory and not description or normative instruction. On this conception, a grammar targets what for the traditionalist passes without comment – the knowledge that constitutes our effortless grasp of a language where we do not fall into error (the very notion of error is questionable, but may serve for the present). In a very real sense, if we have to be told something, then it is simply not part of our language. For example, we might well not have noticed that the sentence, *The shooting of the soldiers scared the tourists*, is ambiguous, but we hardly need to be instructed in its ambiguity, it suffices for it to be brought to our attention. Of course, for some, the singular form of *none* passes without comment, but it is doubtful that such speakers were instructed in its form; they acquired it from mere early exposure to 'good' speakers of English. Further, for other speakers, merely bringing its singular use to their attention does not suffice for them to recognize something they knew anyhow. More vividly, no one needs to be told that *Furiously sleep ideas green colourless* is word salad, while *Colourless green ideas sleep furiously* is deviant in a different respect. A grammar in Chomsky's sense thus offers theoretical explanation of the extant phenomena but not instruction. It seeks to answer the question: What do we know when we know a language, independent of our normative standing, and how come that we have such knowledge independent of explicit instruction?

In a certain respects, however, this explanatory conception of a grammar can be seen as a continuation of the project of traditional grammar, at least when in contrast with behaviourist or taxonomic projects. First, both Chomsky and the traditional grammarian are interested in competent speakers' knowledge of language; that is, both conceive speakers as cognitive agents, systems with knowledge, and not merely as 'behavers' or 'doers'. What the traditionalist takes as an essential given, Chomsky seeks to explain. Second and correlatively, both are concerned with abstract structural description of linguistic forms. A traditional grammar, for example, is concerned with notions of tense, Case, mood, ellipsis, verbal forms, subject/ predicate, clause etc. None of these notions is definable in behavioural terms, nor are they of any obvious taxonomic value; indeed, such notions stand in opposition to taxonomic procedures insofar as they appear to offer an extant vocabulary for linguistic description free of any demand that an accurate description of salient linguistic kinds should be *discoverable* from a given corpus of the language. Chomsky is more than happy to recruit the traditional notions from the grammarian. A crucial difference, though, must be noted.

Since Chomsky's concern is theoretical explanation, the fecundity of the traditional descriptive vocabulary is hostage to empirical fortune and general explanatory virtues. For example, the traditional way for a grammar to describe a sentence is in terms of subject and predicate. A theoretical grammar is not obliged to follow suit. In *Aspects*, Chomsky proposes that subject-hood be understood configurationally; that is, a subject is that element which forms a sentence/ clause when it is the argument of a verb phrase. Similar treatments are now standard across the board for object, indirect object, adjunct etc. In short, such notions are not primitive. Likewise, where a traditional notion appears not to apply, it might still serve for explanation. Case is a prime example. Traditionally, it is judged that English nominals have Case only when pronominal (*he* is nominative; *him* is accusative; *his* is genitive). Now standard accounts treat all nominals as having a Case feature, whether it is morphologically marked or not. More radically still, the traditional idea of a construction type can be seen as an artefact, that is, merely epiphenomenal. We speak, for instance, of the 'English passive'. Descriptively, this is convenient, but it does not follow that a grammar need advert to the passive construction. Perhaps the distinctive features of the passive are derivable from verbal morphology and properties of Case (such explanations are now current). Even the notion of a sentence might be epiphenomenal (see Chapters 7 and 8).

As will be noted, this kind of break with traditional description was not evident in the earliest accounts, which, for example, treat 'Sentence' (S) as a primitive notion and include a specific rule for passive formation. This apparent conservatism, however, can be properly seen as simply the first steps to a richer theoretical elaboration. Since the business of a grammar in Chomsky's eyes has never been mere description according to traditional categories, there was never any essential commitment to the traditional notions. They served well given the state of theoretical development and could be radically developed or dropped, as theory demanded, which is just what later theories do demand.

A further departure from traditional grammar is that the notions a grammar posits are of theoretical kinds and are not of descriptions. The theoretical claim a grammar makes is that competent speakers somehow mentally represent its rules and concepts, and it is such a cognitive state that explains their competence. The notions, therefore, do not describe sentences or phrases as such, but pick out the 'concepts' that enable a speaker to be linguistically competent. It must be said, however, that Chomsky's early account of this cognitive construal of a grammar was ambiguous. To this feature we now turn.

3.2 Systematic ambiguity

Chomsky's 'cognitive turn', as we are calling it, amounts to a construal of the extant framework as an account of the basis of linguistic cognitive capacity. A generative grammar for English, say, becomes an account of the underlying cognitive state that supports speakers' competence with English. In turn, this state is understood to be selected or derived from a general state that is shared across the species, *viz.*, UG. Universal Grammar is a cognitive interpretation of 'general linguistic theory'. Retained under this dual construal is the idea that particular grammars and UG are theory like. Universal Grammar is a general theory that provides the resources (simplicity measure, categories, rule schemata) available for the development of particular theories that account for the competence with particular languages. In this sense, the child and, indeed, the mature speaker are depicted to be unconscious theorists. For a child to acquire a linguistic competence is for it to develop a particular theory following the format of UG that provides an account of language as such.

Chomsky employed the notions of 'grammar' and 'UG' ambiguously. A grammar is both a theory a competent speaker (sub-consciously) knows and a theory of that knowledge. Similarly, 'UG' designates both the universal language endowment of the species and a theory of that endowment. Chomsky (ATS, chapter 1) is explicit about this ambiguity and sees it as being unproblematic, if heeded. Problems arise, substantial or not, with the thought that children are little theorists, and that we have unconscious knowledge, and, indeed, that linguistic competence is a species of knowledge as opposed to a practical ability or know-how of some variety. These issues will be considered as we go along, but something brief should be said now about the theoretical status of a grammar.

The thought that children and, indeed, mature speakers are theorists of language would be patently absurd if the theorization were intended to be conscious. The exercise of linguistic competence is typically effortless, and it is not a theoretical achievement. The notion of theory, then, is employed to suggest a certain structural similarity between linguistic competence and theory construction. First, theories are finite structures of principles, laws or axioms, but have infinite predictive content. Newton's inverse square law of gravity, for example, subsumes any two bodies, regardless of any factors apart from their mass and distance from each other. Similarly, one can think of a grammar as a finite structure that, qua generative, produces an infinity of predictions as to the underlying structure (the T-markers) of the utterances of a language. In this light, it is perfectly rational to think of linguistic competence as being theory-like, for every competent 'creative' speaker is able, on the basis of presumably finite resources, to make an unbounded number of 'predictions' as to the structure of the utterances of her language.

Second, theories are not descriptions of phenomena; they involve the positing of 'unobservables', where it is the relations that hold between the unobservables that account for the surface phenomena. A theory, in other words, explains phenomena rather than merely offer descriptive coverage. Analogously, a generative grammar is essentially an abstract structure some distance from the observed phenomena. The speaker operates, albeit unconsciously, with richly articulated structures (T-makers etc.) that subserve her understanding of the sentences of the language. A speaker does not merely parrot sentences; he has a rich understanding of their structure and how they relate to one another. For example, normal speakers are able to identify ambiguities or recognize them upon them being brought to their attention, but very few speakers are able to say why the ambiguities obtain. Again, it is perfectly natural to think of this competence as being based upon an unconscious theory-like structure of a grammar.

Third, theories are radically undetermined by data. This is not a controversial thesis, but a mere banality. Were a theory to be determined by the data, then it would be nothing other than a description of it. Otherwise put, while a theory should entail available and novel data, it will not do so uniquely; another theory can also be constructed that covers the data equally well. Choice of theory, then, is not determined by data, but data plus general principles of economy, elegance and fit with extant related theories, if any. Of course, this is not to suggest that it is easy to find a theory that covers the data. The point is merely that theory construction is not conceptual analysis or descriptive encapsulation of data. A theory essentially goes beyond the data in its search for explanatory principles from which the data might be entailed only by long chains of inference. A grammar is similarly related to its data. Our interest in a grammar is its *strong* generative capacity, that is, the kind of structures it assigns sentences. There is an indefinite number of choices of how we might construct a grammar that satisfies this demand. We saw a simple example of this in the previous chapter over the AUX rule. We want a grammar to cover the data, but because our goal is explanatory, we are not satisfied with coverage of what is and is not, say, an English sentence. From the view of the speaker, then, we must view her as selecting a grammar not merely on the basis of data, for that would leave her with too much of a choice; the speaker does not merely classify sentences, as if a taxonomist, but assigns structure to them, and so her choice remains undetermined by the data. This relates to the previous point concerning unobservables. If grammar selection is essentially choosing between a set of unobservables (e.g. distinct T-markers), then the data cannot determine the choice in any direct way at all. Again, the grammar, what a speaker knows, is not a mere catalogue of the sentences he has observed.

All of this has been heir to much controversy, especially the last point. My aim here has not been to defend fully the theoretical status of speakers' competence but only to motivate it. Indeed, we shall see that more recent accounts depart from this theoretical perspective in significant ways. Of more philosophical concern is the thought that if a speaker has a theory of language, the language must, apparently, be some external structure for which the theory serves. But what kind of external structure could this be? This will be an issue for later discussion (see Chapter 6). For the moment, let us keep to the theoretical gloss.

3.3 Chomsky's attitude

The achievements of Chomsky's early work, the initial formulation of the generative approach, are denied by none. Chomsky's cognitive turn, on the other hand, has remained highly controversial. In a sense, Chomsky's own attitude appeared to allow for the separation of the two. First, neither LSLT nor SS explicitly commend a cognitive approach to language, still less do they construe the grammars themselves as theories speakers somehow possess. Second, even in the 'Review of Skinner's *Verbal Behavior*' (RSVB), Chomsky does not argue for a cognitive account of language. Chomsky rests content to accuse Skinner of dogmatism for simply ignoring the cognitive contribution native structure makes to our acquisition and maintenance of linguistic competence. The impression given by these two factors, however, is misleading. It is reasonable to think that Chomsky has all along had a cognitive orientation towards language.

In the 1975 'Introduction' to LSLT, Chomsky suggests that the cognitive issues of UG, explanatory adequacy, innateness etc. were central to his thinking in the 1950s; they were in the 'immediate background', 'taken for granted', but their articulation would have been 'too audacious' (LSLT, pp. 13, 35 and 37). Similarly, Chomsky ('Preface to "A Review of B. F. Skinner's *Verbal Behavior*"' (PRSVB), p. 142) expresses regret at the timidity with which the nativist alternative is presented in RSVB. It is not usual for Chomsky to be backward at coming forward. Still, a number of factors bear consideration.

First, it is clear that Chomsky is correct in his thought that cognitive issues were in the 'immediate background'. As earlier remarked, both LSLT (p. 62) and SS (p. 15) view our linguistic 'store of knowledge' and aspects of our creative linguistic behaviour as the object of explanation. Clearly, the task here is not merely descriptive; further, a behaviourist picture was not so much as being entertained, for, as RSVB makes explicit, it does not contain the resources to be so much as descriptively adequate. Chomsky, it is fair to say, appears to have a cognitive understanding of linguistic theory in mind but, albeit temporarily, could not see how to articulate it in a convincing way.

Second, given the task of Chomsky's early work, including RSVB, an explicit cognitive account of grammatical structure was not necessary. The purpose of RSVB is wholly negative; a refutation of Skinner's brand of behaviourism does not require any alternative framework. Likewise, the explanatory goals of linguistic theory are explicitly inconsistent with the descriptive and behaviourist presuppositions of the then prevailing alternative models. Indeed, as Chomsky was soon to argue, the phenomena generative grammar targets simply fall outside of the scope of the extant alternatives. Recall that the weak generative capacity of a grammar was never of immediate interest, a point that was only obscured by the order of explanation in SS. Again, then, it is difficult to see what the complex structures a generative grammar posits could be accounts of other than what a speaker understands or represents. This is inconsistent with the behaviourist framework and simply orthogonal to the descriptive approach of the taxonomists. Given all of this, the absence of an explicit articulation of, say, the explanatory adequacy condition did not constitute a lacuna in the early work.

Third, the works that were immediately to follow SS are all explicit in their articulation of a cognitive model of generative grammars. 'Explanatory models in linguistics' (EML), although not published until 1962, was delivered in 1960. The introductory chapter of ATS, which is often credited as marking the cognitive turn, was in fact written in the late 1950s. In keeping with Chomsky's 1975 remarks, these works introduce the cognitive construal as a natural reading of the generative approach without any declaration of a radical turn. As we have just seen, this is a perfectly honest and coherent move. Consider: since the business of linguistic theory was declared to be explanation from the beginning, and behaviourist approaches were not even judged to be descriptively adequate, it is difficult to see what linguistic theory could be about other than our cognitive capacity. Of course, a number of critics have always judged that linguistic theory should be read as being about language as such or our practical ability to communicate. Chomsky has always seen such approaches as being woefully inadequate. The evidence there is points to Chomsky having such a view in the 1950s, and so as having a cognitive understanding in the 'immediate background'.

It is indeed difficult to think of Chomsky as being less than audacious; in the present case, at least, it would appear that Chomsky had reasons other than a fear of audacity to postpone the articulation of his understanding of linguistics as a branch of psychology.

4 COMPETENCE AND PERFORMANCE

A central distinction of the 'cognitive turn' is that between competence and performance. This is how Chomsky (ATS, pp. 3–4) introduces the distinction:

> Linguistic theory is concerned primarily with an ideal speaker-listener, in a completely homogenous speech-community, who knows its language perfectly and is unaffected by such grammatically irrelevant considerations as memory limitations, distractions, shifts of attention and interest, and errors (random and characteristic) in applying his knowledge of the language in actual performance . . . [N]o cogent reason for modifying [this position] has been offered. To study actual linguistic performance, we must consider the interaction of a variety of factors, of which the underlying competence of the speaker-hearer is only one. In this respect, study of language is no different from empirical investigation of other complex phenomena.

A number of aspects of this passage deserve highlighting and explanation.

(i) Chomsky's appeal to 'an ideal speaker-listener, in a completely homogenous speech-community' is not a suggestion that linguistics is not concerned with the reality of non-ideal speaker-hearers in massively heterogeneous speech-communities. Rather, the thought is that we must idealize away from the complexity of the reality in order to gain theoretical traction on that very reality. For reasons already elaborated at length, it appears that speaker-hearers have a competence with language that is not exhausted by what they do with that competence. Thus, in approaching linguistic behaviour in a broad sense, it is only natural to factor the phenomena into distinct components, where any given linguistic act will be understood as a function from such components.

(ii) As in any other science, issues arise about idealization. Is something central being missed? Is there any reality to the idealization? In the present case, I think such questions can be easily answered. As regards the first one, the worth of any idealization lies in its empirical fecundity and not in its fidelity to an a priori conception of the phenomena (witness Galileo and motion). On the face of it, it is difficult to see the present idealization as anything other than helpful. For example, if we develop an acquisition model for a subject in a homogenous speech-community, and it fails, then such a model would surely fail in the real case, where data are so much more messy. Likewise, if the model works, then we at least know that it is adequate under certain conditions, and we might then finesse such conditions to see where, if at all, it breaks down. More centrally, the idealization is not at the expense of any aspect of the reality, at least not necessarily so. As Chomsky makes clear in the passage, the idealization to competence is not a way of ignoring performance factors but a way of hopefully explaining them, at least to some degree, by factoring the complex phenomena into a modular system. If something central is being missed, it remains unclear what it might be. Furthermore, the idea of targeting linguistic behaviour in toto is surely absurd, for any inquiry would immediately be crippled by the complexity of factors, many of them irrelevant to the inquiry, such as the simple interest or attention of the speaker-hearers.

Is there any reality to the idealization? That is a question for empirical inquiry and applies equally to any science. In the present case, the assumption that there is a competence in distinction to a suit of systems that contribute to performance seems overwhelming. That said, the nature of this competence is not fixed for inquiry; it might be much more paired down than older theories assumed, including that of ATS. Likewise, it might turn out that there is just no system of competence. The modular methodology of competence/performance, however, would not thereby be proved wrong. Quite the reverse! It is only through breaking complex phenomena into discreet units that work in combination that we might begin to understand anything of the phenomena. No methodology dictates the nature of its results.

The picture, then, is that linguistic theory should primarily target competence, or the grammar, that the speaker-hearer possesses as an aspect of her cognitive wherewithal. This competence interacts with other cognitive systems, either general purpose (memory) or dedicated (a parser), which results in the complexity of linguistic behaviour.

5 NATIVISM

Easily the most controversial aspect of Chomsky's 'cognitive turn' was his claim that linguistic competence is native to the human mind/ brain; in a phrase, language is innate. This claim has generated a library of criticism and defence and it would take a much larger book than this merely to summarize it. All I want to do here is respond to some common misconceptions and, in a sense, deflate the issue.

Chomsky (ATS, p. 52) suggests that it is 'heuristically valuable to distinguish . . . [between] different approaches to the problem of the acquisition of knowledge', where the idea is to formulate the approaches clearly enough so that one may 'ask, as an empirical question, which (if either) is correct' (ibid., p. 53) (cf., 'On innateness: a reply to Cooper' (OI)). The two approaches are *rationalism* and *empiricism*. The former position is historically associated with Plato, Descartes, Leibniz, Cudworth and many other thinkers of the seventeenth and eighteenth centuries; the latter position is associated with thinkers from Locke and Hume up to many leading twentieth century philosophers and psychologists, especially Quine (1960) and Skinner. In appealing to these two broad trajectories, Chomsky is not suggesting that the positions are uniform, still less that to commend, say, rationalism involves agreeing with every aspect of Descartes' philosophy. It also bears emphasis that the issue is not so much to decide between the two, but to see, as empirical hypotheses, which one is most fecund, independent of the particular positions articulated by Descartes or Locke, say.

Schematically, then, we can think of the acquisition problem in terms of a diagram.

(AP) $E \rightarrow M/B \rightarrow K$

E is the course of a subject's experience, M/B is the subject's mind/brain (their internal resources) and K is the knowledge at issue, whether of mathematics, language, the physical environment etc. The question for both empiricism and rationalism is how E and M/B give rise to K. To emphasize again, this is an empirical problem and not one to be answered by a mere reflection on what we mean by *mind*, *learning* etc. Now, a caricature of both positions would involve a denial of one or the other of the factors: rationalism involves a denial of the role of experience, while empiricism involves a denial of the internal resources of the mind/brain. As a matter of fact, however, no one has ever seriously entertained such extreme positions; certainly none of the historical figures mentioned have done so. It is still all too common, though, for a nativist or rationalist position to be saddled with the claim that 'language is there at birth', much as Locke attacked rationalism in the opening of his *Essay*, which effectively involves a denial of experience in the acquisition of language. In reality, the difference between the two positions is one of degree. Everyone acknowledges that E and M/B give rise to K; the issue turns on what the respective responsibility is of the two components. Characteristically, empiricism places the burden on E, with M/B merely playing a filtering and/or combinatorial role. On this conception, there is no aspect of K that does not reflect an aspect of E; the differences are due to the novel combinations and abstracting processes that M/B performs on E. On the other hand, rationalism typically places the burden on M/B. K arises from M/B but only given a certain initial stimulus and further shaping from E. In this sense, our knowledge is a reflection of our internal resources and not our course of experience.

As empirical positions, we can see the dispute as being over the nature of M/B given the independent variables of E and K. We may let empiricism be defined by two predictions. First, changes in E will affect K to some significant degree; this must be so, if K is just the output of what the internal combinatorial resources have to hand. Second, an analysis of K will reveal that it involves no principles or concepts that are not derivable from E. Rationalism makes two opposing predictions. First, K is, to some significant degree, invariant over changes in E; this must be so given that K is substantially a reflection of M/B and not E. Second, an analysis of K will reveal that it is organized around concepts and principles that are not derivable from E by mere combination or abstraction. These look like testable empirical claims independent of whether or not the historical figures saw them in such terms. In general, then, empiricism views the M/B as an unformed general purpose device, whose output or knowledge is determined by the experience the subject undergoes; the M/B is not, as it were, designed to produce certain kinds of knowledge at the expense of other kinds. Rationalism, on the other hand, sees our knowledge as being largely determined by the design of our M/B: the knowledge we have is not due to our experience, but the kind of being we are with experience merely stimulating and shaping the *growth* of the initial design.

If we construe these broad claims to relate to language in particular, then Chomsky's rationalist picture is that language acquisition is largely a matter of growth determined by the initial state of the M/B. This position, note, is not meant to be some clear hypothesis; rather, it is sets a research agenda. As Chomsky (ATS, p. 58) puts it, the aim is to develop 'a hypothesis about initial structure that is sufficiently rich to account for acquisition of language, yet not so rich as to be inconsistent with the known diversity of language'. In other words, a nativist agenda involves developing hypotheses about UG that are explanatorily adequate over the descriptively adequate grammars that UG subsumes. In this sense, then, linguistics becomes a branch of psychology and ultimately biology, insofar as the human M/B is a biological object. A central branch of this agenda is the so-called 'poverty of stimulus argument'. I shall turn to this shortly, for it deserves a separate treatment. Before that, let us first consider some general reasons for favouring the rationalist approach.

(i) It is sometimes remarked that nativism illicitly relieves itself of an explanatory burden by simply claiming that what is to be explained is there all along, merely dormant, as it were. While one could imagine a nativist position that was guilty of such a charge, although I cannot think of any extant position that is, Chomsky's position on language is innocent. As the above quotation makes explicit, the task of linguistic theory is to characterize UG in such a way that we can *explain* how individual languages are acquired without those languages themselves being innate. For example, if Smith acquires English, then we want her development to be explicable on the basis of her internal resources (UG) that would, in different circumstances, lead to her acquiring Japanese or Brazilian Portuguese. In this sense, UG is on genuine explanatory duty, for no developmental endstate – competence with a given language – is assumed to be fixed by the initial state. Indeed, as Chomsky, again, makes clear, the real problem is to find UG generalizations that are both abstract and rich enough to cover all acquirable languages.

(ii) Chomsky has never seen his brand of nativism as a controversial claim. At its most minimal, the position is simply that the M/B is a biological object, which is capable of certain developmental trajectories at the expense of others. An acorn seed develops into an oak tree, a shark embryo develops into a shark and a human embryo develops into a human with a suit of capacities not shared by oak trees and sharks. Of course, the details of embryogenesis are very complex and are only just beginning to be understood. Chomsky's claim is simply that we should view language on the same level as our visual or immune systems, or our bipedalism (cf., ATS, p. 59). Whatever else we might think of language, it is a biological artefact that admits inquiry just like any other trait or capacity. One may or may not be interested in this topic, or think that other topics are more pressing, but that does not make the topic go away, still less does it serve as a riposte to on-going theory.

(iii) Traditionally, rationalists have been concerned with forging a connection between the innate, the epistemological a priori and necessary truth. Whatever one might think of these endeavours and their familiar rejoinders, Chomsky's linguistic nativism is not hostage to their fortune. The innate on current understanding is simply the biological/physical structure of the M/B that supports the acquisition and maintenance of linguistic competence. No issue arises as to whether this 'knowledge' is necessarily true (it is unclear what it could be true of) or consciously evaluable. No such issues arise for the visual system, and it is equally unclear why they should arise for language. This is not to suggest that there is not a topic of the epistemology of language; indeed, it is a genuine question how the sub-personal systems of the M/B relate to our conscious judgements about the meaning and structure of our utterances. This issue, however, does not lead inquiry. We should treat our personal knowledge of language as data on the underlying system, but there is no presumption that such knowledge reflects the structure that is the topic of the theory.

(iv) It has been claimed that the very notion of the innate has not been sufficiently clarified and, until it has been, any claims as to the innateness of language (or any other competence or capacity) remain obscure (e.g. Cowie, 1999; Devitt, 2006). First, the notion of the innate is not an explanatory notion, which is rather a theoretical term. It is simply a cover-description for (in broad terms) the experience invariant structure of M/B. In these terms, the study of biology is simply a study of the innate, insofar as biology is not concerned with the unsystematic differences that mark out each individual organism (cf., RR, pp. 185–9). Thus, the crude claim, 'language is innate', is not a hypothesis but simply a recommendation of a research topic, that is, the biological basis of linguistic competence. Hypotheses made under this rubric should be as clearly formulated as possible, for it is them that are explanatory over the data. The topic itself appears to be clear enough and is, anyhow, continuously shifting in detail as new theories are developed. Second, under this broad understanding, there are a number of philosophical elaborations of the concept of the innate that may serve as reconstructions of our common notion. It might be that none of them are ultimately satisfying, but that hardly marks out the innate as unique nor signals trouble for the topic of inquiry as understood via the ongoing theories (we perhaps do not have philosophically satisfying accounts of 'natural law' or 'explanation', but that hardly sounds trouble for particle physics).

(v) To claim that a feature is innate is not merely to say that the feature is universal. This is so in two respects. First, as a general conceptual remark, there might well be universal features of the human species that we would not wish to regard as innate. For example, let us (not unreasonably) suppose that every normal, mature human knows that water is wet. It does not follow that belief in the wetness of water (or any other belief) is innate. Presumably, the universality of the belief is to be explained by the (more or less) universal presence of water in human environments and its crucial salience to all of us. The biological structure of the M/B does not enter into the story, at least not directly (it might be, for example, that we innately possess the concept of water amongst many others). On the other hand, stereoscopic vision is also universal, but here the innate structure of the M/B is clearly pertinent, for such vision is an aspect of the normal development of the human M/B invariant over massive environmental differences. Indeed, it is almost too banal to point out that no one has ever imagined an explanation for the features of mammalian vision that does not appeal to fixed biological structure.

Second, the claim that UG is innate does not amount to the claim that features X, Y and Z are universally exhibited. Universal Grammar provides the resources for any language, but it does not follow that every language uses just the same resources or that a given resource is employed by every language. Universal Grammar defines, in a manner of speaking, every possible human language. Which features are exhibited in the languages of the world at a given moment in time is a complex function of history, not the determination of UG (Jackendoff, 2002; ELF).

I have so far laid out some common misunderstandings that have blighted appreciation of Chomsky's position. None of this, however, is meant to be a positive argument for a rationalist position. For that, we now turn to the so-called 'poverty of stimulus' argument. I say so-called, for, in a certain sense, I do not think there is any such argument and the egregious misunderstanding of what argument there is here has been the source of much needless dispute. Hopefully, this will become clear presently.

6 THE 'POVERTY OF STIMULUS ARGUMENT'

Recall that the acquisition problem shared by empiricism and rationalism is to account for the relation between experience and knowledge (of language) in terms of fixing what the mind/brain (M/B) contributes to the knowledge. Otherwise put, an account of the nature of experience and knowledge should tell us what the character of the M/B is in the sense that if we subtract from knowledge what is provided by experience, then the remainder would apparently be what the M/B contributes. Empiricism places the explanatory burden on experience, with the M/B playing a mere filtering and combinatorial role.

The 'remainder' would thus be minimal conditions of organization. Rationalism places the explanatory burden on the M/B, with experience playing a merely stimulatory and shaping role. On this approach, the 'remainder' would be substantial. Again, it bears emphasis that both parties take experience and the M/B to be essential; the approaches differ only in regard to the placement of the explanatory burden.

An empirical decision, therefore, between these two approaches turns on the character of our experience and knowledge. An empiricist approach predicts that our experience is rich enough to provide us with the content of our linguistic knowledge. Rationalism predicts otherwise: our knowledge of language substantially outstrips what can be plausibly attributed to experience. In its essence, the poverty of stimulus argument (POSA) simply amounts to the argument that the rationalist position here is sound. Why should we, as I suggest, resist the thought that there is an argument here? The matter is perhaps more tactical than substantial. The name of the argument suggests that it has been determined what the nature of the relevant experience is and, upon that basis, determined that it falls far short of that required. Thus, the argument has often been taken to trade on the thought that this or that experience is generally unavailable to children; the assumption being that if such experiences were available, then some empiricist model would be validated, ceteris paribus (Cowie, 1999; Pullum and Scholz, 2002). This is a total misunderstanding of the dialectical situation, bred, no doubt, simply by the use of the term 'poverty'.

Properly understood, the POSA is no more than an invitation to look upon language acquisition as a process of biological development. In this light, Chomsky (AL, p. 50) writes, 'To say that "language is not innate" is to say that there is no difference between my granddaughter, a rock and a rabbit.' In other words, there is a biological property of Chomsky's granddaughter that means that when placed in an environment meeting certain minimal requirements, she develops a language; rocks and rabbits do not. One needs no fancy argument here; what one needs is merely an acknowledgment of the phenomena and an inquiry into the structure and development of this biological property. I should say that there is nothing wrong in substance in presenting these kinds of considerations as an 'argument'. As mentioned, the reasoning goes back to Plato, through Descartes and Leibniz, none of whom appealed to biological development

(RR, p. 37 refers to Descartes' 'poverty of stimulus argument'). The point in resisting the 'argument' label is simply dialectical and to foreclose the idea that the facts at issue are controversial; what is controversial is the particular accounts we give of what is innate.

There is, then, a poverty of stimulus but not in any absolute sense, as if children never experience this or that linguistic structure. The stimulus is poor, rather, relative to that which is acquired, that is, the mature state of linguistic competence. This, trivially, is simply the character of biological development. No one imagines that the growth of a tree is determined by its stimulus, as if we could grow an apple tree from an acorn given the right fertilizer. Likewise, no one imagines that the development of limbs or secondary sexual characterizes or the immune system or vision etc. is determined by the nature of the inputs to the human embryo and later non-somatic experience. In all these cases, it is not so much that the stimulus is not rich enough, as if it *could* be rich enough; rather, we simply understand that biological development is characterized by internal processes of generation and organization free of stimulus determination. In this sense, the development is characterized by a poverty of stimulus not because there is not enough stimulus (whatever that might mean) but because outside of very narrow parameters stimulus is simply irrelevant to the developmental process. Let us consider two quite different scenarios to exemplify this idea.

It is known that different species of song bird have distinct means of acquiring their songs. Some species have a characteristic song that develops independent of song stimulus; that is, the song invariantly develops over other songs (if any) to which the bird has been exposed. Clearly, the song is innate, with its development being characterized by a poverty of stimulus. However, it patently does not follow that the typical bird of the species has not been exposed to the song; it is quite the opposite. The typical bird is inundated with the species song; it is only by radically altering the normal environmental situation of a bird that we discover that the song development is characterized by a poverty of stimulus. Language development is similar. It is not that children lack this or that experience, although they almost certainly do, but that it does not matter whether they have the experience, again, outside of narrow parameters. It is the development that is characterized by a poverty of stimulus, independent of whether the stimulus is rich or not in some absolute sense.

Closer to home, consider the task of the linguist trying to understand English grammar. What the linguist is attempting to theorize is what any normal child can acquire by the age of five. Unlike the five-year-old, however, the linguist has all the data that are possibly relevant. Not only is she already familiar with the target language, she may also have as much data as are required from any other language. She also has the benefit of a mature intelligence, an explicit methodology, and the intellectual cooperation of fellow linguists. The linguist, in short, is in a 'surfeit of stimulus' situation. Nevertheless, we have yet to arrive at a correct grammar for English, what five-year-olds acquire with ease. We can attribute to the child the collective wisdom of 2000 years of thought about language; its acquisition of English would still remain utterly puzzling, for the five-year-old can do what the linguist cannot. Again, then, the issue does not turn towards what data the child has, for we could imagine the child to have all relevant data and the puzzle would remain. The moral of the POSA read aright is that there is no paradox at all here. The child's acquisition of language is an internal developmental process that is largely invariant over experiential differences. Thus, the child's achievement does not depend on data, so, outside of narrow parameters, it is irrelevant whether the child's experience is rich or poor. That is what makes the child's task 'easy', as easy as its development of stereoscopic vision. On the other hand, the linguist is attempting to understand the end-state of a biological process in terms of its effects in combination with a variety of other mental systems.

The proof of this reasoning lies in the development of linguistic theory itself and the known facts about acquisition. I shall not review here all the relevant considerations, for as in any other area of human cognition/biology, the results are partial and as yet too little is understood. My aim is simply to provide evidence for the fecundity of the general rationalist approach.

6.1 Universality and ontogeny

Linguistic competence is a universal species trait, much like binocular vision. Its ontogeny can be roughly broken down into different stages, with all normal children gaining a more or less complete competence (equivalent to mature speakers) by five years of age. That the competence is not present 'at birth' does not suggest that it is not innate. Puberty takes twice as long, but no one imagines that it is anything other than normal biological development. That said, features of linguistic competence are present from the first days of a neonate's life, such as sensitivity to prosody (see Yang, 2006). They are witnessed in deaf neonates in terms of 'hand-babbling' (Petitto, 2005).

The development is also largely invariant over cognitive factors, such as blindness, deafness, low IQ and a range of cognitive dysfunctions. It is also invariant over the amount of explicit tutelage (if any), parental care (apart from extreme neglect) and child-directed speech. Children exposed to a degraded language, such as a pigeon or late-acquired sign, do not learn the 'errors' but develop a language that is consistent in its syntax and morphology. It also appears to be the case that there is a window of opportunity for language acquisition, terminating approximately in the eighth year (see Pinker, 1994, for an accessible overview of these results).

The development of language is also marked by very little 'error' outside of narrow parameters. Familiarly, children have trouble learning irregularity in number and past tense and they make other notable errors, such as leaving *wh*-words in medial positions. Viewed from the perspective of what children *could* get wrong, however, their competence is remarkably consistent with adult understanding. Indeed, adults often stumble over irregularity. Children's competence is so error free that it has been plausibly suggested that children's competence matches the adult speakers; the 'errors' there are performance based (Crain and Thornton, 1998). A striking variation on this theme is Charles Yang's (2002, 2006) claim that, in a sense, children *unlearn* languages; that is, the errors (e.g. medial *wh*) they make are signatures of other languages made available by UG, which the child is sifting through.

Now, a broadly rationalist position is perfectly consistent with this developmental profile; that is, it is just what one would predict if language development is determined by an internal biological process that is largely insensitive to experiential input. On the other hand, the profile looks to be straightforwardly inconsistent with an empiricist position that views the child's development as being largely determined by the character of the experiential input. For example, if language development is highly sensitive to the course of the child's experience, then one would predict that explicit tutelage and, more generally, the amount of child-directed speech, should make a substantial difference to the acquisition profile. This is simply not the case, however. Equally, if children have to learn from experience, then one would predict an error profile that reflects the course of the experience of each particular child. Again, the prediction is false. This is so in two respects. First, the error profile of children appears to be more or less universal. Since child experiences can be radically different without a substantial effect on the acquired competence, the development would appear to be largely independent of those differences. Second, child errors are rare *tout court*. This would appear to demonstrate that children are making 'decisions' about the target language independent of data. If children were being instructed by the data, one would find a preponderance of early mistakes that would gradually decrease as more disconfirming evidence is accumulated.

The facts of development are still very much open to inquiry and the basic empiricist model admits of great variation, including innate mechanisms of a richness that is perceived to be less than the 'official' nativist model. The fact remains, however, that all of the major conclusions reached by empirical research in child development supports the rationalist model against the traditional empiricist model. That is, the general methodological position that language development is a biological process of maturation that is not directly governed by experience is corroborated at the expense of the empiricist model. The precise facts of this development remain unknown, but no one on the nativist side has ever thought the matter was settled. The position has always simply been that approaching language as a biological process is a fruitful line of inquiry, unlike an approach that views language development as directed by the vicissitudes of experience.

6.2 The complexity of syntax

Over the years, Chomsky's favourite example of POSA considerations from syntax is the formation of interrogatives (questions) in English (e.g. RL, chapter 1). I shall follow Chomsky here with the addition of some twists. Two initial points of caution are in order to ward against some common misunderstandings. First, the formation of interrogatives in English (or any other language) is not a settled matter; indeed, their analysis has differed radically over the years, with the old transformational analysis reviewed in Chapter 3 having long been discarded. The point of the interrogative example is just to highlight a general feature of syntax. Second and correlatively, there is nothing especially interesting about English interrogatives; the general rationalist point can be and has been made via any number of construction types and aspects of construal (see, e.g. Crain and Pietroski, 2001; Pietroski and Crain, 2005). Interrogatives are simply a very clear example of the general POS phenomenon. If, then, doubt may be cast on the reasoning from interrogatives, without further ado, that does not essentially damage the general point, unless it can also be shown that the doubt translates to the innumerable other cases. I shall say something more about this shortly.

Polar interrogatives are questions that may be coherently answered with a 'yes' or a 'no'. Let the typical child have data such as the following:

(1) a. Bill can swim
     b. Can Bill swim?
     c. Bill is tall?
     d. Is Bill tall?
     e. Mary will leave
     f. Will Mary leave?

The child's problem is to find the right generalization that covers all cases. On the basis of (1) alone, a hypothesis consistent with the data is as follows:

(A) Alternate the first and second words of a declarative sentence to form the interrogative.

Clearly, no child entertains this hypothesis, for children do not produce (2)b. Plausibly, the child has data on this, anyhow, in the correct interrogative form (2)c.

(2) a. The man can swim
     b. *Man the can swim?
     c. Can the man swim?

A hypothesis that covers all the cases so far is as follows:

(B) Move the auxiliary verb of the declarative to the front of the sentence.

Auxiliary verbs in English are forms of the copula, *have*, and modals. (B) is a fairly rich hypothesis for the child to entertain, for it entails that the child has somehow acquired the means of representing auxiliary verbs. Hypothesis (A) at least has the virtue of appealing to linear order and word segmentation, which might be retrievable from the experiential input without any specific innate competence with linguistic material being presupposed. However, let this complication pass (since the auxiliary verbs are few in number, a child could perhaps learn them as a list, but there are complications here). (B) remains inadequate in two respects. First, it fails to cover a range of cases that feature auxiliary verbs. Second, it does not cover cases of polar interrogatives that do not feature an auxiliary verb, cases that, as we shall see, properly belong to the cases discussed so far.

Consider the following case:

(3) a. Bill, who is blonde, is taller than Bob
     b. *Is Bill who blonde is taller than Bob?

The child's hypothesis thus might be as follows

(C) Move the auxiliary verb of the declarative to the front of the sentence, unless there is a sequence of auxiliary verbs, in which case, move the second verb.

But this is also inadequate:

(4) a. Bill is taller than Bob, who is blonde.
     b. *Is Bill is taller than Bob, who blonde?
     c. Bill, who is blonde and is marring Mary, who is also blonde, is taller than Bob, who is the same height as Mary.
     d. *Is Bill, who is blonde and marring Mary, who is also blonde, is taller than Bob, who is the same height as Mary.

In general, a declarative sentence may feature a sequence of auxiliary verbs of arbitrary length, and there is no generalization based on ordinal position about which verb should move to form the interrogative. Nonetheless, children do not make mistakes in this area; that is, they do not produce the starred cases, even though we are assuming that the data they have available to them are more or less restricted to the examples in (1), which support hypothesis (A). It might be, of course, that some children do hear examples such as (3)a, (4)a and (4)c. However, that is not particularly relevant. Since children do not make mistakes in this area, if they were dependent on such cases, then they had better be preponderant in the typical data set for children (the *primary linguistic data* – PLD). If not, then we would predict that some children make errors in this area either because they were unfortunate enough to miss the crucial data or because they heard the cases alright but treated them as noise, since they occur so infrequently and contradict an otherwise confirmed generalization, such as (B) or (C). It is thus wholly irrelevant whether the crucial cases occur in the *Wall Street Journal* or the works of Oscar Wilde. We would expect them too, for the English sentences are perfectly in order. The crucial issues are whether children hear them and, if they do, what attention they pay them. As it turns out, the best data we have on this tells us that the crucial cases – constructions such as (3)a, (4)a, and (4)c and their respective interrogative forms – occur very infrequently, which is less than 0.1 of the typical PLD (Yang, 2002). Moreover, children lack the negative evidence of (3)b, (4)b and (4)d.

It appears, then, that children are generalizing on the basis of very little data. In a sense, they must be doing so, for as we are seeing, the correct generalization appears to be unstatable in terms of the resources that a child might have to segment the strings of the PLD; that is, the correct generalization can only be stated in terms far richer than word identification and linear position.

The further advertised problem with all of these hypotheses is that polar interrogatives are formed without the movement of auxiliary verbs.

(5)   a. Bill, who is blonde, swims
       b. Does Bill, who is blonde, swim?
       c. *Swims Bill, who is blonde?
       d. The men swim
       e. Do the men swim?
       f. *Swim the men?

Here we see that only auxiliary verbs can move; matrix verbs must stay in situ. Note, however, that the verb morphology changes between (5)a–b. We may also take the morphology to change between (5)d–e, with the tense morpheme zero (i.e. lacking any phonological feature). In general, then, even where there is no auxiliary verb, a matrix tense morpheme moves to the front of the sentence; where it is not an independent word, such as -*s*, it must be supported by the dummy verb *do*. The generalization the child acquires, therefore, must cover both of these cases. Here is a rough version of the accurate 'rule':

Interrogative Rule (IR): To form the interrogative from the declarative, move the matrix tense morpheme to the front of the sentence.

(Interrogative Rule in fact just lays out the features the child must be sensitive to; it is not a rule the child mentally represents.) This rule is a good deal more abstract than the previous hypotheses, for the crucial item that must move is the matrix tense morpheme, which is not an individual word and is also not marked linearly in a string. The rule is *structure sensitive*. In effect, therefore, for the rule to apply, the child must 'chunk' strings according to *hierarchically* organized units that have no discrete signature within the string. For example, the child must, in some sense, represent (6)a as (6)b:

(6)   a. [[Bill [who is blonde]] is [taller than Bill [who is bald]]]
      b. Bill, who is blonde, is taller than Bill, who is bald.

The element that is least embedded is the one that moves, but being least embedded is not a linearly discernable property. It would thus appear that the child must represent sentences to herself as hierarchical structures in order to apply transformations, with neither the structure nor the transformations being discernable independent of the internal resources the child comes equipped with as part of her cognitive-biological make-up.

This conclusion is an empirical hypothesis and not a claim of logical necessity. Still, we can see how quite detailed considerations of the workings of one particular language offer corroboration of the general POS reasoning that holds for language in the round. It should also be emphasized that the reasoning laid out does not so much as suggest that correct interrogative formation could not be learnt in the absence of (IR) or its like. Perhaps it could, perhaps it couldn't. The only interesting issue, at least if one's concern is human psychology, is whether children, given their broad developmental profile and the data they have available, could learn to form interrogatives correctly in the absence of (IR). For example, feeding a neural network masses of data over repeated trials, followed by changes to the network's weightings, *might* result in an output that mimics the five-year-old child, but if the developmental profile of the network and the data made available to it is not the same as the child's, we have no reason whatsoever to take the result as informative about human linguistic competence. No known network development is remotely close to child linguistic development in terms of its freedom from error and general poverty and degradation of data (remember that the child must segment linguistic data from the confusing, buzzing mess of the rest of her experience prior to any greater sophisticated analysis, such as interrogative formation). It is unfortunate that such banalities have to be repeated, for many appear to think that Chomsky and other linguists are attempting to make a priori points as to what is possible, independent of the known facts of human ontogeny. This accusation runs in the face of the very logic of POS considerations. As it is, given the general POS character of linguistic development, we should expect that interrogative formation competence is largely independent of data that might confirm or disconfirm the correct generalization. This is exactly what we do find.

CHAPTER 5

THE REVIEW OF SKINNER

Let me see if I understand your thesis. You think we shouldn't anthropomorphize people?

S. Morgenbesser to B. F. Skinner (apochraphal)

1 INTRODUCTION

We saw in Chapter 4 how in the early 1960s Chomsky offered a cognitive construal of the generative enterprise that had been developed independently of any explicit psychological commitments. In this chapter, I wish to step back a few years to examine Chomsky's review of B. F. Skinner's *Verbal Behavior*. I shall suggest that Chomsky's Skinner review is largely negative and does not offer a positive view of the kind explicitly commended in works from the period of *Aspects*. As we shall see, this view goes against the standard reading of the review. Thus, it is useful for my purposes to have already set out the initial cognitive construal of generative linguistics.

2 TWO READINGS OF CHOMSKY'S REVIEW OF SKINNER

Chomsky's 1959 'Review of Skinner's *Verbal Behavior*' (RSVB) marks the first time Chomsky explicitly approached issues of language acquisition and the psychology of language more generally. His earlier works, including *The Logical Structure of Linguistic Theory* (1955–56/1975), *Syntactic Structures* (1957) and various papers on computational aspects of grammars, do not, for example, offer any explicit argument against empiricism, and they offer still less an explicit argument for nativism. For sure, we need not imagine that it suddenly occurred to Chomsky that the new linguistics was incompatible with the then prevailing empiricism in psychology and the philosophy of mind; some twenty years later Chomsky explains that the notions of innateness and universal grammar were in the 'immediate background', which were too 'audacious' to be then put forward (see Chapter 4). This timidity is even reflected in the Skinner review, where *only after* Skinner's claims are demolished is a nativist account of language acquisition properly discussed (see below). Further, as Chomsky (PRSVB) was to lament, the discussion is far from forthright: nativism is offered as a speculative proposal, albeit one certainly worth considering given the vacuity of the only apparent alternative. We may note, then, two aspects of Chomsky's thought at the time of the Skinner review:

(i) The new linguistics is not premised upon any psychological thesis, including nativism; *a fortiori*, there is no constraint on the nature or status of the new linguistic theories issuing from folk psychology.

(ii) A refutation of behaviourism in the domain of language is possible independent of any particular positive account of language acquisition or the psychological standing of linguistic competence more generally; *a fortiori*, the refutation of behaviourism does not depend on, nor entail, the appropriateness or soundness of folk categories in the explanation or foundation of the new linguistics.

With these two thoughts in place, let us now consider a first reading of the argument of Chomsky's review.

Fallacious Argument (FA):

(i) The behaviourists (Skinner) argue that colloquial mentalistic vocabulary (folk psychology) is non-explanatory of behaviour; it may be fruitfully replaced by learning theoretic vocabulary (*stimulus, response, control, reinforcement, probability* etc.), which place the causes of behaviour in environmental variables, and not in internal states.

(ii) The learning theoretic vocabulary is in fact non-explanatory, or at least the folk vocabulary does a better job.

(iii) Such folksy vocabulary is 'the only president we've got'.

(iv) Therefore, *ceteris paribus*, such a vocabulary provides an appropriate basis for the explanation of behaviour.

This argument reads the review not merely as a refutation of Skinner's behaviourism but also as a defence of folk psychology. Before assessing the premises and the logic of this argument, a question of attribution arises.

I offer Fallacious Argument (FA) as a reconstruction of the received view of the Skinner review. FA has certainly been offered to me numerous times in discussions of Chomsky's review, and no argument that explicitly rejects FA has, to my knowledge, been entertained in the philosophical literature (for texts that seamlessly move from the Skinner review to a folksy-based understanding of cognitive science, see Pylyshyn, 1984; Devitt and Sterelny, 1987; Rey, 1997). More importantly, one can see the argument generally at work in the nigh-on consensus between friends and foes alike that Chomsky is concerned with a propositional conception of knowledge of language (competence) and so is a defender of the explanatory worth of folk categories. If FA has a true father, however, then it is Jerry Fodor. Fodor's *Psychological Explanation* (1968) is, in essence, a spinning out of FA against all of the then current non-mentalist positions. Chomsky is cited only once in an insignificant footnote, but the preface tells us that '[r]eaders familiar with the work of Professor Noam Chomsky will hardly fail to detect its influence on the general approach to psychological explanation taken here. Indeed, this book is in part an attempt to make explicit some aspects of a view of psychological explanation that comports naturally with the generative approach to language' (Fodor, 1968, p. ix). Since 1968, Fodor has continued to read generative linguistics within the framework of folk psychological categories; indeed, he insists upon it.[1] This reading, it must be noted, is not a mere exegetical motif in Fodor's work; it is central to his project that successful cognitive science, for example, linguistics, serves as evidence of the fecundity and soundness of scientific psychology being an extension, at least in part, of our folk understanding. After I have offered an alternative reading of the review, I shall suggest various reasons why, on my understanding, this erroneous construal prevailed.

Although the idea of behaviourism should be familiar from earlier chapters, two points about the first premise bear emphasis. First, while I mean to reject FA, I do not for a moment wish to suggest that Chomsky does not impugn the explanatory credentials of behaviourism; my target is the move from this critique to the conclusion of FA. Second, it is worth noting, if only because of the overdetermined nature of the 'behaviourism' label, that Skinner did not understand himself to be a 'logical behaviourist'. That is, Skinner was not concerned to show that notions of *belief, meaning, intention* etc. can be analysed in terms of a basic behavioural vocabulary. Skinner's position was that mentalistic vocabulary should be swept away, not analysed. This may be seen by considering the paradigm that Skinner was seeking to extrapolate to the human case. An account of the operant conditioning of a rat in a bar pressing regime is not an analysis of an extant intentional explanation; rather, one explains the behaviour simply through an understanding of the process by which the behaviour becomes contingent on certain environmental variables; likewise in the human case, although we do have an extant explanation, the behaviourist program is revisionary in a way it is not when directed at simply organisms. As we shall now see, the chief part of Chomsky's actual complaint against Skinner is precisely that his accounts do collapse into a misshapen analysis of familiar folk modes of description and explanation.

The second premise tells us that learning theoretic vocabulary is non-explanatory. This claim is brought into greatest relief when we consider language acquisition and syntactic competence, although it applies throughout human psychology. Skinner's position on language acquisition is a radical version of the familiar empiricist one, and one which is still widely exemplified within philosophy, if not elsewhere, by talk of 'training' and 'drilling'. The claim of *Verbal Behaviour* is that a child's verbal repertoire can only be developed via fine-grained differential reinforcement from parents and carers. In other words, language develops through, and is a mere reflection of, feedback from the environment. Chomsky (RSVB, pp. 562–5) points to two fundamental flaws in this position. First, it simply gets the facts wrong: children and adults alike show *creativity* with language, where they are spontaneously competent with sentences to which they have never previously been exposed – such as the sentences of the present chapter. This fact is quite inexplicable on Skinner's model. Likewise, competence appears to be on a fixed developmental trajectory that is broadly insensitive to feedback variation. Again, these facts are inexplicable if we follow Skinner. Second, it is clear that feedback alone will not produce mature competence, for, presumably, not *any* creature can acquire language given the right learning regime. In other words, some native structure must be in place. Chomsky expresses neutrality about what such structure might be. The structure might be specific to language – what was soon to be dubbed

Universal Grammar – or be simply greater and more complex processing capacity than Skinner allows, although this would just be to nod in the direction of a more complex story. Either way, Skinner's account is in the explanatory red, for native structure surely has a non-trivial role to play in language acquisition, but it is difficult to see what non-trivial role such structure could play in Skinner's overall methodological framework. The verdict is equally grave in the area of syntactic competence.

The theory of syntax or sentence structure presented in chapter 13 of *Verbal Behavior* is based upon the idea of sentences being the incarnations of skeletal frames, where what incarnates a given frame are verbal response types keyed to certain environmental types (nouns to objects, verbs to actions, adjectives to properties etc.). A further set of responses compose the basic elements. These are what Skinner called *autoclitics*, and they include order, predication, tense, quantification, agreement etc. as marked within morphology. It is a curiosity that, even to this day, variations on Skinner's theme are played as if they were novel ideas struggling free of dogma. On the contrary, the falsity of all such approaches was *demonstrated* nearly fifty years ago in Chomsky's early work.[2] In his review of Skinner, Chomsky restricts himself to pointing out that grammaticality is not, in general, preserved under substitution of lexical items within fixed frames. Consider:

    (1)   a. Struggling artists can be a nuisance.
               b. Marking essays can be a nuisance.

Both sentences have the same 'frame' and autoclitic features, but the grammatical properties of the sentences are clearly distinct. The subject of a. is plural, for we can substitute 'are' for 'can be' to produce an acceptable English sentence. The insertion of 'is' produces deviance. The situation is reversed in b., where the subject is singular, a gerundive, as may be noted by the following:

    (2)   a. *Bill's struggling artists is a nuisance.
               b. Bill's marking essays is a nuisance.

The fact that lexical insertion into frames does not uniformly produce grammaticality is not an isolated feature of certain English structures; it is the norm throughout the world's languages. Chomsky

(RSVB, p. 574) concludes, 'It is evident that more is involved in sentence structure than insertion of lexical items in grammatical frames; no approach to language that fails to take these deeper processes into account can possibly achieve much success in accounting for actual linguistic behavior'.

FA then concludes that given the transparent worthlessness of the learning theoretic approach, and the apparent absence of another alternative, the original folk categories remain in the field, as it were. This leads to the final conclusion that, *ceteris paribus*, such categories provide an appropriate basis for the explanation of behaviour.

The principal problem with the logic that leads to this conclusion is that the inadequacy of learning theory adds no credit to folk psychology's account. This can be missed if one is fixated on the revisionary dialectic, which goes from the apparent inviolability of folk psychology to the learning theoretic approach as its usurper. However, of course, FA does not provide any initial good reason to think that the folk categories were explanatorily in order. Otherwise put, we have no good reason to think that any extant framework is apt to explain verbal behaviour or rational action more generally. As it stands, the argument of the review is wholly negative and gives us no warrant whatever to infer anything about familiar mentalistic vocabulary, *pro* or *con*.[3] It may be further noted that the above arguments from acquisition and syntax do not in any way depend on folk categories. The arguments, for instance, do not credit speaker/hearers with propositional knowledge or belief-desire reasoning; they go through on data alone without an accompanying favoured explanatory framework. This is just to repeat one of the key points from the beginning of this section: the review is officially neutral on the correct explanation, if any, of linguistic behaviour.

This criticism of FA is further buttressed if we consider the competence/performance distinction. The distinction is not in play in the review, although it is implicit in both LSLT and SS. In essence, as Chapter 4 described, the distinction is between verbal behaviour and its interpretation (performance) and the cognitive resources (competence) necessary to account for such performance. Alternatively, 'performance' covers the processes of linguistic action and 'competence' covers the 'information' such processes access. Chomsky has never offered a theory of performance, and is neutral or sceptical on whether any adequate theory will be forthcoming, although a theory of competence will clearly form the basis of any such theory might one ever come along. In this light, the argument of the review may be read as saying that the problem with Skinner's model is that it wholly neglects competence. As Chomsky (RSVB, p. 574) quoted above puts it, 'no approach to language that fails to take these deeper processes [read: competence] into account can possibly achieve much success in accounting for actual linguistic behavior'. So, to think that folk psychology *qua* a general account of behaviour (*inter alia*) is supported by the failure of the learning theoretic account is simply to conflate performance with competence. Folk psychology appears not to enter into our understanding of competence at all, just as learning theory does not. The fact that the latter is therefore wholly inadequate to account for verbal behaviour should lead one to think likewise of the former. We shall return to this point in the following section, for many do think that competence is a state that falls under a folk understanding. Before that, as an alternative to FA, consider the following Eliminativist Argument (EA):

(i) The behaviourists (Skinner) argue that colloquial mentalistic vocabulary is non-explanatory of behaviour. It may be fruitfully replaced by learning theoretic vocabulary – *stimulus, response, control, reinforcement, probability* etc. – that places the cause of behaviour in environmental variables and not in internal states.

(ii) However, the terms of the new nomenclature are 'mere homonyms, with at most a vague similarity of meaning' to the vocabulary defined in the lab. In fact, the terms are 'metaphoric' of our 'mentalistic' ones, which 'simply disguises a complete retreat to mentalistic psychology' (RSVB, pp. 552–3).

(iii) Therefore, the 'terminological revision adds no objectivity to the familiar *mentalistic* mode of description' (ibid., p. 556), especially when 'used with the full vagueness of the ordinary vocabulary' (ibid., p. 559).

(iv) However, it just does not follow that the mentalistic vocabulary is explanatory. 'It is futile to inquire into the causation of verbal behavior [or any other type of behaviour] until much more is known about the specific character of this behaviour' (ibid., p. 575).

Evidently, this is a quite different argument from FA: it does not offer any support whatsoever to – let alone vindication of – our colloquial mentalistic vocabulary; in fact, the argument claims that the very failure of the learning theoretic vocabulary to advance beyond mentalism is its principal failing – a rose by any other name would smell as foul. Given the history of Chomsky's Skinner review, EA bears some elaboration. The first premise is agreed upon by all and may pass without further comment. The second premise and its conclusion in (iii) reflect the heart of the review's argument. Chomsky (RSVB, pp. 251–2) presents a dilemma for Skinner. Skinner sets out to show that behaviour in general is *lawful*; that is, it is under stimulus control. Of course, as our knowledge stands, we really have no hope of describing such laws under the strict conditions that the learning theoretic vocabulary is used in the lab. So, the behaviourist must either admit that, as things stand, behaviour cannot be understood as lawful or else he may restrict himself to those areas of behaviour that *appear* to be lawful, such as the bar pressing behaviour of trained rats. Either way, we have no reason to think that learning theory should replace folk psychology. Skinner, however, evades the dilemma by metaphorically extending the technical language of the laboratory to cover any piece of behaviour as required. Yet, this 'metaphoric reading . . . is no more scientific than the traditional approaches to the subject matter [*viz.*, folk psychology]' (RSVB, p. 552). That is to say, the new vocabulary is merely a misleading paraphrase of familiar modes of description, and does not constitute an insight into the actual causal antecedents of behaviour, let alone an appropriate vocabulary for the natural kinds of human behaviour. A nice example of Chomsky's critical method is provided by his response to Skinner's notion of a proper noun being a response under the *stimulus control* of a person or thing (RSVB, p. 553). If taken literally, that is, as the term *stimulus control* is used in the laboratory, this means that one is more likely to use a proper noun – its use is *reinforced* – when one is in the presence of the controlling thing or person. This is transparently absurd. First, we do not tend to utter a name repeatedly with increasing frequency when in the presence of its referent. Second, we use names all the time without being in the presence of their referents. Third, it is hard to see how one could generally be under the control of 'things' picked out by proper nouns such as *England, Henry VIII, Sherlock Holmes* etc. So, as Chomsky (RSVB, p. 554) notes, it 'appears that the word *control* here is merely a misleading paraphrase for the traditional *denote* or *refer*'.

As the theoretical situation stands, then, we are still in the domain of folk psychology: the new vocabulary of the laboratory extends to cover verbal behaviour only by metaphorical extension. In itself, of course, this does not signal the inadequacy of folk psychology; minimally, it shows that the new vocabulary is at best equal to the traditional mentalistic one. Chomsky assumes, however, that folk psychology does not constitute an adequate basis for the explanation of behaviour, verbal or otherwise. Two factors need to be separated here: performance and competence. First, although folk psychology covers verbal behaviour, Chomsky claims that no adequate account of behaviour is so much as on the horizon. Throughout the 1960s and continuing up to the present, Chomsky has claimed that free action, such as intentional verbal behaviour, is potentially a *mystery* beyond our understanding. If this is so, then we might be fated never to move beyond folk psychology, even though it is constitutively incapable of providing explanatorily deep, predictive generalizations (CL; *Problems of Knowledge and Freedom: The Russell Lectures* (PKF); RL, chapter 4; NHSLM, p. 72/95). Second, Chomsky does not so much as consider the thought that traditional mentalism may cast light on, or constraint, syntax and its acquisition.[4] Again, his position has not changed in the intervening years. Chomsky (ATS, p. 4) has, for sure, described his position as a species of 'mentalism' but only in a 'technical sense'; that is, '[m]entalistic linguistics is simply theoretical linguistics that uses performance as data . . . for the determination of competence, the latter being the primary object of its investigation' (ATS, p. 193, n.1). Further, in the same work, Chomsky reiterates his earlier censure of Skinner in the context of a note on Quine:

> [W]hat is proposed [by behaviourism] is a mentalist account differing from *traditional* ones *only* in that many distinctions are necessarily obscured because of the poverty of the terminological apparatus available for paraphrase of the *traditional* mentalistic notions. What is particularly puzzling, then, is the insistent claim that this paraphrase is somehow 'scientific' in a way in which *traditional* mentalism is not. (ATS, p. 204, n. 25) (my emphasis)

Clearly, Chomsky is here dealing with two construals of 'mentalism': a technical, methodological sense, premised on the competence/performance distinction and the traditional sense embodied in our familiar psychological idioms. Inquiry governed by mentalist principles in the former sense is in no way constrained, a priori or otherwise, to validate our folk conception. Further, the undue claim that the behaviourist vocabulary is 'scientific' in comparison with the traditional vocabulary does not suggest that the latter is 'scientific'; the clear implication is that neither is deserving of the epithet. Indeed, since behaviourism differs from 'traditional mentalism' 'only' in terms of relative obscurity, it would seem that technical mentalism marks a substantial departure from its traditional namesake.[5]

So, for reasons independent of the particular failure of behaviourism, folk psychology is not adequate for scientific employment. The failure of both is an instance of the putative failure of every theory of behaviour. The failure of folk psychology in particular follows from the thesis of meta-scientific eliminativism: folk theories do not make for science. Of course, this meta-thesis is entirely independent of any claims concerning behaviourism in particular.

3 ISSUES OF INTERPRETATION

A chief component of the argument so far is that folk categories are not essential to the development of theories of linguistic competence. Such categories might well be essential to our understanding (as far as it goes) of linguistic behaviour/performance, but such an aspect of our linguistic wherewithal is, or so it seems, beyond the reach of scientific inquiry. Linguistic competence is not so recalcitrant. Thus, if the eliminativist reading is to be maintained, then folk categories had better not be central to our understanding of linguistic competence. Yet the *prima facie* problem with this demand is that since the early 1960s Chomsky has readily appealed to *knowledge of language* as the object of linguistic inquiry. If Chomsky's position as early as 1959 was as I have depicted it, how come Chomsky spent the next few decades apparently claiming just the opposite? It is hardly surprising, in this light, that the significance of the Skinner review should be seen as positively supporting a certain mentalistic conception that is happily square with our ordinary notions. Rey (2003a,b), in particular, has recently expressed critical bemusement that Chomsky no longer appears to believe what he once did, that is, that propositional knowledge of grammar is computationally instantiated in the neuronal substrate such that it may enter into the aetiology of linguistic performance, just as our folk theory has it. Chomsky's (RR) response that the apparent intentional commitments were merely motivating glosses or metaphors might seem to some as 'creative' as my own reading of the Skinner review.

Chomsky exegesis is a complex matter, if for no other reason than that he has said many different things to many different audiences over the past 40 years. Still, I think a good case can be made that Chomsky has been as consistent as my portrayal depicts him to be. Of course, the particular psychology of a particular person is not that important. Who cares if, of late, Chomsky has changed his mind? The crucial issue is how we should understand and interpret the dominant theories in linguistics. In this regard, I think it has been an error to see them as essentially being a progression on, or even a vindication of, our ordinary folksy understanding. I shall briefly assess three factors that have led to the misconstrual in these matters. I do not, suffice it to say, intend the following remarks to be definitive, but they do carry a significant weight, I believe.

3.1 A grammar as a theory

From the mid-1950s to the late 1970s, Chomsky suggested that a generative grammar was best thought of as a *theory*. For example, in the Skinner review, we find the following passage from the final section that briefly elaborates Chomsky's positive view:

> The speaker's task is to *select* a particular *compatible* set of optional rules. If we know, from grammatical study, what *choices* are available to him and what conditions of *compatibility* the choices must meet, we can proceed meaningfully to investigate the factors that lead him to *make one choice* or another. The listener (or reader) must *determine* from an exhibited utterance, what *optional* rules were *chosen* in the construction of the utterance. [. . .] The child who learns a language has in some sense *constructed the grammar for himself on the basis of observation* of sentences and non-sentences (i.e. *corrections* by the verbal community). Study of the actual observed ability of a speaker . . . apparently *forces us to the conclusion* . . . that the young child has succeeded in carrying out . . . a remarkable type of *theory construction* . . . The fact [of remarkable rapidity] suggests that human beings are somehow specially designed to do this, with *datahandling* or '*hypothesis-formulating*' ability of unknown character and complexity. [. . .] In principle it may be possible to study the problem of determining what the built-in structure of an *information-processing (hypothesis forming)* system must be to enable it to arrive at the grammar of a language

from the available *data* in the available time. (RSVB, pp. 577–8) (my emphasis)

The italics mark the expressions that appear to show Chomsky being committed to an intentional framework of explanation. Similar passages can be found throughout Chomsky's works from the 1950s to the 1990s.[6] If we take Chomsky at his apparent word, then it is difficult not to see him as being committed to an intentional framework. Theory construction is an intentional activity *par excellence*. The language acquiring child must *represent* a hypothesis, *compare* it to the available data, *evaluate* its fit with the data, *assess* other possible hypotheses and *arrive at a judgement* as to the best hypothesis. In sum, acquiring a language on this model is a *rational achievement*.[7]

Upon closer examination, however, I think it is questionable that Chomsky was seriously considering this model as a genuine theoretical account. I think we can see Chomsky as employing 'theory' as a trope or metaphor. As we saw in Chapter 4, what was crucial about the 'theory' talk was not the appeal to hypothesis testing or the other explicitly intentional notions, in general, that would make acquiring a language a rational achievement. What the theory talk did, rather, was to capture the *formal* and *structural* features of competence and its development in such a way as to place it far beyond the reaches of any empiricist/behaviourist account. Talking of theories did this well enough, but it is a quite separate issue whether the linguistic theories developed required any answers to the philosophical problems that arise once one employs intentional vocabulary. Thus, when the principles and parameters model was developed in the late 1970s/early 1980s, linguists of the generative tradition saw how to ditch theory talk and took this to be an advance.

Note, in support of this reading, that in the passage quoted, 'hypothesis-formulating' occurs in 'scare quotes'. In the same section, Chomsky (RSVB, p. 576) writes, 'It is *reasonable* to regard the grammar of a language L *ideally* as a mechanism that provides an enumeration of the sentences of L in *something like* the way in which a deductive theory gives an enumeration of a set of theorems' (my emphasis). Similarly, 'What [the child] accomplishes can fairly be described as theory construction of a non-trivial kind . . . a theory that predicts the grammatical structure of each of an infinite class of potential physical events' (EML, p. 528). A few years later, 'It seems plain that language acquisition is based on the child's discovery of what *from a formal point of view* is a deep and abstract theory – a generative grammar for his language – many of the concepts and principles of which are only remotely related to experience by long and intricate chains of unconscious *quasi-inferential* steps' (ATS, p. 58).

It would seem that Chomsky is using 'theory' and the attendant terminology in a specific sense; he is not depicting the child to be a little scientist *as such* but rather suggesting that aspects of the capacities generative theory attributes to the child may be fruitfully conceived as being theory like. Again, what is crucial here is that there is a formal correspondence, which usurps the then prevailing empiricist models. In this light, theory talk might well be properly seen as a motivating gloss on the generative theories of transformational structure that is radically undetermined by data available to the child.

There are roughly four related senses in which a grammar might be understood to be a theory.[8] First, a grammar is a quasi-deductive structure (at least on the early model), with T-markers or deep/surface structure pairs serving as the predictions the theory makes as derived from the base given a specified set of generalizations or transformations. Second, a grammar is underdetermined by the data. In this sense, like a theory, a grammar is not a mere description of, or generalization over, the data. Third, a grammar deals with unobservables (concepts indefinable in experiential terms) and generalizations that go far beyond any data set. Fourth, grammars are evaluated not merely in terms of empirical coverage; some measure of simplicity and economy is also relevant.

Now, these features are 'formal' in Chomsky's sense; he is perfectly happy to describe a grammar so understood as a 'mechanism' or a 'device' (in a sense familiar from computability theory). Further, the child who constructs a theory-like grammar need not be viewed as an agent in any sense. In a note to the long passage quoted above, Chomsky writes, 'there is nothing essentially mysterious about this ["hypothesis formulation"]. Complex innate behaviour patterns and "innate tendencies to learn in specific ways" have been carefully studied in lower organisms' (RSVB, p. 577, n. 48). In *Aspects*, Chomsky writes, 'the structure of particular languages may very well be largely determined by factors over which the individual has no conscious control . . . [A] child cannot help constructing a particular sort of transformational grammar to account for the data presented to him, any more than he can control his perception of solid objects or his attention to line and angle' (ATS, p. 59).

Thus, it seems that Chomsky is using 'theory' to designate 'formal' features of generative grammars that distinguish them from empiricist models. On this basis, one *can* understand the child to be a theorist, yet such a theorist is not a rational agent, but a 'device', whose state resembles in relevant respects the achievements of rational agents. In this light, it is perfectly reasonable for Chomsky to motivate the generative model by treating the child *as if* he were an agent who manages the 'rational achievement' of acquiring a language. Of course, humans *are* agents, but not *qua* acquirers of language.

It bears noting that Chomsky's analogy of generative grammars to theories has ceased due to two related factors. One is the development of the *principles and parameters* model that depicts language acquisition as a non-theoretical switching mechanism. The other factor is a change in the character of the theories themselves, which now describe a uniform computational process and the factors that constrain it (see Chapters 7 and 8). In this respect, there are no conceptually rich laws specific to each language (Collins, 2004; 'Three factors in language design' (TFLD)). These developments, however, are not outside of the generative tradition's inquiry into the native human linguistic capacity. Of course, it might be that Chomsky has changed his mind, but that is irrelevant, for the developments show that the apparent commitment to children as rational theorists was not an essential part of the generative model of a science of language.

3.2 Cartesian linguistics

From the early 1960s on, Chomsky (CILT, ATS, CL, ML, RL) has consistently appealed to the 'Cartesian' tradition for motivation and fruitful antecedents to the generative enterprise (the tradition goes from English neo-Platonists (Cudworth) through Descartes and Port Royal up to Kant, Schlegel and Humboldt). For Chomsky, the 'Cartesian' epithet is a loose descriptive term, not intended to cover only Cartesians or all facets of Cartesian philosophy.[9] Still, it is very easy to see Chomsky as aligning himself with Descartes in the sense that his concerns are primarily epistemological, and he has been read in this way by Fodor (1983, 2000a), who was perhaps the most influential reader of Chomsky. On this view, Chomsky is concerned with 'innate knowledge of language' much as Descartes, Leibniz and others were concerned with our peculiar knowledge of geometry and the Deity. None is, in the first instance, if at all, making any claims as to the structure of the human brain; their concern is for the epistemic standing of our knowledge. I have responded to this reading at length elsewhere (Collins, 2004); here, I only want to point to some contrary evidence.

First, Chomsky's initial appeal to the notion of innateness was made on the basis of the work of Lenneberg (RSVB, p. 577, n. 48, EML, p. 529, n. 2), and not on the works of Descartes or Leibniz. Chomsky saw linguistic competence or knowledge as a factor that enters into linguistic behaviour, although one that cannot be accounted for in terms of the control of behaviour via external variables. The concern here is not for epistemology but a theoretical factorization of the components that *might* explain our linguistic behaviour (especially see RL, chapter 1). Thus, Chomsky (RSVB, pp. 548–9 and 577, n. 48) accuses Skinner of wholly neglecting the 'biological structure' of the organism. Skinner is not accused of getting the epistemology wrong.

Second, Chomsky's concern was to offer an explicitly formulated version of the 'rationalist/Cartesian' strain of thought in a particular domain, the explicitness enabling empirical testability (ATS, p. 53). In this sense, the old theories were 'reconstructed as empirical theories' (OI, p. 77). Again, as we saw above, the epistemic standing of the speaker is not at issue. It is not lost on anyone, of course, that the knowledge at issue, however, construed, need not be conscious. My present point is that, for Chomsky, as soon as we dispense with a condition of 'conscious accessibility' epistemological issues of warrant or justification cease to be relevant. The 'knowledge' theoretically attributed is a structured state to which the speaker stands in no external relation at all, although the state does contribute to the linguistic judgements of the speaker, which may thus serve as evidence for the nature of the state (ATS, pp. 8–9). We may rightfully call such states 'cognitive' as a reflection of the phenomena that concern us (phenomena picked out as being mental as opposed to chemical or pancreatic or whatever), but the designation does not mark them out as being essentially different from other kinds of states studied in science or, perforce, as demanding a distinct methodology. In sum, Chomsky does not separate the cognitive state from what is known in virtue of being in that state. In this light, for a child to be a little theorist is simply for the child's cognitive state to stand in relation to her experience in certain formal respects that can be modelled on the reflective relation a scientist has towards data. The 'metaphor', whether enlightening or not, was never a substantial explanatory commitment.

3.3 Common cause

Throughout the period that concerns us, Chomsky (ATS, ML, RL) was at pains to establish linguistic inquiry as a genuine naturalistic pursuit; in particular, he sought to spike philosophical claims that linguistics was infected with various dubious rationalist philosophical assumptions about innate knowledge or conscious access. In this regard, Chomsky made common cause with 'intentional realists', such as Fodor and Katz, against the various species of anti-realism that claimed that 'there is no fact of the matter' about either semantic or syntactic properties or that the only facts are dispositional or behavioural (most centrally, Quine, 1960, 1969, 1970). Chomsky's concern, however, may be rightly seen as a commitment to a properly formulated rationalism as an empirical research programme. As we have seen, this does not involve an essential commitment to the explanatory status of intentional vocabulary; the commitment, rather, was to the empirical integrity of the domains commonly picked out by 'knowledge' and 'meaning'. In other words, Chomsky sought to secure an area of empirical research, not to establish that the explanations in that area are to be framed in an intentional manner. The fact that those who doubted the empirical integrity of the intentional idiom also doubted that there were facts of the matter was not Chomsky's chief concern; he only sought to show that empirical inquiry could be conducted; that is, there are facts of the matter beyond behaviour, no matter how one chooses to describe them. This approach is explicitly set out in section 8 of the opening chapter of *Aspects* and rearticulated throughout the later *Reflections on Language*.

To repeat, I neither intend the above considerations to be decisive, nor even to speak to much of Rey's (2003a,b) careful discussions. One issue, in particular, is untouched: the apparent intentionality of 'representational' states of the brain; how it is, for example, that the human brain represents verb phrases, case features etc. This issue, I think, is independent from the present one. It might be, for example, that some notion of representation is essential to the idea of computation, but that would not establish that every computational theory of a cognitive competence trades in propositional

attitudes (see NCMP; RtR). Indeed, it might well be that the operative notion of representation is quite distant from the folksy idea of
a proposition. It is doubtful, for example, that the idea of *mis*representation has any application to the language faculty; this forecloses
the duality of a representation and what it represents, as if a syntactic structure were an image of something beyond it.[10] More formally,
I think we can understand the idea of representation as used in
linguistics as that of a *transparent object*. Let us say that an object is
transparent when operations can apply to it that change the constituent relations that hold between its parts. So, the formulae of a theory
of arithmetic are transparent objects because rules of inference apply
to them. A formally defined space is also a representation in that
topological transformations warp it, and the data store in a computer is representational in that it can be accessed, erased etc. The
particular notation or encoding is ultimately irrelevant, for we can,
for example, take the same set of relations to be encoded geometri-
cally or algebraically, as Descartes showed us. What is crucial is that
the same relations are preserved, which is reflected in the set of operations permissible on the given objects. The operations, we may say,
define the representations much as they do in mathematics when we
define groups, rings etc. and their various sub-species. A representation, then, is a structure made up of opaque objects (e.g. points,
numbers, lexical features) that is transparent to operations.

4   CHOMSKY'S CURRENT VIEW

Consider the following recent remarks by Chomsky (OINC, p. 397):

> [I]n English one uses the locutions 'know a language,' 'knowledge
> of language,' where other (even similar) linguistic systems use such
> terms as 'have a language,' 'speak a language,' etc. That may be
> one reason why it is commonly supposed (by English speakers)
> that some sort of cognitive relation holds between Jones and his
> language, which is somehow 'external' to Jones; or that Jones has
> a 'theory of his language,' a theory that he 'knows' or 'partially
> knows.' . . . One should not expect such concepts to play a role in
> systematic inquiry into the nature, use, and acquisition of language,
> and related matters, any more than one expects such informal
> notions as 'heat' or 'element' or 'life' to survive beyond rudimen-
> tary stages of the natural sciences.

Chomsky here is not denying that we *know* languages; his point is
that the locution simply reflects English collocation, and facts of
collocation do not make for theoretical insight, although they often
make for metaphysical and epistemological confusion. So, the epistemic locution is perfectly appropriate to pick out, albeit informally,
the object of linguistic inquiry. For instance, the linguist is primarily
concerned with the *judgements* made by competent users of a language rather than with acts of usage *qua* performance.[11] It might seem
that putting matters this way places the folksy notion of judgement
at the heart of linguistic theory. We must, though, distinguish between
theory and data. Linguistic judgements are the preponderate data
and so informally mark out the object of inquiry, but this is only
contingently so; it *might* be that advances in neuroscience will enable
richer direct data from brain structure, even if it is wholly unclear at
the moment what such data would look like.[12] In general, there is no
restriction on what the relevant data are, for the genuine object of
inquiry – what our theories are about – is arrived at *a posteriori*: our
theoretical conception of language is *whatever* serves to explain most
coherently what we determine to be the relevant data – there is no
a priori constraint from folk notions of language. Presently, and
perhaps forever more, we have no way of identifying the relevant
data apart from using folk notions. However, data and theory are not
the same. The theories we develop will *not* attribute to the speaker/
hearer *beliefs* about our theoretical technology. That is, the present
theories are about the structure of speaker/hearers' brains; they are
not about an independent 'something' of which the speaker/hearer
has knowledge. In other words, intuitive *judgement* is included in the
explananda of our theories; it is not part of the *explananas*. Nothing
would change, at the level of theory, if we were incapable of reflective
judgement on what our utterances mean. Self-consciousness is one
thing, linguistic capacity is another (NH, pp. 142–3).

So, there is nothing wrong at all with our folksy way of talking;
indeed, it is, and may ever be, indispensable to our picking out the
relevant phenomena. Consider:

> There is no problem for ordinary language . . . But there is no rea-
> son to suppose that common usage of such terms as *language* or
> *learning* (or *belief* and numerous others like them), or others
> belonging to similar semantic fields in other linguistic systems,
> will find any place in attempts to understand the aspects of the

world to which they pertain. Likewise, no one expects the commonsense terms *energy* or *liquid* or *life* to play a role in the sciences, beyond a rudimentary level. The issues are much the same. (LBS, p. 23)

Chomsky is decrying any suggestion that our common theory-free idioms are under threat from scientific advance. However, the fact that their mere presence might be inviolable offers no reason to think that they are likely to partake in a genuine scientific understanding of the phenomena they currently pick out. As Chomsky makes clear, one requires no advancement at all in the science of the mind to arrive at this judgement in regard to folk psychology; the judgement follows from a simple generalization from the cases of physics, biology and chemistry. The burden is on those who see the science of the mind as dependent on folk categories to make clear how scientific – as opposed to philosophical – advancement relies on such dependence. At least in the case of linguistics, Chomsky's judgement is that the burden cannot be met.

CHAPTER 6

LANGUAGE: INSIDE OR OUTSIDE THE MIND?

I don't want to give a definition of thinking, but if I had to I should probably be unable to say anything more about it than that it was a sorting of buzzing that went on inside my head. But I don't really see why we need to agree on a definition at all. The important thing is to draw a line between the properties of the brain, or of a man, that we want to discuss, and those that we don't.

Turing (1952/2004, p. 494)

1 INTRODUCTION

We have seen how, for Chomsky, linguistic theory is a branch of psychology (ultimately biology). On this conception, the two leading questions are as follows: (1) What does a speaker/hearer know when she knows a language? (2) How does the normal speaker/hearer acquire that knowledge? In other words, linguistics is concerned with competence and its development. On the face of it, however, linguistics cannot be a wholly cognitive enterprise; for language, it seems, is one thing, and our knowledge of it is another. After all, it looks like an egregious category mistake to say that English is a type of cognitive state. In this chapter we shall lay out and defend Chomsky's reasoning that, in a certain sense, the very notion of language is redundant for theoretical inquiry; linguistics is concerned with internal states alone, what Chomsky calls 'I-languages', and not with languages as external 'objects' ('E-languages'), if such there be.

2 DOUBTS ABOUT THE VERY IDEA OF A LANGUAGE

In an interview from the late 1970s, Chomsky (GE, p. 107) made the following remarks:

> I do not know why I never realized before, but it seems obvious, when you think about it, that the notion of language is a much more abstract notion than the notion of a grammar. The reason is that grammars have to have a real existence, that is, there is something in your brain that corresponds to the grammar . . . But there is nothing in the real world corresponding to language.

A few years later, Chomsky ('On the representation of form and function' (RFF), p. 7) wrote:

> The shift of focus from language (an obscure and I believe ultimately unimportant notion) to grammar is essential if we are to proceed towards assimilating the study of language to the natural sciences. It is a move from data collection and organization to the study of the real systems that actually exist (in the mind/brain) and that enter into an explanation of the phenomena we observe. Contrary to what is widely assumed, the notion 'language' (however characterized) is of a higher order of abstraction and idealization than grammar, and correspondingly, the study of 'language' introduces new and more difficult problems. One may ask whether there is any reason to try to clarify or define such a notion and whether any purpose is served in doing so. Perhaps so, but I am sceptical.

Essentially, a 'language' is an 'epiphenomenon' determined by the grammar, 'perhaps in conjunction with other systems of mind, or even other factors, depending on how we choose to conceive of the notion "language"' (RFF, p. 5). Before we unpack these remarks, some historical considerations are worth broaching.

Although it is true that only in the late 1970s/early 1980s did Chomsky begin to speak explicitly of grammars being more 'real' than languages, this inversion of (philosophical) commonsense had been implicit for many years. First, as we have seen, Chomsky's chief concern was never for languages understood as a set of well-formed symbol strings independent of the mind of a speak/hearer. This is reflected in the explanatory goals of linguistic theory as set out in LSLT and SS. Furthermore, the concern for *weak generative capacity*, as defined over such a set of strings, was always a mere minimal condition to exclude certain types of grammar; it was never an end in itself (see Chapter 2 for discussion). If the goal of linguistic theory were a characterization of a set of strings independent of the mind of the speaker/hearer, one would expect weak generative capacity to be of inherent importance.

Second, Chomsky had made a number of remarks in the 1970s that indicated the relative 'reality' of grammars and languages. For example: 'Since the language has no objective existence apart from its mental representation, we need not distinguish between "systems of belief" and "knowledge"' (LM, p., 169, n. 3). Chomsky's point here is that since language is simply an abstraction from the mental states of speaker/hearers, which are the real concern of the theory, a subject's 'knowledge' of language is not knowledge of an external 'object' she might go right or wrong about in her beliefs. Hence, 'knowledge' is simply a stand-in for mental states and carries no presupposition of an external object as our colloquial notion often does. In other words, the 'knowledge' at issue is not relational but more a state of the speaker/hearer. Chomsky writes:

> The basic cognitive notion is 'knowledge of grammar,' not 'knowledge of language' . . . Knowledge of grammar, like knowledge of mathematics, of biology, of the behaviour of objects in the physical world . . . is not expressible as some variety of true belief . . . Knowledge of language, so understood, involves or perhaps entails particular instances of *knowledge-that* and *belief-that*. . . . But knowledge is not constituted of such elements and no atomistic, element-by-element account of the character of growth of knowledge of this sort is possible. A system of knowledge in this sense is an integrated complex represented in the mind . . . We might say that each such cognitive system pertains . . . to a specific domain of potential fact, a kind of mentally constructed world. If there is a domain of actual fact that is not too dissimilar, the cognitive system can be effectively used. The case of language is unusual in that, there being no external standard, the domains of potential and actual fact are identical; *X*'s grammar is what *X*'s mind constructs. (RFF, p. 6; cf., RL, pp. 164–6)

Our knowledge of language, therefore, is not answerable to an external reality; *pace* Fodor (1983, pp. 4–6), the knowledge is not of 'truths' about language. It is more that 'knowledge of language' picks out those states of the mind/brain that enter into an explanation of what we normally call 'knowledge of language': 'Linguistics is simply that part of psychology that is concerned with one specific class of steady states, the cognitive structures that are employed in speaking and understanding' (RL, p. 160). Again, the domain of linguistics is the internal states of speaker/hearers; language is of no concern, at least if the notion is understood independently of cognitive states (Chomsky (RL, *Knowledge of Language: Its Nature, Origin, and Use* (KoL)) introduced the term 'cognize' as a neologism to replace the confusing 'knowledge', but the new term seemed to generate more problems than it is worth).

Chomsky was soon to codify this distinction between internal states and external languages as a difference between 'I-languages' and 'E-languages'. Before we turn to these notions, let us consider the opening quotation from Chomsky and adduce some reasons to be suspicious of our inchoate notion of language, at least from the perspective of theoretical inquiry.

Chomsky's charge is that the notion of a language is abstract and probably does not correspond to anything in the real world. A grammar, on the other hand, is real, for, ex hypothesi, a grammar is simply a steady state of the mind/brain of the speaker/hearer. The substance behind Chomsky's claim has a number of aspects.

(i) *Variability*. Colloquially, we think of languages as things such as English, German, Italian etc. But a moment's reflection will tell us that there is immense variability between speaker/hearers' competence in any given language. The variability is most obvious in phonology, but applies equally to our lexical competence, in regard to the words we understand and how we understand them (e.g. 'livid' for some means 'white', for others 'red'). There is even great variability in syntax between dialectics; compare urban African-American, Ulster, Scottish and southern English. The same pattern applies as one moves north up the Italian peninsula, or across Germany, or as one criss-crosses the vast array of dialects in China. That we speak of 'English', say, rather than a myriad of dialects appears to be a matter of convenience and historical contingency. Such factors are fascinating in their own right, but they do not tell us that there is 'English' beyond the heterogeneity we find.

One might be tempted by the thought that languages are to be classified on the basis of peoples who can verbally communicate with one another or by way of some intersection of properties that populations share. The problem for any such strategies is that variability goes right down to each individual language user; we might as well say we each have our own language or that we all speak one single language with regional differences. Either option is vacuous if our concern is to characterize the idea of a language as a mind-independent object. The notion of communication offers no assistance either, for the notion is too nebulous in itself and fails to classify languages according to our expectations. For example, people on the Dutch/German boarder communicate with an ease neither would enjoy were they speaking to an Austrian or a native of Amsterdam. In general, whether two populations use the same language is analogous to asking whether two cities are near each other. The answer depends on one's interests, if one is flying or driving, say. There is no sense in which cities are near each other in absolute terms.

Two points are worth making to guard against potential misunderstanding. First, the variability of language does not mean that it is impossible to devise some notion that classifies languages in a non-vacuous way, and, for many practical purposes, loose definitions work well enough for language as they do for any other area (Newton's approximate laws put a man on the moon). Still, even if some classification of mind-independent languages were to be available, we have no reason whatsoever to expect it to play a role in theoretical inquiry. The key empirical issues of the nature of linguistic competence and how it is acquired appear to be independent of the dubious task of defining languages. Second, the variability of language does not mean that there might not be significant commonalities within and between the ways populations of humans speak and understand one another; indeed, there clearly are such commonalities. The task of discerning such shared structure, however, neither presupposes nor leads to the idea of a language independent of the cognitive states of speaker/hearers. We may, of course, abstract the notion of a language from whatever clusters of common features we find, and such an abstraction might prove convenient, but there need not be any more reality to it than that. (We shall return to this issue below.)

(ii) *Normativity*. One reason we unthinkingly speak of languages is that we have a notion of linguistic error and readily think of some people being better or worse with language, as well as people acquiring a language or only having a partial grasp of one. Although such ideas play a significant role in our everyday thinking about language, they are inherently *normative* or *evaluative* and so do not establish that there are languages to be right or wrong about; they reflect our interests, conceptions of group belonging and structures of authority (e.g. educational institutions, media) rather than matters of fact.

A human simply speaks and understands the way she does, with deviation and quirks, as is expected in any complex system. Error can only be assessed relative to some external standard. On this perspective, error is in the eye (ear) of the beholder, and not an aspect of the system understood as an object of theoretical inquiry. For sure, we need not be told that we have made an error; we may recognize it ourselves. There is, then, deviation either from one's own standards or those of others, but such standards merely reflect the constraints we place on each other, willingly or not. It does not follow that there are facts of the *right* language independently of our choice of standards. Sometimes, as in the case of Ebonics (African-American vernacular), there are political controversies as to whether a population should be educated out of a way of talking. There should, however, racist assumptions apart, be no question about whether the vernacular is a perfectly correct way of speaking from the appropriate standard, that is, not the standard of a racist culture. Similar issues arise in many countries based on class and region. The decisions to be made are political or moral, and are not factual.

More complex considerations arise in the case of language development or second-language learning but with much the same conclusions. It is perfectly appropriate to speak of a child as only having a partial grasp of English, but this is from the perspective of an understanding of the child's expected mature competence. An external language is not required to make such talk coherent. For example, if all adults were to disappear, children would still have a complex of mental states with their particular properties as theorized by a grammar, and those state would then develop in a different way, no better or worse than they would develop otherwise. Similarly, the second-language learner has a partial grasp of a language from the perspective of native speakers of the target language, but, again, if there is no external language that the native speakers fully grasp, then there is nothing the learners are only partially grasping. The evaluation of second-language learners is based on a comparison with a second class of speakers, and not an independent language.

(iii) *Irrelevance*. Lastly, the very notion of a language independent of speaker/hearers seems to be irrelevant to any empirical inquiry. Many philosophers have assumed that, in some sense, a language must exist apart from individual agents in order to allow for communication (see, e.g. Davidson, 1990; Dummett, 1993; Devitt, 2006). On the face of it, however, an independent language appears to be neither necessary nor sufficient for communication. It is not necessary, for communication clearly proceeds across 'languages' or even in the absence of language. Moreover, if communication is minimally understood as the eliciting of an understanding for another, then this may come about through various cues and suggestions without the understanding being encoded in a shared public form. An independent language is not sufficient for communication, for if the language were independent, then a complex story must be told of how interlocutors orientate themselves in the same manner towards the language.

It is not to be denied, of course, that linguistic communication involves an arbitrary association of meanings with signs, either in speech or orthography or hand gestures. Two points, however, are crucial. First, what might be said to be external to the speakers, such as words on a page, do not inherently possess the properties that concern linguistics (semantic, syntactic, phonological). Second, it is the mental resources of speaker/hearers that, as it were, animate the external items; it is thus the mental resources that are the proper target of inquiry. Consider, for instance, the mimicking of a parrot. It is a mere matter of decision whether we want to take its mimicking as tokens of English ('Whose a pretty boy, then?'). Equally clear, though, is that it is only the human mind that can invest the tokens with semantic and syntactic properties. One is free, of course, to take whatever class of items the human mind may project semantic, syntactic and phonological properties onto as a language, but this is an empty exercise, for, again, the proper target of inquiry remains the mental resources that underlie such a projection.

It can seem peculiar that, in a sense, linguistics is not about language, as if physics is not really about the physical, or as if biology is not really about the biological. There is, in fact, nothing peculiar at all. No science is constrained by inchoate common-sense conceptions of its proper domain. Sciences are about whatever successful theories discover. For example, we do not constrain physics to cleave to a commonsense conception of objects and their properties. Similarly, if linguistics, qua empirical inquiry, has no explanatory recourse to languages as shared, mind-independent entities, then so be it. Whatever our common-sensical conception of language is, empirical inquiry need pay no heed to it, just as physics pays no heed to our commonsense take on material objects. For example, physical objects at every level are mainly empty space; 'solidity' is an interaction effect of one physical system in reaction to another. A neutrino, unlike my hand, could happily pass through my computer.

Chomsky ('Human language and other semiotic systems' (HLSS), pp. 32–3) sums up these points in the following passage:

> The question, what is a language, is not, as it stands, a question of science at all just as the question, what is a visual system, or a system of locomotion, is not as it stands a question of science. Rather, these questions pose problems of conceptual analysis . . . Suppose, for example, that I meet a biologist who is studying the flight of birds, and I suggest to him the following line of inquiry; 'What is "flying"? It is an act in which some creature rises into the air and lands some distance away, with the goal of reaching some remote point. Humans can 'fly' about 30 feet, chickens about 300 feet, Canada geese far more. Humans and chickens "cluster" (only an order of magnitude difference), as compared with geese, eagles, and so on. So if you are interested in the mechanisms of bird flight, why not pay attention to the simpler case of human "flight".' The biologist is not likely to be too impressed.

The point of the analogy is simply that real phenomenon do not come packaged in ways that correspond to our intuitive concepts, whether of language, vision, flying, swimming or whatever.

Our intuitive categories are largely irrelevant to empirical inquiry and only become relevant if they are sufficiently sharpened to reflect the actual phenomenon of our inquiry, in which case, though, again, their intuitive standing becomes irrelevant. That linguistics is not about 'language' turns out to be quite banal. To see the point here, consider Devitt's (2006) suggestion that a grammar is about an external language; a separate inquiry is required to figure out how such a grammar relates to our cognitive states. In a phrase, 'linguistic reality' is not 'psychological reality'. The thought can seem obvious; indeed, Devitt is bemused that anyone would deny it. But now ask the question: *What non-cognitive phenomena would an adequate grammar explain?* It is difficult to think of any such phenomena. For example, is a sentence ambiguous in itself independent of any interpreting mind? The very thought is a category mistake. A sentence is ambiguous just when it robustly supports two or more construals. The construals are what the grammar targets. A sentence understood as a concrete token could no more be inherently ambiguous than it could be inherently meaningful. More generally, a phrase structure is not a description of the properties of a sentence, as if we already have a clear idea what such an abstract object could be. The structure is a hypothesis about the mental states that enter into understanding and production of what we commonsensically think of as sentences. In this light, a grammar is thoroughly psychological.

3   E-LANGUAGES AND I-LANGUAGES

In *Knowledge of Language* (KoL), Chomsky codified much of the above reasoning in terms of a distinction between two conceptions of language that have animated inquiry, at least in the modern period (from Descartes onwards): *E-language* and *I-language*.

'E-language' designates conceptions that take language to be *external* and *extensional*. There are two broad respects in which language might be seen as external. First, language might be seen to be essentially public or social, where, although human cognitive resources might be essential to the character of the language, the language itself has an independent existence and can be theorized independently of theorizing speaker/hearers' mental states. Hence, analogies with games are often employed (after Wittgenstein, 1953). If there were no humans, then there would be no game of chess, but it does not follow that the rules of chess apply to mental states, or that chess theory is a branch of psychology. The point applies to any designed 'object'. Furniture depends upon human beings, but chairs and wardrobes are not therefore in one's head. In short, it can seem that taking language to be mental involves a confusion of *dependence* with *constitution*. Language depends upon mentality, but language is not therefore mental, no more than chess is or a bedside lamp is.

Second, language can be conceived to be external on analogy with mathematics. Based on this conception, languages are abstract objects that humans represent but do not create. Just as in mathematics, although it is perfectly legitimate to inquire into the psychology of a linguistic (mathematical) competence, the object of our competence is independent. When we prove a theorem, we are not making a psychological discovery; just so, when we hypothesize a certain syntactic structure, we are not making a psychological claim (Katz, 1981; Katz and Postal, 1991).

The notion of language being *extensional* means that a language is conceived as a set of symbol strings, understood concretely or abstractly. English, one may say, might be understood as the set of sentences that would be understood by a certain population under various idealizations. As we saw above, it is difficult to find the correct conditions to make this notion non-vacuous. Still, if one is convinced that language is external to the mind/brain, then the extensional conception appears to be mandatory, for one could not identify language with the states that constitute speak/hearers' understanding of their sentences, which is an aspect of the human mind/brain.

'I-language' designates what Chomsky had previously called a 'grammar'. The notion of a grammar had been ambiguous between the linguist's theory and what the theory was of – a class of mental states. The new term removes the ambiguity, where an I-language is the states of the speaker/hearer and not what the linguist produces.

The 'I' of 'I-language' is intended to suggest *internal, intensional* and *individual*. As a conception of language that animates linguistic inquiry, this means that the focus is on internal states of the speaker/hearer's mind/brain and not on their behaviour or any public, abstract object. The states are understood as *intensional* in contrast to *extensional*. Based on this view, a language is not a set of symbol strings, but the generative procedure (or function computed) that maps from lexical items to structures that might be taken to underlie our linguistic performances. Of course, one could always characterize the input/output pairs of the function computed as a set. Chomsky's point is simply that this would be an abstraction from the competence; after all, no mind/brain realizes an infinite object. Furthermore, an extensional characterization of the function, while formally permissible, of course, would not correspond to any language as conceived on the E-language conception (this will become clear shortly). Finally, an I-language is individual in the sense that we each enjoy various peculiarities of competence. Any theory, for sure, will seek the broadest generalizations, but we should not lose sight of the fact that if our object is the mind/brain, rather than an ideal external object, then much individual variation will have to be accommodated. In essence, the 'individual' condition is simply making explicit that, strictly speaking, there are no languages from the theoretical perspective; there are only individual mental states that share whatever properties prove to be theoretically salient.

4 I-LANGUAGES AND LINGUISTICS

The leading questions for linguistics, according to Chomsky (MP, pp. 1–2), are

  (i)   What does a competent speaker/hearer know?
  (ii) How is that knowledge acquired?

Three ancillary questions are

  (iii) How is the knowledge put to use?
  (iv) How did linguistic competence evolve in the human species?
  (v)   How are the structures identified in answer to question
        (i) realized in neuronal structure?

The latter three questions are ancillary, not because they are unimportant or somehow misplaced, but because they only make sense relative to answers to question (i). If one doesn't know what structures and features linguistic competence involves, then it is impossible to say how they are used, how they are evolved or how they are physically realized. Furthermore, it is difficult to see how inquiry into the latter three questions might aid inquiry into question (i), at least at the present state of knowledge. Assuming, then, that these are legitimate lines of inquiry for empirical linguistics, let us consider how the E and I conceptions of language fair at animating the inquiries.

4.1 Knowledge

On the face of it, the 'knowledge' question appears to presuppose an E-language conception, with language as the object of knowledge independently constituted of the mental states that represent it. As we have seen, however, the 'knowledge' locution harbours no substantive epistemology; in particular, it does not presuppose any external relation between the mind/brain and language. In inquiring after what a speaker/hearer knows, we only need to have in view the structure of the subject's internal states, regardless of whatever presuppositions our colloquial notion of knowledge carries. There has been a good deal of confusion on this issue. Many philosophers have imagined that there is a fallacious argument in the offing here, as if the interest in cognitive states is meant to show that there is no E-language (e.g. Soames, 1984; Devitt and Sterelny, 1987; Katz and Postal, 1991; Devitt, 2006). The 'argument' is meant to be fallacious on the basis of the aforementioned difference between *dependence* and *constitution*; that is, while the existence of language might well depend on human mentality, a language itself is not a psychological kind. As we shall see, this very idea amounts to nothing more than an a priori insistence on the sovereignty of commonsense over science. In truth, there is no internalist argument against the existence of E-languages; there is only a cluster of theoretical and evidential considerations that show the notion of an E-language to be redundant in linguistic inquiry, regardless of what commonsense might sanction. There are three basic lines of argument that are meant to show the relevance of E-languages.

First, in general, relations of dependence do not make for theoretical demarcation. For example, presumably, every natural domain of inquiry depends on the underlying physical substrate, but it does not follow that every inquiry is a branch of physics. We should not be biological or economical *eliminativists* just because the kinds in both domains supervene on physical properties.

Second, if language were of a psychological kind, then one would expect linguistic evidence to come from psychology; as it is, the preponderant data come from speaker/hearers' judgements *about* language. Worse, it is difficult to see how psychological data, understood in terms of internal processes and states, could even bear on syntax. Could we discover that *Visiting relatives can be boring* is not ambiguous after all?

Third, many have appealed to what we might call the 'Martian Consideration' (see Katz, 1981; cf., Quine, 1969, 1970; Stich, 1972 and the references above). Imagine that Martians landed and, to all appearances, spoke English; we could, surprisingly enough, communicate with them just as well as we do with our English-speaking fellow humans. In such circumstances, we would consider the Martians to be English speakers. If, however, Chomsky is right, then the Martians' internal states are crucial in deciding whether they speak English or not, that is, whether they should be classified as speakers of the same language as us. Now, of course, the Martians' internal states might differ from ours as wildly as logic permits, but the fact that we would, independently of any internalist inquiry, be able to discern shared properties between the Martians and ourselves *shows* that external 'symbols' have a whole host of linguistic properties, precisely those we share with the Martians.

These three lines of argument share a peculiar insistence to treat linguistics as if it were not a genuine science; that is, on each count, linguistics is presented as being essentially constrained to cleave to distinctions that are involved in our commonsense reasoning about language. They also share an a priori conception of disciplinary boundaries. Let us take them in turn.

There is, for sure, a difference between dependence and constitution. The existence of my computer depends upon the mental states of various designers and engineers, but the computer is not therefore mental; once produced, it has a life of its own, as it were. It is difficult, though, to see how such a difference is meant to play out in the case of language. Let us presume that the linguistic properties that concern us are those revealed by generative theories. Well, clearly, such properties of hierarchical organization and transformational relation (movement) are not to be found in sound waves or inscriptions, indeed, nor are phonological or semantic properties. There is nothing about /eager/ and /easy/ that tells us that they are adjectives, and still less that the first assigns an obligatory theta role to an external argument while the second does not. To find that out we must inquire into the judgments of speaker/hearers; that is, we must inquire into their minds. In short, it is just obscure where the relevant properties are supposed to be if not in the minds of the language users.

Now, it is perfectly legitimate to talk *as if* inscriptions have all of the relevant properties, but our theoretical interest is in how the human mind/brain can 'project' such properties; how it is that it can utilize sounds and inscriptions in ways unavailable to rabbits or trees. Although it might be overly concessive, we could say that linguistics is only concerned with the dependence issue, leaving the existence of E-language as an idle issue of how one wants to construe the metaphysics of commonsense. In this light, to insist that there are E-languages, albeit dependent on psychology, is to miss the very inquiry linguistics is pursuing, namely, one into the character of the mind/brain. If we are to take seriously the E-language idea, it must be shown how the notion might fruitfully enter into linguistic explanation.

Consideration of the relations of dependence between sciences is also irrelevant. Linguistics is an autonomous science just to the extent that its modes of explanation and results are not properly integrated into the other sciences, much as biology is (largely) independent of physics. But this is simply the norm and is hardly a virtue. There is no argument, due to Chomsky or anyone else, from dependence to constitution. To say linguistics is a branch of psychology is to say nothing more than that its concern is for linguistic cognition. Only an a priori conception of disciplinary boundaries would lead one to question this, as if any inquiry must come labelled with an appropriate discipline, or that disciplines cannot cover a host of different domains, methods and data sources. This leads us to the second argument.

The second argument presented above seeks to show that language is not a psychological kind from the premises that linguistics is not evidentially rooted in the psychological. There is much confusion in this line. First, data do not come labelled with the hypotheses for which they might be relevant. All data are potentially relevant to any hypothesis; relevance is determined by inferential connection and not by an a priori conception of what the data signify. Thus, even if linguistics does not depend upon psychological data, which is not the case anyhow (see below), it wouldn't follow that the linguistic hypotheses were not cognitive ones. Second, the argument appears to trade on the presumption that psychology is solely concerned with processes, and so if linguistics is to be part of psychology, then it must be a theory of processes, that is, the mechanisms of production and perception. But this is simply a stipulation as to the nature of psychology. Chomsky conceives linguistics as being primarily concerned with competence, or the function computed, without venturing into, at least in the first instance, hypotheses about performance.

On the face of it, far from not being part of psychology, such a competence theory looks like a prerequisite to any performance theory (Chomsky, ATS, chapter 1). The matter, however, is academic, for no one (university administrators and librarians apart) should waste a moment wondering whether linguistics is really psychology or not. If linguistic theories prove fruitful in the explanation of cognitive phenomena, then a priori stipulations of disciplinary boundaries are empty. As it happens, linguistic theories are very fruitful in psychology.

Third, it is simply not true that linguistics is detached from broader psychological research. Psycholinguistics is highly informed by linguistic theory (Crain and Thornton, 1998; Guasti, 2002). As are many parsing studies (Berwick and Weinberg, 1984; Pritchett, 1992) and also deficit studies (Grodzinsky, 1990). Moreover, even much of the technology of syntactic theory, such as categories that lack a phonetic register (so-called empty categories – see chapter 7), submit to psychological investigation (Fodor, 1995; Grodzinsky and Fintel, 1998; Philips and Lasnik, 2003). In general, we may hope and expect for closer integration as the sciences of the mind develop in unison. If linguistic theory proves to be fruitfully involved in many paradigmatic areas of psychology, it becomes a mere matter of semantics whether one wants to call linguistics a branch of psychology.

Correlatively, both the preponderate data for linguistic theories and the phenomena the theories seek to explain are psychological, rather than E-linguistic (to do with external 'symbols'). The main data for linguistics are the kind of intuitions elicited by the examples presented in previous chapters concerning ambiguity, referential construal, acceptability, inferential connection etc. (There is, of course, no necessity for this data source. All data are potentially relevant, but the intuitive data are readily available, not obviously misleading and face no serious competitor in their richness.) In all cases, we are concerned with how speaker/hearers *interpret* the sentences offered; the sentences themselves, understood as symbol strings, are not data. Nor is the linguist interested in the informants' *opinion*, as if they were fellow linguists. It is often convenient to present data in a manner of speaker/hearers finding a certain sentence ambiguous in three ways, but we do not thereby attribute to the informants the concept of ambiguity and still less a relation of passive transformation. The data are how the informants manage, if at all, to interpret a string or find it acceptable; they need not have an opinion on the strings that deploy linguistic concepts; they need not even have a concept as simple as ambiguity. It is thus misleading to say that informants have judgements *about* language, as if we are interested in their reflective deliberation. Likewise, linguistic theories are explanatory of the interpretations informants make; it is difficult to make sense of the idea that the theories are explanatory of the language as such. For example, the kind of structural analysis a sentence receives is meant to depict how the speaker/hearer understands the sentence; it is not a description of the sentence as an external object. Hence, the whole point of transformations is to record relations of interpretability between sentences as understood by speaker/hearers (e.g. passive/active). If our concern was an E-language, it would be difficult to see why one analysis should be preferred over another, for, absent the mind/brain that interprets the sentences, a given class of analyses (a theory) would just be one classification among innumerably many others. The E-language conception appears to denude linguistics of any explanatory power. It comes as little surprise that the E-language conception is often married to a scepticism about the scientific credentials of linguistics (Quine, 1969, 1970; Stich, 1972). The inference is fine, albeit utterly trivial given the restricted conception of linguistic explanation ('Quine's empirical assumptions' (QEA), RL, RR).

Finally, it is quite true that we should not expect psychological inquiry to overturn most of the data of linguistics, just as we do not expect physics to overturn apples falling to the ground. No science overturns data as such, but often the data are interpreted in quite radical ways (the earth is rotating; that's why, *inter alia*, terrestrial objects fall in parabolas); just so, in the case of linguistics. For example, that informants find a string ambiguous or unacceptable is a datum, but it is a theoretical matter to explain it. It might be a semantic phenomenon, or a syntactic one, or a pragmatic one, or simply stylistic. It is not obvious, prior to any theory, what the answer will be, and the ultimate answer might well depend upon the integration of linguistics into the other cognitive sciences.

Let us now turn to the 'Martian Consideration'. The argument, recall, seeks to show that there are E-linguistic facts on the basis that we could discern that a Martian and a human speak 'English' even though their respective internal states might radically differ. The reasoning, of course, does not depend on the science fiction. The general import of the argument is that internal states, whether the same or different, do not enter into the individuation of linguistic types, including languages. Hence, at the very least, not all properties that concern linguistics are properties of internal states.

First off, as previously explained, the concern of generative theories has always been only for *strong*, not *weak*, generative capacity. In other words, a generative theory seeks to *explain* linguistic phenomena by offering analyses that constitute hypotheses as to the mental structures that underlie speaker/hearers' linguistic understanding, as evidenced in their intuitions, and whatever other data are available. A linguistic theory is not meant to classify strings as belonging to this or that language. In this light, the 'Martian consideration' shows nothing whatsoever.

Let us imagine that the Martians land and they appear to speak English. In this case, any theory for English would be equally explanatory over the Martians, for, let us presume, there is no evidential difference, that is, all linguistic intuitions come out the same within bounds that are the same for human English speakers. Let us further imagine, however, that due to a closer integration of linguistics and neuro-cognitive science we discovered that the Martians lack a human UG; their linguistic competence is realized in quite a different way utilizing calculations over probabilities that are way beyond our powers. In this circumstance, we would have made a discovery on the basis of novel data, that is, while the human UG is evidentially sufficient for humans, it is not so for the Martians. Still, given the great overlap in data from the two cases, we would have to establish how the internal states of the Martians manage to respect the same syntactic, semantic and phonological features as found in human English. At a certain level of abstraction, therefore, one theory would still serve, but the shared properties between the Martians and humans would not therefore be in the language in some external sense; on the contrary, much of the cognitive data would be the same for the two populations.

Do the Martians speak English or not? The decision is of no scientific interest, for we have never been concerned with what language populations speak but only with what explains the linguistic phenomena of the populations. Scientific interest ceases where there is no explanatory or evidential difference. For sure, commonsense would decree that the two populations both spoke English, or Marlish, as it were, but we knew already that commonsense classifications of language in themselves are of no concern for linguistics. The 'Martian consideration' simply shows us that linguistics departs from commonsense. If, by all evidential criteria, Martians and English speakers come out the same, then they are the same for all theoretical purposes. If there is some evidential difference that requires the hypothesis of distinct structures, then they are not the same. In sum, the 'Martian consideration' amounts to nothing more than an insistence that linguistics should answer to a commonsense conception of language, regardless of the pattern of evidence. Of course, so put, no one would commend the argument, but it is difficult to see what substance remains.[1]

4.2   Linguistics and mathematics

As previously noted, a brand of the E-conception is motivated by apparent similarities between mathematics and linguistics (e.g. Katz, 1981; Katz and Postal, 1991). According to this conception, just as the domain of mathematics is numbers and their properties, so the domain of linguistics is sentences and their properties. In both cases, the inquiry is directed at a mind-independent realm of entities and not at the psychological states of those who know or think about the entities. No one imagines, for example, that the proof of 'Riemann's hypothesis' was a result in cognitive science. Sentences, like numbers, appear to be causally inert abstract entities outside of space–time that exist independently of anyone thinking about them.

There is something correct about the analogy insofar as linguists can happily study constructions without caring for particular speaker/hearers. Furthermore, as noted in Chapter 5, it is difficult to think of, say, neurophysiology overturning the apparent results of linguistics, and it is practically inconceivable, after we find out more about the brain, it will turn out that *The duck is ready to eat* is not ambiguous. The analogy, however, between mathematics and language is very strained and ushers in more problems than it resolves, if any.

First, Platonism about numbers is not a result of mathematics; it is a particular philosophical construal of mathematics. For sure, most mathematicians are Platonists, not in any developed sense, but merely because the philosophical issues are largely irrelevant; Platonism is the default attitude. It makes no difference to the status of a theorem whether its truth is based upon an independent mathematical reality or not. Indeed, when philosophical issues have intruded into mathematics, as in the so-called foundational disputes in the first half of the twentieth century, it is noteworthy that the mathematicians were as divided on the issues as philosophers have always been. What is certainly the case is that mathematics is not psychological in the sense of being subjective, or personal, but no one is proposing that linguistics is the study of such first-person mental states. In sum, even if we were to accept the analogy between linguistics and mathematics, it is not obvious that we should thereby be Platonists about linguistics.

Second, a chief problem for any species of Platonism is to account for how we are in touch with the entities in questions. It appears that some mysterious channel is required to connect our all-too physical brains with the all-too incorporeal entities that exist outside of space and time. In the case of mathematics, the bullet can seem worth a bite, for mathematics is, well, mysterious anyhow, but we should not generate a mystery where none is required. It can seem mysterious that we have access to an infinite set of sentences, but that is a tendentious way of construing the relevant phenomenon. What each of us enjoys is an unbounded competence. This requires explanation, but the positing of an infinite set of sentences does not contribute to the explanation; it simply obscures the phenomenon. The case is different in mathematics, where the very 'phenomenon' one is concerned with is the infinite, in say analysis or set theory. Some mathematicians (so-called formalists and intuitionists) have attempted ways of relieving themselves of commitment to 'actual infinities'. However forlorn such attempts might be, it remains opaque why linguistics is required to trade in actual infinities. This point can be missed by the universal applicability of set theory. A set is indifferent to the character of its members. An infinite set of sentences (or anything else) is thus a perfectly kosher mathematical object, but it does not follow that the object has any relevance to linguistics anymore than the infinite set of possible tigers is of any interest to zoology, or the infinite set of possible electrons is of any interest to physics. Likewise, a recursive definition can be reformulated as an explicit definition of an infinite set. For example, one can characterize the infinite set of natural numbers as formed from 0 and the operation of the successor function. Again, we have a kosher mathematical object, but the set qua object is of no interest beyond its cardinality (and the ordinal type to which it belongs); it is the structure of the set that is of particular interest to mathematics (Hilbert once quipped that the natural numbers could be beer glasses, so long as there were an infinite number of them and they could be well-ordered). In sum, one can turn linguistics into a study of abstract objects by simply importing available mathematical techniques, but it remains opaque what the explanatory value is. The empirical phenomena remain as they were, although now obscured by idle formalization. Formalization, in any area, is supposed to aid understanding; one does not formalize merely for the sake of it (cf., 'On formalization and formal linguistics' (OFFL); GE, pp. 100–3).

Third, one can be concessive. Let us grant that there is an inquiry akin to mathematics that deals with language as an abstract object. Now we can evaluate the discipline on formal criteria. Are there any interesting theorems, that is, answers to questions that are independent of a particular choice of formalization? Whatever the answer is, and I am unsure, it does not adversely affect the bio-cognitive inquiry animated by our leading questions; indeed, such inquiry progresses without being mathematics, just as physics, chemistry and biology have. As Chomsky (KoL, pp. 4–5) writes:

> Generative grammar is a topic, which one may or may not choose to study. Of course, one can adopt a point of view from which chemistry disappears as a discipline (perhaps it is all done by angels with mirrors). In this sense, a decision to study chemistry does stake out a position on matters of fact.

In other words, whatever one thinks language is in some metaphysical sense, the topic of generative linguistics remains, and the metaphysics sheds light or it does not. In the present case, turning linguistics into a branch of mathematics appears to cast only shadow.

We can now turn to the remaining leading questions and continue our comparison of the I- and E-conceptions.

4.3 Acquisition, use and the other questions of linguistics

We may be brief with the other leading questions of linguistics (as conceived by Chomsky), for it is pretty obvious that the E-language conception is ill suited to animate the inquiries. Still, sometimes, the obvious needs to be stated.

4.3.1 Acquisition
The principal fact of language acquisition is that every human child (barring some children with specific neurological deficits or later trauma) develops a linguistic competence that reflects the competence

of the conspecifics in her community. This relation, however, is contingent, for each child could have acquired any of a range of distinct competences with equal ease. Expressed colloquially, each child acquires at least one language, but could have acquired any other language. Two immediate consequences are (i) that no child is innately predisposed to acquire one language rather than another and (ii) that what the child does possess innately must be general enough to cover any possible language. This gives rise to a tension between descriptive and explanatory adequacy (see Chapter 3). On the one hand, languages appear to vary greatly, and so what is innate must be rich enough to encode such particularity in the resulting grammars or I-languages. On the other hand, since every language is equally accessible, the initial state must be general enough not to favour one language over another. We shall see in Chapter 7 how this tension is resolved; *pro tem*, let us consider how our two conceptions of language fair in shedding light on this acquisition problem.

An E-language conception, however understood, looks to be simply a spinning wheel. The acquisition problem is how to understand the development of a general (non-language specific) state into one that is particular in the sense of excluding other options. If languages exist outside of the mind in any substantive sense (not merely as a reflection of mental projection), then the problem becomes one of how the child manages to learn of these external properties and their organization. But what can we say of the child's initial state? If we attribute to the child UG, then we are faced with the general development problem as outlined and no issue arises of the child learning the properties of the external language, for they are mostly already encoded, given the facts of poverty of stimulus. Thus, the external language is an empty posit, for UG, understood as a general theory of external languages, sheds no light at all on the acquisition problem unless the child *knows* the theory. If we don't attribute UG to the child, then language acquisition becomes a mystery in the face of poverty of stimulus considerations.

Thus, it is not so much that the very idea of an external language is inconsistent with the facts of acquisition, but rather that the idea is wholly otiose insofar as a child's acquisition of knowledge of an external language presupposes an internal developmental based upon UG, if we are not to fall foul of poverty of stimulus considerations.

The move to the I-language conception does not solve the problem of acquisition, but it allows us the right perspective on it by jettisoning the free-spinning idea of an external language. The notion of an I-language is not constrained by any pre-theoretical conception of language; the notion simply designates any state of the language faculty understanding as an aspect of the mind/brain that subserves linguistic competence. In this light, the problem of language acquisition becomes one of the internal development of a series of I-languages or states of the language faculty. Thus, we may innocently construe UG as the initial I-language, an internal state (shared by the species) of sufficient generality to encompass every 'language'. Rather, then, UG being a theory of the set of grammars, it is a state of the mind/brain, which may thus enter into an explanation of language development. Acquiring a language, on this model, is an internal developmental process going from an initial state (UG) to a final steady state, which we may take to be the state that underlies mature competence. As I said, the problem remains of how to theorize such an initial state, its various transitions and how they are triggered, but at least the model is coherent, of the right shape, and uncorrupted by the dangling idea of an external language.

4.3.2 Language use

Language use is essentially a cognitive phenomenon. The problem is to figure out how the mind/brain manages to integrate varied sources of information to deploy language to express and organize our endless stream of thoughts. As with the previous considerations, it is not that the bare phenomenon is inconsistent with an external language; it is, rather, that the notion looks to be explanatorily redundant. Using a language is not like using a hammer or a chess piece. Linguistic items (words, sentences) are not ready to hand, but only exist with the relevant properties as produced by speaker/hearers. The problem is thus to figure out how the underlying systems bring about such a complex integration. The I-language conception allows for a perspective on one component of the integration. Three features of Chomsky's understanding of language use are worth noting.

First, for Chomsky (RL; 'The evolution of the language faculty: clarifications and implications' (ELF)), language use does not necessarily involve a process of externalization, such as in speech or writing. On reflection, this is obvious, for most of our employment of language is a 'silent' use to organize our thoughts and plan and rehearse our actions, linguistic or otherwise. For sure, the relation of thought to language is obscure, but if we insist on an external conception of language, it becomes simply opaque how to begin to understand the purely cognitive use of language.

Second, Chomsky has suggested that language is not essentially usable. The thought can seem incoherent from the perspective of the common philosophical dogmas, but the claim is perfectly intelligible from the empirical view of the I-language conception. Language use involves an integration of systems, including the language faculty. To say that language is not essentially usable, then, is simply to claim that the design of the faculty is such as to preclude a class of its outputs being legible to wider systems. If we take recursion to be an essential design factor of the faculty, then unusability trivially follows, for by recursion, the faculty admits structures of any finite bound, that is, structures that exhaust general memory limitations. Indeed, even simple multiple embedding makes for unusability, as in *Sailors sailors sailors fight fight fight*. Of course, we can understand such 'unusable' structures off-line, but they remain noiselike for our on-line use of language. What, from an E-language perspective, can seem like a nonsensical claim, from the I-language perspective looks to be an important insight into the design of the human mind.

Third, Chomsky (CL) has characterized language use as *creative*: it is typically novel, stimulus-free and appropriate to context. Chomsky has suggested that such creativity might be *mysterious*, that is, intractable to human theoretical understanding (see Chapter 5). It is crucial to note, however, that mystery does not shroud the whole of linguistic behaviour; in particular, a generative grammar is intended precisely to explain the novelty aspect of creativity (Chomsky, CL, pp. 77–8, n. 8). On Chomsky's view, linguistic behaviour is not reflexive, for we typically *decide* what to say; indeed, we might decide to say nothing at all. In this sense, our behaviour is stimulus-free (even when we speak unthinkingly, for no particular reason, our utterances are not under any stimulus control). However, it is not random, in that what we do say is expressive of our mutual recognition of intentions and beliefs that form the background of appropriateness to our linguistic exchanges. Still, such free appropriate action has a reflexive structure to it. Children do not decide to acquire a language, anymore than a mature monolingual English speaker could *decide* to speak French or Mohawk. Likewise, we cannot help but interpret utterances in a familiar tongue and we cannot help but fail to interpret utterances in a foreign tongue, even though understanding what our interlocutor is intending in both cases is a more or less an affair based upon the prevailing shared context. A generative theory makes explicit this fixed structure without hypothesizing about the mechanisms (if any) that allow for free expression, which is not to say, per our second remark, that there is nothing more to the structure than is revealed in our linguistic behaviour.

4.3.3 Evolution

Linguistic competence looks to be a property unique to the human line. Precisely what is unique to humans is currently unclear, but the arrangement of capacities enjoyed by the human is certainly different from any other species. From the I-language perspective, linguistics is a straightforward biological inquiry, much as if our concern was for the mammalian visual system or the auditory capacity of bats. An I-language is a biological structure, albeit one whose properties are as yet salient only from an abstract perspective; as such, it has an evolutionary history, as all biological structure does. Of course, this leaves every option open as to the phylogeny of language, and this does not mean that language is an 'adaptation' for some particular purpose.[2]

From an E-language perspective, the question of evolution is difficult to so much as approach. The perspective might simply co-opt the internal/biological resources of the I-perspective, but this would render the notion of an E-language a useless appendage. Alternatively, it might be thought that language is some kind of external resource that the human mind exploits or even something that has co-evolved with the human mind. Ideas along these lines have recently gained some popularity (Dennett, 1995; Clark, 1997; Deacon, 1997). On the face of it, however, the thoughts do not even rise to the level of speculation, for none of the thinkers have felt it necessary to learn the first thing about linguistics. It is difficult to know, therefore, just what resources are meant to be external to the human mind/brain but, apparently, not accessible to rabbits, toads or chimpanzees. If generative linguistics is even remotely on the right track, then the kind of properties that are essential to an explanation of linguistic cognition are simply not witnessed in external patterns; language, if construed as external, only exists as a projection from the human mind. Of course, anyone is free to disagree with the generative theories, but first they must be understood. Simply assuming an E-language in the absence of any story as to how external structures could possess the relevant properties that enter into linguistic explanation is not a serious position.

4.3.4 Neurological realization

An I-language is a state of the mind/brain or the brain from an abstract perspective. We should obviously like to see a closer integration of cognitive neuroscience and linguistics leading to an understanding of how neuronal organization supports the distinctions and features made at the abstract level of linguistics. It is true that at present it is the linguistics that is constraining the neuroscience, but many startling discoveries have been made. Of special note is the fact that the same brain centres are active in deaf signing (including 'hand babbling') and spoken language. This finding supports the modality independence of the language faculty and further buttresses the claim that 'speech is not special' (Petitto, 2005). More generally, the peculiar specificity of language deficits suggests that the realization of language is found in dedicated circuitry, as opposed to more general levels of organization.

An E-language, by definition, cannot be neurologically realized. It would appear, therefore, that the results of the neurosciences, on the E-conception, are completely independent of linguistics. In the face of current research, the E-conception expresses a mere lack of interest in the biological foundations of language. Again, it is not that the very idea of an E-language is inconsistent with any science of the mind/brain; the problem is that the conception precludes integration of understanding from various disciplines without any conceivable off-setting value save for the upholding of commonsense, which should, anyhow, be abandoned in any serious inquiry.

CHAPTER 7

DEVELOPMENTS IN SYNTAX

But again and again nature still proved itself to be the superior to the human mind and compelled it to shatter a picture held final prematurely in favour of a more profound harmony.

Weyl (1949, p. 159)

1 INTRODUCTION

From the 1960s to the present, the developments in generative linguistics have been far reaching in the detail and scope of analysis offered across the world's languages. There have also been great developments in the study of language acquisition, linguistic processing and, more generally, the place of language within the mind/brain. In the space available, even a cursory overview of this history is impossible; besides, this is a volume about Chomsky and not generative linguistics in general. Fortunately, the main changes in the conception of the *architecture* or *design* of the language faculty may be reviewed without our getting bogged down in technicalities. I shall give some indication of the analyses that have proved most central, but I do not affect any kind of empirical coverage – every analysis remains controversial. Moreover, many of the architectural changes have a theoretical motivation, which brings into relief the general logic of the generative enterprise. For the non-linguist, therefore, the architectural changes may be appreciated in the absence of a detailed understanding of any particular class of analyses.

The moral of this chapter will be that the developments in linguistics from the time of *Aspects* to roughly the end of the 1980s have been coordinated by a drive for great simplicity in basic principles and more economical explanation. I shall largely neglect the cognitive conception of linguistics that has been presented in the previous few chapters; the point of this chapter is to see how the theory developed internally, as it were. In Chapter 8, we shall see how this pursuit of economy relates to the broader cognitive issues in the guise of the *minimalist program*.

2   THE INTERFACES: DEEP STRUCTURE AND SURFACE STRUCTURE

Let us begin by recalling some of the salient features of the LSLT framework. A grammar consists of two parts. The *base* consists of phrase structure rules (incorporating a lexicon as a set of rules that rewrite labels as lexical items). The *transformational* component consists of a set of rules that apply to the output of the base. The output of the transformational component is a set of T(ransformational)-markers that record the transformational histories or derivations of the structures underlying a given language. The structural description of a given sentence can be understood as a reduction of its T-marker so that it only records the unique *is a* relations. The purpose of the transformational component is to explain a host of 'felt relations' that constitute our linguistic competence. The transformational component is also the seat of recursion in the shape of *generalized* transformations that allow for clausal embeddings and coordination. In a sense, the base simply feeds the transformational component, for no base structure underlies a sentence; the most transformationally simple structures are those to which only obligatory transformations have applied: the phrase markers for the *kernel*. The kernel consists of mono-clausal active declaratives with auxiliary morphology fixed by the number transformation. This choice is not principled; it simply makes for the most convenient explanation, although there are reasons to find it plausible (see Chapter 3).

The 'big fact' about language that this model brings into relief is that there is a mismatch between the apparent structure of sentences and how we understand them. On the one hand, sentences that look the same structurally can express quite distinct relations between their parts. Ambiguity is the most obvious case, but the phenomenon is much wider. Consider:

(1)   a. Bill is easy to please
      b. Bill is eager to please

    c. The picture was painted by a real artist.
    d. The picture was painted by a new technique

In (1)a, *Bill* is the understood object of *please*; thus, it has the paraphrase *It is easy for someone or other to please Bill.* In (1)b, *Bill* is not
the understood object of *please*, but is the subject of *eager*; thus, it
lacks the paraphrase *It is eager for someone or other to please Bill.*
Also note that the content of (1)b can be expressed as a nominal,
while that of (1)a cannot be.

    (2)   a. Bill's eagerness to please
           b. *Bill's easiness to please

In short, the sameness of apparent form misleads as to the semantically significant relations between the words. The second pair of
(1) displays the same phenomenon, where *a real artist* is the understood subject of *paint*, but *a new technique* is not. Of course, no
competent speaker/hearer is actually misled by these differences,
quite the contrary: it takes some thought to appreciate how distinct
the semantic relations are precisely because we so effortlessly understand the differences notwithstanding the sameness of apparent
form.

On the other hand, we find sentences of distinct apparent form
that are closely related semantically, such as active/passive pairs,
declaratives and interrogatives and numerous other constructions:

    (3)   a. Bill wants a car
           b. What Bill wants is a car
           c. It is a car that Bill wants
           d. A car is what Bill wants

The principal explanatory burden of the transformational component is to account for this mismatch by unearthing an underlying
pattern of structures, recorded in the T-markers, that allow us to trace
relations of sameness and difference of understanding to relations
of sameness and difference in the T-markers. In this light, as emphasized in Chapter 2, it really is bizarre how Chomsky has been read as
somehow ignoring semantics. The early work, for sure, is cautious on
the issue of semantics, but the fundamental relevance of structure to

meaning is never in doubt. Chomsky (SS, p. 92) offers the following reasoning:

> [I]n order to understand a sentence it is necessary to know the kernel sentences (more precisely, the terminal strings underlying these kernel sentences) and the phrase structure of each of these elementary components, as well as the transformational history of the development of the given sentence from these kernel sentences. The general problem of analysing the process of 'understanding' is thus reduced, in a sense, to the problem of explaining how kernel sentences are understood, these being considered the basic 'content elements' from which the usual, more complex sentences of real life are formed by transformational development.

The suggestion here is that since transformations are purely structural, defined by the relation between their structural analyses and structural changes, the 'process of understanding' boils down to accounting for the kernel. It is this idea that coordinates the changes from the early framework to that of *Aspects*.

In *Aspects*, Chomsky adopts a version of what has since been dubbed the *Katz-Postal hypothesis* (Katz and Postal, 1964), which may be phrased as follows:

(KPH) Transformations are semantically inert.

Note, first, that KPH is a substantive hypothesis. While it is true that transformations are purely structural, on the face of it they do effect changes of meaning even though they are not specified in terms of semantic properties (e.g. there is no transformation that targets sentences about cities as opposed to rivers). For instance, interrogatives appear to be semantically distinct from declaratives; more broadly, generalized transformations clearly effect semantic changes in allowing clausal subordination. The thought behind KPH, then, is that these apparent changes can be accommodated by the underlying base structures. If this is so, then the object of interpretation is not the T-markers at all, for transformational histories cannot be pertinent to understanding if they do not effect any semantic change. On this model, therefore, a grammar produces a pair of structural descriptions for each sentence; one base structure that determines properties of semantic significance and one structure that determines the apparent form that codes for phonological interpretation. Chomsky dubbed these two levels *deep structure* and *surface structure* respectively. Schematically, a grammar has the following design:

Deep Structure → Semantics
↓ ← Transformations
↓

Phonology/Morphology ← Surface Structure

The job of the transformational component is to map from deep structures to surface structures. Construed cognitively, what a competent speaker/hearer knows is a particular pairing of 'sounds' with 'meanings' over an unbounded range, where the transformations are mere mechanisms to effect the pairing. Separate components of phonology and semantics *interpret* the respective syntactic structures, without such components not intruding into the derivation.

As we shall see, Chomsky came to reject KPH and with it the above model, although the interpretive model of semantics was retained. One reason for commending KPH, however, was the status of generalized transformations in the early model. The base of the old model was non-recursive and the transformational component consisted of two types of rules: singular rules that successively targeted transformed structure in a specific order of application and (unordered) generalized rules that targeted two or more structures. On the face of it, this looks odd. If the base is to determine the set of *is a* relations, then surely it should determine clausal subordination and coordination. This is easily achieved by allowing rewrite rules that feature 'S' on their right-hand sides. If this is permitted, then only singular transformations are required, so long as they operate cyclically to build a multi-clause structure with the right relations of subordination. Here we see a natural economizing of the grammar lending weight to KPH.

The nature of deep structure was to prove very contentious. The so-called *generative semantics* movement that developed in the late 1960s had many strands to it, but the core idea was that deep structure was semantic structure itself. On this conception, there really is no deep structure at all, if understood as a level of syntax; transformations map from semantic structure to structures that code for phonology. A grammar is purely mediational, that is, merely coordinating 'sound' with 'meaning'. In many respects, this debate still rumbles on; indeed, Seuren (2004) has claimed that Chomsky's most recent (minimalist) architectural model is close to a generative semantics one. As we shall see, this is not the case, at least not if we are supposed to think of the latest model as being a step back to the *Aspects* model. If anything, the latest model harks back to the earliest model. Whatever the case might be, Chomsky at the time of *Aspects* did not identify deep structure with semantic structure itself; deep structure was a level of syntax. It is useful, though, to think of deep structure as determining certain formal properties of meaning. Deep structures *interface* with semantics in the sense that they encode relations between words that determine a minimal level of semantic interpretation. Let us encapsulate this thought as the deep structure hypothesis (DSH):

Deep structure is the level of representation where grammatical position corresponds to the understood semantic role of the lexical item in that position relative to other items in the grammatical structure.

Consider two of the sentences discussed earlier:

(4) a. Bill is easy to please
  b. Bill is eager to please

In (4)a, *Bill* is the grammatical subject and the infinitive clause lacks both a subject and object. It is understood, however, that the sentence means that it is easy for someone or other to please Bill. In a sense, then, (4)a departs from (DSH) in three respects; that is, (4)a is not the terminal string of a deep structure representation. First, *Bill* is not the understood subject; after all, Bill is not easy, whatever that might mean. There is no understood subject. Second, there is an understood subject of *please* – the agent who does the pleasing – that is elided. Third, there is an understood object of *please* (*Bill*), but it occurs in grammatical subject position. We can, therefore, think of the deep structure corresponding to (4)a as a structure that cleaves to DSH by having elements in the grammatical positions that correspond to our understanding of the semantic roles the sentence expresses, as stated in the three points made above. Simplifying, then, we may take the deep structure (more precisely, the terminal string of the deep structure phrase marker) to be

(5) It is easy for X to please Bill

Transformations target the structure, substituting *Bill* for *it* and deleting *for X* to produce the form of (4)a.

By analogous reasoning, we may take the deep structure of (4)b to encode the string

(6)   Bill is eager for Bill (himself) to please X

Here we see the deep structure much closer to the surface structure and so less transformational work is required. The phrase *for Bill* is deleted as is the object of *please*. The job of a grammar, then, is to detail the relations between deep structures and surface structures in the way exhibited, with each sentence of the language having a deep and surface structure related to it that code for its semantic and phonological interpretation.

Many issues arise here. One crucial problem is the *recoverability* of the deep structure. For example, if one hears (4)a, then one immediately understands the relations encoded in its deep structure, but how is that possible given the displacements and deletions made by the transformational component? In a sense, the transformations should not loose information if it is to be recovered after all. On the other hand, given the mismatch between semantically relevant position and surface grammatical position, the information, if retained, must be encoded differently. That is what the data show us. We shall return to this problem later. Let us now, though, consider another major change.

2.1   The place of the lexicon

The LSLT model includes the lexicon within the base component, that is, lexical items (words and formatives) are included within the phrase structure rules that allow for the rewriting of non-complex categorical labels as terminal symbols. For example,

(7)   a. N → Bill
       b. P → on
       c. V → kiss

The motivation for this move appeared to be that it allowed for a smooth derivation of terminal strings: the base component directly derives the kernel sentences under their various structural descriptions. There is, however, good reason to detach the lexicon from the base and *Aspects* follows this course (ATS, pp. 86–7). Lexical items relate to deep structure via rules of *lexical insertion*. We can think of deep structure as a pure syntactic form with dummy symbols (Δ) in place of lexical items in a structural description. A lexical insertion rule permits a rewriting of Δ as lexical item *L* in a phrase marker *K*, if *K* meets the usual kind of transformation analysability condition indexed to the features inherent to *L* (ATS, p. 122). Let's turn to these features.

We can understand the lexicon of a language to be essentially a list that packages various kinds of information into words and other formatives. The packages are largely idiosyncratic in that there are obvious differences between the items in terms of their semantic, phonetic and syntactic properties. The rules of a grammar, however, are meant to be productive and perfectly general. The detachment also simplifies the application of the transformational component. For example, some transitive verbs allow for object deletion (*read*, *eat*), while other others do not (*keep*, *allow*). If we allow this idiosyncratic information to be stored lexically, then a deletion transformation may apply or not without the difference redundantly being duplicated in the base phrase marker. This means, of course, that some of the lexical information must be visible to the transformations in order to determine their applicability. We should expect this, anyhow, for words clearly impose conditions upon one another. Let us go into this in some more detail.

Aspects takes a lexical item to be a pair [D, C]. D denotes a distinctive phonetic matrix that codes for the item's phonological articulation within a phrase. C denotes a complex of features, both syntactic and semantic. Centrally, C includes *selection* and (strict) *subcategorization* features (ATS, pp. 94–5). The former express what we might think of as abstract semantic features that determine what other kind of words a given word selects to produce a literal interpretation of the words in co-occurrence (this will be explained). Here is a simple example for N (noun):

(8)　a.　N → [+N, ± Common]
　　　b.　[+Common] → [± Count]
　　　c.　[+Count] → [± Animate]
　　　d.　[-Common] → [± Animate]
　　　e.　[+Animate] → [± Human]
　　　f.　[-Count] → [± Abstract]

(9) a. *boy* [+N, +Common, +Count, +Animate, +Human]
   b. *democracy* [+N, +Common, -Count, -Abstract]

Subcategorization features record restrictions on the grammatical occurrences of items, essentially, in what grammatical contexts they may occur. For example,

(10) a. *believe* [+V, +–NP, +–CP]
   b. *grow* [+V, +–NP, +–#, +–ADJ]

(10)a carries the information that *believe* is a verb that can take an NP as a direct object (e.g. *Bill believes Dave*) or have a clausal phrase as a complement (e.g. *Bill believes that Jim is tall*). Likewise, (10)b carries the information that *grow* can take a direct object (e.g. *Bill grows tomatoes*) or occur with no object (e.g. *Tomatoes grow*) or occur with an adjective (e.g. *Tomatoes grow big*).

One immediate question we may ask here is whether two sets of features are required. Chomsky's principal argument in *Aspects* for the distinction is the difference between the acceptability of deviations (ATS, pp. 148–53). Consider the following:

(11) a. Bill found sad
   b. Bill elapsed that John would come
   c. Bill compelled
   d. Bill became John to leave
   e. Bill persuaded great authority to John

(12) a. Colourless green ideas sleep furiously
   b. Golf plays Bill
   c. Bill might frighten sincerity
   d. Misery loves company
   e. They perform their leisure with diligence

Both sets of sentences are deviant in some sense. Those under (11) are clearly unacceptable to the point of being gibberish. The sentences under (12), however, are acceptable, but only under a figurative reading; we *impose* an interpretation on them. Chomsky expresses this difference as one between 'degrees of grammaticalness' (ATS, p. 150; see Chapter 3). The subcategorization and selection features help explain this difference.

The sentences under (11) deviate from the subcategorization restrictions of the respective verbs. For example, *find* has the feature [--ADJ], *elapse* has the feature [--CP] etc. The sentences under (12) do not deviate from such restrictions but do deviate from selection restrictions. Briefly, the verbs *sleep*, *play* and *love* are marked to take [+Animate] nouns as subjects; *frighten* is marked not to take [-Animate] nouns as objects and *perform* is marked to take [-Abstract] nouns as objects. (Chomsky (ATS, pp. 164–5) adopts a convention that subcategorization features are marked positively and selectional features are marked negatively. I ignore this convention for the sake of convenience.)

Thus, it appears that deviation from subcategorization restrictions creates a higher degree of unacceptability than deviation from selection ones. To be more precise, the features in coordination create a hierarchy, running from failure of selection of the most dominant category to failure of the least dominant subcategorization restriction, which corresponds to our intuitive ranking of deviance. Chomsky (ATS, p. 152) offers the following example:

(13) a. Sincerity may virtue the boy
      b. Sincerity may elapse the boy
      c. Sincerity may admire the boy
      d. Sincerity may frighten the boy

(13)d is perfectly acceptable; (13)c less so, as *admire* requires a [+Animate] subject. (13)b is worse still, as *elapse* is a [+-#] verb, that is, intransitive. Worst is (13)a, which does not feature a verb at all. Assuming that such data comes under the purview of descriptive adequacy, then we have a justification of the grammar being sensitive to such lexical features; thus, the lexical features should be open in the structural descriptions so that the grammatical rules may operate in accordance with them.

2.2 The depth of deep structure

The notion of deep structure caught the imagination of theorists across a range of disciplines. In this light, it is important to bear in mind that Chomsky intended the notion to have a precise meaning, which we encapsulated in DSH. We can now be more precise and say that deep structure is (i) where lexical insertion applies; (ii) where basic *is a* relations are determined; (iii) where lexical restrictions are satisfied in such a way that grammatical position corresponds to the subcategorization of the item in that position; and (iv) where transformations initially apply. So understood, there is nothing *deep* about deep structure. It is simply a level of syntactic representation with certain defining properties. It does stand in distinction to surface structure, but, likewise, there is nothing superficial about surface structure; it is just another level of representation that meets other demands. Chomsky (LGB) was to drop the 'deep/surface' notions in favour of 'D-Structure' and 'S-Structure'. The crucial point is simply that, given the mismatch between apparent structure and what we understand the structures to express, there should be two levels of representations; just what we call them is irrelevant. The confusion, however, is forgivable.

Chomsky was certainly not the first person to hypothesize a level of structure distinct from apparent form. Indeed, Chomsky is very happy to give that credit to the post-Cartesian grammarians of Port-Royal (ATS, pp. 198–9; cf. CILT, pp. 15–6; CL). Further, the twentieth century saw a general diagnosis of philosophical and other conceptual problems as being due to the apparent form of language being systematically misleading as to the structure of thought. A simple and foundational example is the difference between proper names and quantifier expressions (terms of generality). On the face of it, the sentences in (14) have the same form:

(14)   a. [$_S$ [$_{NP}$ Bill] [$_{VP}$ is happy]]

      b. [$_S$ [$_{NP}$ Everyone] [$_{VP}$ is happy]]

Semantically, however, they appear to differ greatly. In (14)a, happiness is predicated of an individual, but not in (14)b. The class of humans can be neither happy nor sad. In terms of Chomsky's selection restrictions, happiness can only be predicated of animate things and the class of sentient beings is not animate. In short, (14)b is read as predicating happiness to each individual of a class, making the NP an operator over a class rather than a designator of a class (i.e. 'Every member of some class is such that it is happy'). We shall return to this kind of example. The present point is simply that there appears to be a level of analysis that captures the thought expressed that is concealed by the apparent form, at least if we pre-theoretically take grammatical constituency to be a strict guide to semantic interpretation. In the philosophical tradition, this basic insight led to a variety of different approaches. To simplify greatly, on the one hand there was an approach that disregarded natural language as irredeemably messy, to be abandoned in favour of the formulation of precise formal languages. On the other hand, there was an approach that highlighted the inordinate complexity of natural language and saw the development of formal languages as constitutively unsuited to capture the witnessed richness of the colloquial idiom. Whatever the virtues or vices of these two attitudes, it bears emphasis that neither was primarily interested in language for its own sake. The approaches were animated by long-standing philosophical concerns with the nature of judgement, truth, logic, meaning etc.

If we were to situate Chomsky in the philosophical landscape, he would be someone who travelled a course between the two extreme peaks. On the one hand, Chomsky employed formal techniques that radically departed from a mere description of language as it appears or is used; on the other hand, the whole point of the formal exercise is to account for language as we find it and not to create a substitute for it to satisfy non-linguistic demands.

Chomsky understood D-structure as a level of syntax and not as meaning or thought. This meant that the properties of deep structure are to be determined by linguistic data of acceptability, of the kind exemplified above, rather than a freewheeling analysis of whatever might be plausibly construed as an aspect of meaning. Further, the goal of generative theory has always been to link the two levels of structure (via transformations) and not merely to dismiss S-structure as superficial. The richer D-structure becomes, in accommodating all that might plausibly fall under the label of meaning, the more complicated and arbitrary becomes the transformational component that must map the now baroque D-structure to S-structure. If the goal is to understand thought in its full panoply, then such complication might be required. If the provisional goal is to understand the narrow structure of language, understood as the map between two levels of structure, then the governing methodological assumption must be that grammatical processes only have access to a restricted set of features that explain the narrowly construed linguistic data. This is not a principled argument, of course. It is simply an assumption that there is a peculiar linguistic competence in distinction to thought in general. The truth of the assumption lies in its explanatory fecundity and not merely in its coverage of more and more linguistic phenomena. Such coverage, for sure, is ideally sought, but the real goal is to explain the structure and development of the witnessed competence.

3   DEVELOPMENTS IN SYNTAX: AN ECONOMY DRIVE

The theory of *Aspects* sketched above became known as the *standard theory*. By the mid-1970s, the model had changed to the *extended standard theory* (EST). By the 1980s, the model was *Government and Binding* (GB). The 1990s saw the emergence of the *Minimalist Program* (MP), which has since gone through various developments. To theorists outside of the field and, for that matter, many in the field, such changes can be alienating. The changes might even suggest that generative linguists are flapping about not having made any genuine discoveries. Worse, it could be thought that the field turns on the latest whim or suggestion emanating from MIT; the changes call for a sociological or ideological explanation. Such accusations are unwarranted; the remainder of this chapter will explain why. First, though, let us make some remarks on theoretical change.

First, theoretical change in itself is neither a virtue nor a vice. If a sequence of changes increase a framework's explanatory depth, enable greater empirical coverage or make for a more economical explanation, then the changes are obviously a good thing. A theoretical framework that resists simplification and modification both in relation to external data and internal demands for economy should not be valued, unless, miraculously, we had discovered the right theory. The truth is that scientific frameworks change constantly, and it is no more a vice in linguistics than it is in physics or chemistry. Besides, as we shall see, the changes have not been arbitrary or revolutionary. Science is only as conservative as the latest best theory.

Second, no discipline worth pursuing inherits its value from another. Interdisciplinary integration is to be valued, but it is not an a priori constraint. One of Chomsky's favourite examples is the development of modern chemistry and physics (see Chapter 6). Prior to the development of quantum theory, it is was impossible to see how the apparent laws of chemistry could be physically realized. This led many to view chemistry as merely taxonomic or descriptive, much as many now see linguistics. After the radical developments in physics, however, which made a theory of the chemical bond possible, it was understood that the chemistry had been right all along; it was the physics that had been wrong. Of course, current linguistics is not as established as early twentieth century chemistry, but the moral remains. If developments in linguistics appear to lead the field further away from current thinking in supposedly lower-level sciences, such as psychology, then that is not a signal of degeneration. It might well be that it is the lower-level sciences that must change. Of course, there is no way of knowing this a priori: we dream of all the sciences catching up with each other, but at no point do we know who is in the lead. Equally, if developments in linguistics appear to speak less and less of philosophical concerns, then that might well signal that such concerns are misplaced. As we saw in Chapter 5, it is not the business of linguistics or any other science to support or be constrained by philosophical presuppositions about the nature of mind or language. Such presuppositions might well simply be false.

Third, it is an insult to many linguists to imagine that they blindly follow Chomsky's lead. First, there are many disagreements within the generative camp, just as one would expect in rational inquiry. Second, many of the major developments we shall survey came about through cooperation, with Chomsky often not leading the way. That said, this is a book about Chomsky, so my focus will be on his ideas.

3.1   X-Bar theory and the demise of the base

In 1972, Chomsky (*Studies on Semantics in Generative Grammar* (SSGG), pp. 124–5) wrote:

> The gravest defect of the theory of transformational grammar is its enormous latitude and descriptive power. Virtually anything can be expressed as a phrase marker . . . Virtually any imaginable rule can be described in transformational terms. Therefore a critical problem in making transformational grammar a substantive theory with explanatory force is to restrict the category of admissible phrase markers, admissible transformations, and admissible derivations.

Prima facie, it may seem that a grammar of 'latitude and descriptive power' is to be commended, for it promises to cover more of the phenomena. As Chomsky explains, however, and as we have been stressing throughout this book, the goal is explanation and not mere description. Each part of a grammar should embody generalizations that are simpler or more economical than the phenomena they cover, for this enables the theory not only to encapsulate the relevant phenomena descriptively but also to make predictions and show that otherwise disparate phenomena follow from the same basic principles. A theory as rich as the phenomena it targets is no theory at all. For example, to take up Chomsky's first point, if a theory of phrase markers (the base) allows for a structural description of any string of words at all, then the theory would not capture what is shared by the well-formed strings. Likewise, if any relation between sentences whatsoever could be expressed transformationally, then the transformation component would only accidentally capture the set of peculiar structural relations found in natural language. Furthermore, since the theory is meant to account for language acquisition, a rich or non-restricted theory would allow the child too much latitude; she would, as it were, have too many options. Poverty of stimulus considerations tells us that the child lacks the data to exclude many options. In this state, the child had better be able to make the right generalizations from the data she has, which just means that her options had better be restricted. Such considerations led, first, to the elimination of the phrase marker base of the *Aspects* model in favour of what came to be called *X-Bar Theory*. Rather than go through the growing pains of this theory (first formulated in Chomsky's *Remarks on Nominalization* (RN), 1968), let us motivate it abstractly.

As we saw, transformations were first proposed, because a phrase marker grammar lacks the resources to capture many salient relations. The result was the standard theory wedded a phrase marker base with a transformational component. Here, the base is meant to capture, *inter alia*, the set of *is a* relations; that is, it embodies categorical information about what constitutes a sentence, a verb phrase etc. It does indeed do this job but with far too much latitude; that is, every construction on an individual basis can be described by a phrase marker, but generalizations are missed and so unwanted constructions are derivable. Let us see this by a comparison of verbs, which nouns and adjectives.

A phrase marker grammar of the *Aspects* kind allows the following three sets of rewrite rules:

Verb	Adjective	Noun
VP → V	AP → A	NP → N
VP → V PP	AP → A PP	NP → N PP
VP → V S	AP → A S	NP → N S
VP → V PP S	AP → A PP S	NP → N PP S

Clearly, there are generalizations to be had here. For example, each major phrase (VP, AP, NP) includes or dominates a category of its type; the lexical item corresponding to this category is called a *head*. So, we can say that all phrases have heads. Also, heads are initial, with their complements following. We can *see* that these generalizations hold, but the rule system does not encode the generalizations. This is evidenced by the fact that the rewrite rules do not exclude rules such as the following.

(15) a. VP → A PP
      b. AP → VP PP N
      c. NP → S N

These putative rules contravene the generalizations. As Chomsky says, the rules allow for structural descriptions of any string. What is desired, then, is a restricted theory of the phrase markers that simultaneously captures the right generalizations and, by so doing, excludes cases such as those in (15). X-bar theory does just that.

X-bar theory is a general account of phrase structure that says that all phrases follow the same pattern (express the same relations), with complex phrases simply being iterations of the same simple general pattern. This pattern is given below:

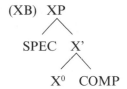

Or, in bracket notation

(XB*)   [XP [[SPEC] X' [X⁰ COMP]]]

As a set of rules, the pattern is expressed as

(XBR) a. XP → SPEC X'
       b. X' → X'
       c. X' → X⁰ COMP

(Here I exclude the position of adjuncts that extend the X' level with an X'.) 'X' is a variable that ranges over the categories, with 'X⁰' being the label for the head and 'X'' being its intermediate projection (this notion will be explained below). 'SPEC' stands for 'specifier'.

The notion was initially introduced to cover items that specify the following head, but the notion should be understood as simply marking out a structural position in the X-bar schema. So, for example, the above phrase marker rules – (14) – fit into the schema as follows (the reader can see how the rest follow):

(16) a. [VP [[SPEC] V' [V^0 sleep] [COMP]]]
  b. [AP [[SPEC] A' [A^0 proud] [COMP that Mary won]]]
  c. [NP [[SPEC The] N' [N^0 destruction] [COMP of the city]]]

Here we see that positions (SPEC, COMP) are optional but can be filled. The X-bar schema intends to give the general form of structure rather than a mere description of instances. To check its worth, let's see how it deals with the two problems, exemplified in (15), that beset the phrase structure rules.

First, as presented, the X-bar schema captures the two generalizations mentioned. The first generalization concerned heads, which may expressed as follows:

(END) All phrases are endocentric, that is, an XP phrase contains an X (head) which projects to define the categorical status of the phrase.

This is easily confirmed. If all phrases realize the X-bar schema, then all phrases require X^0, which is simply the head of the phrase.

The second generalization concerned linear order:

(LO) (In English) heads precede their complements.

Again, trivially, we see that the X-bar schema captures the generalization. It should be noted, however, that other languages differ in this regard. Japanese, for instance, is head final, unlike English, which is head initial. We shall return to this issue later.

Given that the schema captures the generalizations, we should expect it to exclude the deviant phrase structure rules and indeed it does. For example, (15)a, b are non-endocentric and (15)c is not head initial.

A further attractive feature of the X-bar schema is that it allows us to define structurally the familiar grammatical functions of *subject*, *predicate* etc. In *Aspects*, Chomsky (ATS, p. 71) defined them as follows:

(16) a. Subject-of: [NP, S]
  b. Predicate-of: [VP, S]

    c. Direct-Object-of: [NP, VP]
    d. Main-Verb-of: [V, VP]

If we let [X, Y] mean 'X immediately dominated by or included in Y', then subjects are SPECs of S, predicates are V's (Ss without SPECs), direct objects are the COMPs of V X^0s and main verbs are V X^0s. Thus, X-bar theory allows for the smooth definition of grammatical functions.

Associated with the development of X-bar theory was a realization of a massive redundancy, which Chomsky noted in *Aspects* but ignored until LGB. If we take lexical items to have subcategorization features, then the items themselves determine their combinatorial operations. However, the phrase structure rules appear to state exactly the same information, that, for example, a transitive verb must have a direct object, information that is already recorded in each transitive verb. The question arises, therefore, of what must go? The answer is not difficult to fathom. First, lexical items are subcategorically idiosyncratic; that is, there are no generalizations over their co-occurrence on the basis of their categories. We shall discuss some examples below, but just consider a verb such as *eat*. It is both transitive and intransitive. Also contrast *ergatives*, such as *boil, spill, clear, fry* etc., whose objects can also be their subjects (e.g. *Bill boiled the soup* → *The soup boiled*), with true intransitives (unergatives), such as *run, sleep die* etc., or unaccusatives, such as *arrive, die, fall, melt*, where their subjects are not agents, or true transitives, such as *spread, sieve, fix* etc. Phrase structure rules to capture all these differences and more would appear to be simply a description of the phenomena, with no generalization at all. Second, if lexical items did not contain syntactic information, then how would rules apply to them? It would be as if the application of a rule made an item an intransitive verb, say. This is absurd, for nothing would preclude any item being of any category. Again, phrase structure rules look to be purely descriptive. If we reason in the other direction, and dispense with phrase structure rules, the problems do not arise. First, the idiosyncrasy of lexical items is respected. Second, it will be the inherent properties of lexical items that determine their combinatorial options. Of course, we still need generalizations about the structure of clauses, but X-bar theory now provides that by presenting a uniform structure that admits variability, either through options, as exemplified, or via movement (see below). Here is a beautiful example of how linguistics pursues economy of principle and, by so doing, captures the right generalizations.

So far, X-bar theory appears to be a great improvement on the old phrase structure base. Its development, however, brought into relief a fundamental problem with the old phrase marker system that, so far, we have inherited in our presentation of the X-bar schema.

As presented, the X-bar schema misses out the AUX category and complementizers, that is, items that introduce clauses, such as *that*, *if*, *whether* etc. In RN, Chomsky does fill these lacunae with the following two rules, where 'C' is the generic label for complementizers and 'I' is the generic label for items falling under the old AUX, that is, inflectional items, including tense:

(17) a. S' → C S
      b. S → NP I VP

(17)a says that S' is a complementizer followed by a sentence (i.e. a subordinate clause), such as *that Mary is tall*, *if Bill arrives*, *whether Bill is happy* etc. (17)b says that a sentence now includes an obligatory item 'I' that encodes tense. On the face of it, the rule in (17)a fits the X-bar schema, with S being the head of S' and with C as its SPEC, but when we look at the analysis of S in (17)b, we find a complex structure without a head. Thus, S looks like a headless category, with S' inheriting the affliction. This should be obvious really, for heads (X^0s) are lexical items, but S is not. The problem, then, is twofold. First, the rules in (17) are exceptions to the X-bar schema, which is intended to give the universal form of phrase structure. Second, the exception is not innocent. The rules contravene (END).

In effect, a headless phrase amounts to a stipulation of the theorist, or, at best, an intuitive generalization. Headedness *explains* the behaviour of a phrase (its co-occurrence with other phrases) by its inheritance of category features from its head (the head projects) and so the phrase can be understood as being selected by such features. Without a head, we are simply stipulating that, say, phrases of a certain kind are what we shall call 'sentences'.

It is surprising that Chomsky was stuck with rules such as (17) for nearly twenty years, until he (KoL) made the natural rectification.

(18)   a. CP → C IP
      b. IP → NP I VP

Here, CP is a complementizer phrase and IP is an inflectional phrase. These two rules resolve the problems with (17). CP is headed by C and IP is headed by I. I say these rules are natural, for they provide heads that are lexical items, that is, complementizers and inflectional items, such as auxiliary verbs and tense morphemes. The rules also fit smoothly within the X-bar schema.

(18)   a. [CP [[SPEC] C' [C⁰] [COMP IP]]]
      b. [IP [[SPEC NP] I' [I⁰] [COMP VP]]]

(Note: These schemata involve a change in our earlier definitions of grammatical functions. A subject now is the SPEC of IP and a predicate is the complement of IP.)

The ditching of S and S' in favour of IP and CP also has empirical support, quite independently of the theoretical concerns. This is just what we should expect: increasing theoretical simplicity converging with increasingly deep explanation of phenomena. For example, C appears to be the head of subordinate clauses rather than S, for C is both selected by the verb and C selects IP. Consider the following data.

(19)   a. Bill believes that/*if/*whether Mary is tall
      b. Bill believes *that/*if/*whether to leave
      c. Bill knows that/if/whether Mary is tall
      d. Bill knows *that/*if/whether to leave (or not)
      e. Bill asked *that/if/whether he could leave
      f. Bill wondered *that/*if/whether to leave (or not)

Here we see that some verbs, such as *believe*, only select C *that*, which in turn selects a finite IP alone (witness (19)b, d, f). Other verbs, such as *know*, select any C, but only *whether* can select infinite IP. Still other verbs, such as *ask* and *wonder*, do not select *that*; they require an interrogative C, but only *whether* selects infinite IP. The generalization here is that verbs differ in regard to what C they can select (co-occur with), but the Cs, as selected, do not differ in what IPs they can select. This pattern is explained if verbs select CPs, for, qua C headed, the selected IP or sentence will not project its features to the phrase head and so the verbs will be, as it were, blind to the status of the IP; they can only see the head. That is exactly what we find.

Also note that CPs can *move* as units in ways IPs cannot. For example,

(20) a. That Bill is so tall intimidated the crowd
     b. *Bill is so tall intimidated the crowd
     c. Whether Mary should leave or not is what bothered Bill
     d. *Mary should leave or not is what bothered Bill

Empirical data also supports (18)b. We have already seen this with respect to polar interrogatives, where the I head is displaced by a transformation, that is, the transformation targets the least embedded item for displacement, which is equivalent to saying that it targets the head. The reverse process is witnessed. Consider:

(21) a. Murder JFK, Oswald did
     b. What Oswald did was murder JFK

In (21)a, the VP *murder JFK* has been topicalised (displaced to the front of the sentence). However, note that the past tense morpheme -*ed* is left in situ and is *do*-supported. That tells us, just as polar interrogatives do, that the inflection carrying item is independent of the NP and VP, that is, not included in either of them. Thus, it is the head. (21)b exhibits the same effect.

Here we reach a lovely conclusion: in a real sense, there are no sentences! The notion of a sentence, both as a subordinate clause and as self-standing, gives way to CP and IP. This provides a beautiful example of how empirical inquiry can lead us to reject the most central notions of our pre-theoretical conception of phenomena. This kind of theoretical development is very familiar in the hard sciences, but it should be recognized as a general trait of empirical inquiry even where the inquiry is most intimate to us. In the present case, it looks as if the concept of a sentence is simply a descriptive notion, for, if all phrases are headed, and the full phrase is a projection of the head, then there is simply no room for sentences; they are explanatorily otiose.

In conclusion, by the mid-1970s, X-bar theory had replaced the phrase marker base. This was a great economizing, which both captured the right generalizations and better accounted for the extant data and unnoticed data.

3.2 The lexicon and theta theory

So far, then, deep structure consists of X-bar schemata. Two immediate questions arise. How do lexical items relate to X-bar theory? How, if at all, do transformations affect the X-bar structures? As we shall see, the two questions are intimate. In this section, we shall discuss the first issue.

The lexicon is understood as a list of exceptions, that is, packages of information that differ from each other in at least some respect, either phonetically, semantically or syntactically. Let us just focus on the syntax. A lexical item must, it seems, carry at least the syntactic information that determines its grammatical category, a noun rather than a verb, say. In *Aspects*, as we saw, Chomsky considered there to be two distinct syntactic features: subcategorization features and selection features. Chomsky quickly dropped the latter notion and with it the concomitant notion of degrees of grammaticalness. Chomsky's reasons are not explicit, but the natural explanation is that while selection clearly does affect acceptability, (i) the features have no affect on syntactic processes (X-bar schemata or transformations) and (ii) much of their work can be accommodated by an otherwise required mechanism (theta theory, which we shall come to shortly). Notwithstanding this, it is worth noting that something akin to selection still holds, an aspect of what Uriagereka (2002) has dubbed 'vertical syntax'. Nouns appear to form into an inclusion hierarchy:

(VS) Proper name ← Count ← Mass ← Abstract

So, all proper names have construals as count, mass and abstract; all count nouns have mass and abstract construals, but not proper construals, and so on. This curious fact is mostly ignored in philosophy of language. The debates there have been dominated by the attempt to figure out how proper names have their unique reference in distinction to the other nouns; how, that is, *Mary* refers to Mary alone, the actual Mary, as it were. On the basis of (VS), however, we can see how the endeavour is at best confused, for *Mary*, as a freestanding proper name, does not refer to Mary at all. It only acquires a unique construal when so used (see PP, NH). To see the point here, consider the following:

(22)　a.　Mary believes in ghosts
　　　　b.　All the Marys in the class passed

   c. After the steamroller had finished, Mary was spread all over the road

   d. What this party needs is a Mary

The data in (22) give examples corresponding to the (VS) hierarchy. Mary can be a unique thing, a plurality of things, the stuff of such things or an abstraction from such things. We clearly do not want to say that *Mary* is four ways ambiguous. However, if there is a single lexical item, [Mary], then distinct features of the item appear to be triggered in different contexts. This is an intriguing area of research that I simply wish to flag. Let us now get back to the main thread.

With selection features eschewed, we are left with just an item's subcategorization features, as understood on the *Aspects* model. Each lexical item carries information on other items with which it can co-occur. As we just saw above, distinct Cs subcategorize distinct IPs. Here are a few examples:

(23)   a. *destruction* [N+, _PP]
       b. *believe* [+V, _NP, _PP, _CP]
       c. *proud* [+N, -V, _PP]
       d. *on* [-N, -V, _NP]

As well as subcategorization, lexical items also appear to impose other conditions related to what we might call the internal *logic* of an item. Let us take verbs. Familiarly, verbs are intransitive, transitive or ditransitive.

(24)   a. Bill sleeps
       b. Bill saw Mary
       c. Bill gave Mary flowers

Let us say that *sleep* has one argument, *see* two arguments and *give* three arguments. An argument is another item or phrase that, in this case, a verb must *mark* in relation to itself. If we take verbs to describe an event or state, then the verb's arguments mark the different participants in that event or state. For example, *sleep* marks just one argument, for sleeping requires just one person and not two things. Similarly, *see* marks two arguments, for there must be someone who sees and a thing seen. A person cannot see and not see something, and something cannot be seen unless there is someone doing the seeing. The same reasoning applies to *give*. Any event of giving requires someone giving something to someone. As should be evident, these arguments play different roles within the event or state the verb describes. These roles are termed θ(theta)-roles and we say that lexical items mark other items as playing a certain θ-role. (Chomsky adopted this approach in LGB (1981), although a similar approach was discussed in *Aspects* under the (confusing) name of 'case' due to Fillimore. Theta theory, as it has become known, was developed by many theorists during the 1970s). The precise number of θ-roles is a theoretical matter, but the following are the main candidates:

(TR) AGENT: The thing that initiates an event or performs an action.
THEME: The thing affected by an action or event.
EXPERIENCER: The thing that experiences the event or state.
BENEFACTIVE: The thing that receives or benefits from the event or action.

So, in (24)a, *sleep* assigns its single AGENT role to *Bill*. In (24)b, *see* assigns a EXPERIENCER role to *Bill* and a THEME role to *Mary*. In (24)c, *give* assigns an AGENT role to *Bill*, a BENEFACTIVE role to *Mary* and a THEME role to *flowers*. In LGB (p. 36), Chomsky adopted a θ-*Criterion*:

(θ-C) (i) Each argument of a θ-assigner is assigned one and only θ-role.
(ii) Each θ-role a θ-assigner has to assign is assigned to one and only one argument.

This tells us that there is a 1:1 map between θ-roles and arguments, where an argument cannot have more than one θ-role and each θ-role must be assigned to just the one argument. (θ-C) has been controversial since its inception, but let us adopt it as a hypothesis.

(θ-C) makes some obvious predictions that are borne out. Consider:

(25)   a. *Bill sleeps Mary [argument without a θ-role]
       b. *Bill saw [a θ-role without an argument]
       c. *Bill gave [two θ-roles without arguments]

Theta theory also accommodates much of the selection data. Consider the following:

(26) a. Golf plays Bill
      b. Sincerity saw Bill
      c. Bill travelled to democracy

These sentences are fine as far as selection goes and they also keep to (θ-C). The problem arises due to a misalignment in the *kind* of θ-roles assigned. So, *play* assigns an AGENT role, but golf is not the kind of thing that can affect another thing in an event. Likewise, *saw* assigns an EXPERIENCER role, but sincerity cannot have experiences. Let *travel* assign a LOCATIVE role to its selected PP. Here, the problem arises with democracy not being a place. If we compare the unacceptability of the sentences under (25) with the figural construals those under (26) admit, we have the prediction that contravention of (θ-C) results in unacceptability, while mis-assignment of roles produces constructions that require an imposed construal. Thus, it looks as if we can adequately capture the basic thought behind selection without any special features, just θ-roles that look to be independently required.

There are many ongoing issues concerning theta theory that are way beyond my present scope.

3.3 Semantics, the projection principle and the demise of transformations

Recall that by the Katz-Postal hypothesis, transformations are semantically inert; that is, transformations apply to deep structures to produce surface structures, but they do not alter semantic interpretation. A sentence's meaning, in other words, is determined by its deep structure and not its apparent structure. As we saw, Chomsky had something like this thought in mind as early as SS, and he provisionally adopted the articulated principle in ATS. By the late 1960s, however, he came to question the thesis and fully rejected it in the articles collected as SSGG (published in 1972). The K-H hypothesis is very attractive for it cleanly articulates a way of handling the chief phenomenon the generative enterprise sought to explain: the mismatch of semantically relevant structure with apparent structure. It bears emphasis, then, that Chomsky's change of position was less motivated by theory and more by troubling data. As the range of semantic analysis mushroomed in the late 60s to include many discourse related aspects, such as focus, topic, presupposition, stress and especially quantification structure, the more a defender of K-H had to enrich deep structure to accommodate it. On the face of it, however, such phenomena are essentially post-transformational; that is, the interpretations are not determined by structure that determines grammatical functionality. The data here quickly become complex, so let us just consider two chief examples.

Assume there is a passive transformation that maps from a deep structure that determines the active form. By K-H, this means that there is no semantic difference between the passive and the active. Consider the following (see Chomsky's EFI, pp. 39–40):

(27)   a. Beavers build dams
       b. Dams are built by beavers
       c. Fools write poems
       d. Poems are written by fools
       e. Fools climb mountains
       f. Mountains are climbed by fools

We do not interpret the active (27)a as making a claim about every dam; for example, it remains true notwithstanding the Hoover dam. Likewise, (27)c may be taken as true even if one thinks that Elliot was far from a fool. The interpretations appear to alter with the passive counterparts. It would be perfectly natural to rebut utterances of (27)b,d by appeal to the Hoover dam and Elliot respectively. In other words, in the passive cases, the grammatical subject takes on a universal reading; (27)a is not about every dam, (27)b is. The passive transformation alone, however, is not responsible for this change, as is witnessed by (27)e,f. It appears that the change is due to the transformation in combination with the verb. 'Creative verbs', such as *create, build, write, make* etc. semantically affect their subjects in ways other verbs do not, such as *climb*. However, we are to account for the difference; the passive transformation appears to result in a semantic difference, even if it is not solely to blame.

Consider now quantificational ambiguity:

(28) a. Every student admires some teacher
       b. Two students in the class know three languages

Both of these sentences look to be *structurally* ambiguous; that is, the readings are not dependent upon any lexical ambiguity. (28)a has the following two readings:

(29) a. Every student is such that some teacher (or other) is admired by them
       b. (every student x)(some teacher y)(x admires y)
       c. Some teacher is such that every student admires them
       d. (some teacher y)(every student x)(x admires y)

The same kind of dual interpretation holds for (28)b: two students might know the same three languages, or they each might know three different languages. This difference is referred to as a *scope* ambiguity, where one NP (*every student, three languages* etc.) is interpreted in the scope of another; that is, it is interpreted relative to the first. The schematic structures of (29)b,d depict the difference. In (29)b, *some teacher* is in the scope of *every student*, and so it is interpreted relative to *every student*, giving us a reading where teachers map individually onto the class of students. The situation is reversed in (29)c; *every student* is now interpreted relative to some given teacher. The important thing to note here is that the changes in scope are not recorded at D-structure, at least not as we have been understanding that notion. If the only structural relations deep structure determines are those of grammatical function via something like an X-bar schema, then it should be impossible for the sentences in (28) to admit differential scope relations at deep structure; after all, there is just the one structure and not two.

Suffice it to say, these issues were complex then and are more so now. My present intention is just to depict Chomsky's reasoning at that time. The natural conclusion Chomsky drew (along with Jackendoff (1972)) was that deep structure is not the sole determiner of structural semantic significance. This resulted in the extended standard theory, whose architecture is given below.

[X-bar, θ-roles, lexical insertion] Deep Structure → Semantics

$\downarrow$

$\downarrow$ ← Transformations

$\downarrow$

Phonology/Morphology ← Surface Structure → Semantics

On reflection, one should see something odd about this model as a response to the two cases discussed. While it is not in itself incoherent for semantics to interface syntax at two levels, if the split interface is designed to capture scope relations (*inter alia*), then they appear to be still free, for surface structure is as incapable of structurally reflecting the differential relations interpretable in (28) as is deep structure. In other words, while topic, focus and presupposition might be 'surface' phenomena, scope is not. Scope appears to involve the differential domination or inclusion of grammatical subjects and objects in a way that is not reflected by any transformation to surface structure. In RL, Chomsky designated the result of transformations as 'Surface Structure/Logical Form', but this seemed to be a mere labelling of the problem.

Robert May, who worked with Chomsky in the mid-70s, offered a natural solution by way of a particular transformation – *Quantifier Raising* (QR) – that raised quantifier NPs out of their grammatical function positions to adjoined positions outside of the IP (then still called 'S'). QR is a *covert* transformation in the sense that it applies to surface structure; that is, its effect is not phonologically registered. It is interesting to reflect that at this moment in the development of linguistics, neither Chomsky nor anyone else reflected on the possibility of a threefold split interface with semantics: deep structure reflecting θ-assignment and basic structural positions, surface structure reflecting discourse effects and Logical Form reflecting scope. It seemed that the split interface of the extended standard theory was bad enough; a threefold split would be rubbing salt into the wound. But why? Well, the interpretive component (semantics) appears to be unitary in that our understanding of a sentence reflects all semantic properties; we should, therefore, seek a single level of structure in the syntax that precisely encodes those properties. In this light, we can view the split-level model as reflecting a problem. No single level appears to be able to encode all semantically significant structure; if, however, transformations could retain structure, then a single post-deep structure level could encode all relevant structure, if it picked structure up along the way, as it were. This is just what Chomsky proposed by way of three innovations: trace theory, the incorporation of Logical Form as a distinct level and the projection principle. Let us first look at trace theory and how it enabled a massive streamlining of the transformational component.

Trace theory is way of accounting for the retention of structural information within a derivation from one level to another. So far, we have understood transformations as operations that alter deep structures in various kinds of ways. The only apparent constraint on what transformations we may posit is just the demand for descriptive adequacy. As we saw in Chapter 6, however, that constraint itself is in tension with the demand for explanatory adequacy as a condition on UG. The more transformations we posit to account for variation within a language the more distant a plausible account of UG becomes, for now the child is called upon to select the right group of transformations, which is an apparently impossible task under conditions of poverty of stimulus. All else being equal, then, it would be best if UG contained the most minimal set of transformations that applied to any possible language. Beginning with John Ross's brilliant PhD in the late 1960s and continuing throughout the 1970s, linguists attempted to constrain transformations to meet certain conditions and also to satisfy *filters* that held at levels of syntax. Space precludes discussion of this rich tradition (see EFI and 'Filters and control' (FC)). The upshot of this reasoning, though was the most minimal conception of transformation that Chomsky articulated in LGB (1981). There, the transformational component is reduced to a single rule: *Move α*. This rule says, in effect, move any constituent of a structure anywhere else. The notion of transformation thus becomes one of *movement* or the displacement of a constituent. The importance of this development is that it frees the idea of transformation from the structure types particular to individual languages. For example, English exhibits passive and raising constructions, both of which appear to require their own transformations particular to English. *Move α*, on the other hand, is general as regards displacement across and within languages. Thus, we can attribute it to UG, which we cannot do for the construction particular transformations. Of course, if unconstrained, the rule is a garbage machine. The constraints come into play at the syntactic levels: each level marks a set of conditions that must be met by the composed structure. So, D-structure must meet X-bar and theta theoretic requirements; surface structure must meet Case conditions and other requirements. With so much in place, let us turn to trace theory.

A trace is a result of movement. A moved constituent leaves behind a trace of itself in its original structural position. Let us take the simple example of the passive:

(29) a. $[_{IP}$ was $[_{VP}$ defeated $[_{NP}$ France]]]

      b. $[_{IP}$ France$_i$ was $[_{VP}$ defeated $[_{NP}$ t$_i$]]]

Here, the NP *France* has moved from its D-structure position to the SPEC IP position at S-structure. The operation leaves behind a trace that marks the position in which *France* acquires its THEME. We can, therefore, think of movement as an operation that forms a *chain* of a lexical item and its traces, and it is such chains that are interpretable. Here is a more complex example:

(30) a. $[_{CP}$ $[_{IP}$ Mary $[_{I'}$ $[_{I}$ –s] $[_{VP}$ love WH]]]]

      b. $[_{CP}$ do–s$_i$ $[_{IP}$ Mary $[_{I'}$ $[_{I}$ t$_i$] $[_{VP}$ love WH]]]]

      c. $[_{CP}$ WH$_j$ do–s$_i$ $[_{IP}$ Mary $[_{I'}$ $[_{I}$ t$_i$] $[_{VP}$ love t$_j$]]]]

The derivation proceeds from a D-structure corresponding to *Mary loves whom* to a S-structure corresponding to *Whom does Mary love?*. The head I first moves to the C head and then the WH object of *love* moves to the SPEC CP position.

Now, the great virtue of traces is that they allow a derivation to retain its information. Just as T-markers encoded the history of a derivation, so now a given structure can encode its derivational history by way of its traces or, better, its constituent chains. There is, therefore, no need for a split interface, for just because certain features are initially encoded at a level, it does not follow that those features cannot be carried through a derivation to higher levels. All one requires is a mechanism to record those features and that mechanism is trace theory.

Traces might strike the unwary as odd. Remember, though, that a phrase structure is not intended to be a description of a sentence; rather, it is a hypothesis about the information a speaker/hearer possesses that enables her to understand the sentence in question, and there is no reason to think that all that goes into understanding a sentence is recorded phonologically. In fact, we know this already, for the very idea of the mismatch between semantic structure and apparent form tells us that there is more to understanding a sentence than classifying its 'visible' parts. Traces are aspects of our mental structure that simply lack phonological interpretation; they are a species of *empty category*.

In LGB and subsequent work, the kinds of empty categories expanded beyond traces. Here I can just mention one other signifi-cant case. Consider:

(31)   a. Bill seems to be happy
       b. It seems that Bill is happy
       c. Bill tries to be happy
       d. *It tries that Bill is happy

In (31)a, *Bill* is in grammatical subject position (SPEC IP), but it appears to have been displaced there; that is, its deep structural position is not SPEC IP. This is so for two reasons. First, the infini-tive IP – *to be happy* – requires a subject or, better, a θ-role assigned by *be* (a thing in the state of happiness), and the only available item is *Bill*. Second, (31)b shows that the subject position of (31)a is not theta marked; that is, *it* is an expletive here and not referential: there is no AGENT of seeming; there is a seeming (to someone or other) that Bill is happy. One can see the contrast with the verb *try*. In (31)c, *Bill* is the AGENT of *try* as is evidenced by (31)d, which shows that *try* assigns AGENT to its subject. How, then, do we explain this difference?

With trace theory in place, it is natural to analyse (31)a with *Bill* originally (deep structurally) in the SPEC IP of the infinitive from where it acquires its θ-role as the experiencer of happiness, which it retains once it moves to the SPEC of the higher IP to become the subject of *seem*. However, now we appear to have a problem with (31)c, in which *Bill* is both the AGENT of *try* and the EXPERI-ENCER of *happiness*. How can Bill acquire both roles at D-structure unless the item is in both positions at that level? If *Bill* is in the lower position at deep structure, then the item must have moved, but it couldn't have moved to the higher position, for that must have already been occupied by AGENT *Bill*; nor could *Bill* have somehow been erased, for then we would loose a required θ-role. In short, it appears that *Bill* has two roles, which not only contravenes our θ Criterion, but seems impossible to account for structurally (Chomsky first broached this problem in FC). The answer Chomsky proposed is that there is a kind of empty category beyond trace: PRO. We can think of PRO as a phonologically null pronoun, whose possible structural position is complementary to phonologically realized pronouns. An anaphoric link (termed *control*) between a phonologically realized item and PRO enables the higher controlling item to be understood as if it had two θ-roles, even though, structurally, the distinct roles are assigned independently. Thus, we should analyse (31)c as

(32) $[_{IP}$ Bill$_i$ tries $[_{IP}$ PRO$_i$ to be happy]]

It bears emphasis that while empty categories are perfectly legitimate posits (we are dealing with mental structures and not descriptions of sentences), they cannot simply be plucked from the air to account for otherwise anomalous data. First, their positing should accord with otherwise sound principles. In the present case, we can see how this is so. Second, we might try to seek psychological data on their existence. Third, their positing should allow for simpler and more elegant explanation of extant and novel data; this would show us that they are not merely ad hoc. A nice case of this is contraction data.
Consider:

(32)   a. Who do you want to visit?
       b. Who do you wanna visit?
       c. Who do you want to visit Bill
       d. *Who do you wanna visit Bill

(32)a is ambiguous between a reading that questions which person is such that you want to visit them and a reading that questions which person is such that you want them to visit you. The difference is accounted for by distinct D-structure positions open to *who*: either the object of visit or the SPEC of IP *to visit*. If we contract, as in (32)b, so that the verb attaches to the infinitive marker *to* ('wanna'), we loose the second reading. On the assumption that *who* must move and is interpreted in its original position, it appears that contraction over the original D-structure position blocks the construal that depends upon that position. This is further supported by the next two sentences. (32)c is not ambiguous; it can only mean, which person is such that you want them to visit Bill. In other words, since *Bill* is in situ as the object (THEME) of *visit*, that position cannot be questioned, and so *who* can only have moved from the SPEC of the infinitive IP. If this is correct, then the prediction is that we should not be able to contract over the only possible D-structure position of *who*, the position in which it is interpreted as the AGENT of the visit. (32)d confirms the prediction. One hears (32)d as if one were asking Bill (= *you*) who he wants to visit, but one cannot hear it as if one were asking someone or other who they want to visit Bill. The WH trace appears to have an affect on interpretation, which is just what we would expect if the item is a real aspect of mental structure and not just a piece of taxonomy. Interestingly, the affect of covert material on contraction holds generally. Consider:

(33) a. Bill is intending to arrive the same time as I am <intending to arrive>.
      b. *Bill is intending to arrive the same time as I'm <intending to arrive>.
      c. Do you know where$_i$ the meeting is t$_i$ tomorrow?
      d. *Do you know where$_i$ the meeting's t$_i$ tomorrow?
      e. Do you know what$_i$ that is t$_i$ up there?
      f. *Do you know what that's t$_i$ up there?
      g. What$_i$ do you think that is t$_i$?
      h. * What$_i$ do you think that's t$_i$?

Just how such data and many other cases are to be accounted for remains unclear; my present point is simply that empty categories are not mere ad hoc descriptive devices. They earn their explanatory keep, which is all that science requires.

With trace theory, it becomes possible to see how a syntactic derivation can retain information, and if derivations can retain information, then it becomes plausible to think that there is just the single level of semantic interface that retains all previously assembled information relevant to semantics. If a rule of QR is required for scope relations, then that level must be LF, which is just what Chomsky concluded in LGB. Consider our earlier example:

(34) a. Every student admires some teacher
      b. [$_{IP}$ [$_{NP}$ Some teacher]$_j$ [$_{IP}$ [$_{NP}$ every student]$_i$ [$_{IP}$ t$_i$ admires t$_j$]]]

Via QR, both NPs can move from their surface positions to successive adjoined positions outside of their original IP to give us the reading where *some teacher* scopes over *every student*. Also note that the NPs retain their θ-roles through their respective trace positions; that is, *every student* remains the admirer of *some teacher*. To capture the other reading, we reverse the movement, so that every teacher scopes over some teacher, with the respective traces remaining the same (May (1985) changed his position on this so that just the structure in (34)b is legitimate at LF, but we may sideline the somewhat complex reasoning). It is also important to note that QR comes with no cost; it is just another species of *Move* α analogous to WH movement, which also results in scope relations.

Finally, we come to the projection principle, which should now be fairly obvious (I simplify somewhat from Chomsky's (LGB, p. 38) presentation):

(PP) (i) If α selects β in γ as a lexical property, then α selects β in γ at L_i

   (ii) If α selects β in γ at L_i, then α selects β in γ at L_j

(PP) express a general relation between lexical features and syntactic levels via X-bar schemata. (i) says that all selection (grammatical and theta) determined by lexical features is realized at a certain level L_i. (ii) says that whatever is determined at a given level is retained at higher levels. Thus, if we set L_i to be D-structure, then information is retained at S-structure (L_j). In turn, we can set L_i to be S-structure, and information is retained at LF (L_j). In short, syntax projects a structure from the properties of lexical items that determine the kinds of other items with which each can occur. For example, the verb admire selects two NP arguments as a lexical property that, according to the X-bar schema, must be positioned as SPEC and COMP; that is, grammatical functionality is fixed. However, no particular NPs are required. Theta theory requires an AGENT and THEME; let *every student* and *some teacher* be suitable arguments. We now have an approximate D-structure (ignore inflection) whose properties are fixed. Post S-structure, the NPs covertly move to adjoined positions, but there is no loss of information, for the traces remain to realize theta interpretation and the selection requirements of the verb. In effect, then, PP says that syntactic derivations do not loose information.

In LGB and subsequent work up to the early 1990s, the following T-model was proposed.

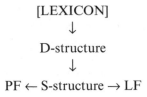

Lexical items enter the derivation at D-structure. Move α transforms the structure to produce an S-structure. This constitutes a point of spell-out, where the derivation splits. PF codes for phonology and LF for semantics. The model gives us the design for how the mind – the language faculty – pairs structures of 'sound' and 'meaning' via the structuring of lexical items into complex units in accord with the X-bar schema.

CHAPTER 8

THE MINIMALIST PROGRAM

[T]he grand aim of all science . . . is to cover the greatest possible number of empirical facts by logical deduction from the smallest possible number of hypotheses or axioms.

Einstein (1954, p. 282)

1 INTRODUCTION

In this chapter, we shall look at Chomsky's (and many others') current approach to the generative enterprise: the minimalist program (MP). As with all of our discussions so far, we must be selective and there is no space to defend any of the many analyses that have been proposed under MP. Still, we shall see how the current ideas promise to deepen the issues that have characterized the generative enterprise from its inception. Before we get down to the substance of MP, let me ward off three common misconceptions. First, as 'program' indicates, MP is not a particular theory but a way of approaching linguistic theory: 'There are minimalist questions, but no minimalist answers, apart from those found in pursuing the program' (MI, p. 92). Indeed, the various developments that simplified the standard theory may be happily described as minimalist in spirit, if not letter. In this sense, MP simply pushes certain explanatory goals to the forefront of inquiry. Second and correlatively, MP does not essentially involve ditching any previous analyses or theoretical principles. For sure, as we shall see, much of the work surveyed in Chapter 7 falls foul of MP scruples, but one requires an argument or data or a better alternative before one may rightly reject an aspect of a previous theory. No one thinks (*pace* Lappin, et al. 2000a,b) that merely branding an analysis non-minimalist suffices for its rejection. Equally, no one should now think that a scientific theory is led by data; sometimes, even though a theory might fit the data, it is just too ugly to be true. Third, Chomsky and others involved in MP speak of '(virtual) conceptual necessity'. To some, it has appeared as if such appeals mark a descent into a priori speculation, where data are ignored (Postal, 2004). In a sense, the opposite is the case: the 'necessities' give us a set of minimal conditions in terms of which we can hopefully understand the general shape of the mass of data; any departure from the conditions might then be fruitfully considered anomalous, a spur to better theorizing as opposed to a sign to further complicate the theory. Again, the intent is programmatic. As we proceed, these ideas will become clearer.

2   THE MINIMALIST PROGRAM AND THE NATURE OF SCIENCE

To understand MP, we first must retrace some steps.

We have seen in previous chapters how the developments in linguistics from its initial conception have been animated by a philosophy of science. We can think of Chomsky's early work as motivated by the thought that linguistic phenomena should be explained and not merely classified. Likewise, the 'cognitive turn' was animated by the desire to understand language acquisition and the cognitive basis of mature competence. It is not enough to think of language as a form of behaviour. These motivations led to an explicit internalism, where the job of linguistics is not to understand language, as if it were a disembodied phenomenon, but to understand the internal system that gives rise to the observable phenomena. The object of linguistic theory is thus the set of I-languages, which mark out the developmental trajectories of speaker/hearers. We assume that the initial state is a species wide property (UG); under the influence of experience, this state develops along certain permissible pathways that terminate in states that support what we loosely think of as the world's (possible) languages. UG sets the possible menu of languages, as it were, and experience selects from the available options. This model is called *principles and parameters*, where the principles are fixed and the parameters are open, to be fixed one way or another, in potentially complex relations of dependence, by the data the subject receives. For Chomsky, this model solves the acquisition problem. Of course, the theory is not fully developed and many problems remain.

What the model does do, however, is remove the mystery from acquisition. Let me explain.

On the face it, UG is simply the set of principles that hold for each possible I-language. As we saw, this creates two problems. First, there is the tension between (i) the constraint of descriptive adequacy on individual grammars (theories of I-languages), which appears to demand richer and richer resources to account for all of the linguistic differences and (ii) the simplicity required of UG by the constraint of explanatory adequacy; that is, a child's initial resources must not be so specific as to exclude a possible steady state (a mature language) from developing under poverty of stimulus conditions. Second, if we take UG to be the initial state, then how are we to understand its relation to later states of the language faculty? How does the faculty develop? The P&P model deals with both problems simultaneously: variation in language is restricted to the open parameters making developed languages not so very different after all, and I-languages develop by the setting of these parameters.

Everything looks fine. The acquisition problem is domesticated and each I-language can now be viewed as a particular realization of the T-model of the GB framework, a quadruple, if you like, of a set of D-structures, S-structures, phonetic forms (PFs) and logical forms (LFs). Far from casting doubt on this success, MP is premised upon this success. Given what we appear to know, MP asks: Why is language the way it is?

'Why' questions are notoriously ambiguous. Chomsky's question is not after a *purpose* to language (at least not in any teleological sense) nor a theory of its evolution (at least not directly). The question is seeking a fundamental basis from which we can explain why languages exhibit the features they do. Why is language the way it is as opposed to any other way? An analogy (Chomsky's favourite example) is quantum mechanics and chemistry. The physics explains, at a fairly broad level (not the detail), of why we find the stable chemical molecules we do. In other words, we know that at a certain level chemical explanation gives way to physics, which explains the broad shape of the chemical realm, even if no one is much concerned with working out the calculations which take us from the field equations to each particular compound. Suffice it to say, I am not suggesting that linguistics is anywhere near such success; my point is only to explain the relevant and perfectly legitimate notion of 'why'. Of course, if linguistics were a mere formal taxonomy with language understood as a more or less arbitrary pattern of behaviour, which just happens to be the way it is, our 'why' question would be senseless. It only becomes meaningful to ask 'why' (in the relevant sense) once one has a systematic body of doctrine that explains a range of phenomena by way of a small set of principles, that is, once one has figured out a certain design of a natural realm. Again, the question is predicated on success. The 'why' question in linguistics, then, carries the presumption that the design of language has an explanation in more fundamental, non-linguistic properties.

Now, of course, it might be that there is no such explanation to be had. Evidence for this sceptical conclusion appears to be rife; after all, linguistic explanation appeals to primitive principles that look to have no correlation to anything outside of linguistics; indeed, such language specificity of the principles was a common reason to think that language is a biologically isolated system. On the other hand, if it turns out that linguistic explanation increasingly depends upon resources that are conceptually natural and non-language specific, then this would lend credence to the thought that the design of the language faculty might be explainable in terms of more fundamental properties. This is precisely what Chomsky believes is happening: a methodological minimalism is supporting an ontological minimalism, that is, the language faculty might be a mechanism so simple as to admit to explanation. Let us be clearer about some of the details here.

Let us agree on some '(virtual) conceptual necessities', that is, properties that look to be essential to any conception of language.

(i) *Lexical items*. Every language has a set of lexical items that form the basic atomic units of all complex structures in the language. A lexical item is the smallest unit that carries phonetic, syntactic and semantic information.

(ii) *Combinatoriality*. Every language contains an unbounded range of structures built out of lexical items.

(iii) *Interfaces*. Every language produces a pairing of 'sound' and 'meaning' over an unbounded range (let 'sound' also cover gestures of sign languages).

Translating these facts into a view of the language faculty, we can say that the faculty is a computational (combinatorial) procedure that maps from selections of lexical items to pairs of structures that code for properties of 'sound' and 'meaning'. Following Chomsky

(NH, MI), let us call such pairs *expressions*. From the side of the faculty, an expression is a pair, <PF, LF>, that determines, from the other side of the interfaces, the pair, <PHON, SEM>. Minimally, then, any theory of the faculty must account for the computational operation that maps from the lexicon to expressions that are legible or interpretable at the interfaces. By itself, this bare design specification explains nothing. If, though, we set this design as a minimum, we can ask: How well is language designed? How *perfect* is language? Of course, these questions are not directed at what we use language for; in that regard, language is far from perfect. The question of good design or perfection is asking, rather, how well designed is the language faculty as we find it at computationally mapping from the lexicon to expressions. Chomsky (*The Architecture of Language* (AL), MI) invites us to think of it as a problem for a super engineer: How would an ideal engineer have designed the language faculty to meet the minimal design specification?

This can seem like a very odd question, but, really, it is just another way of asking how far the language faculty departs from the simplest theory one can tell that meets the necessities and is empirically adequate. This might seem to be an equally alien inquiry, but such approaches characterize fundamental physical theory, as Chomsky has often remarked, from Galileo to the present *On Nature and Language* (ONL). One aspect of this is the familiar thought that good theories should be simple and beautiful. This in itself is not trivial, for getting a simple theory that explains a lot is a rare thing indeed. A more fundamental thought, however, is that theories should have a certain necessity to them, what Steven Weinberg (1993) has called *rigidity*. A rigid theory is one that cannot be alerted without it leading to absurdity, either making impossible predictions (e.g. elementary particles with infinite energy or the calculation of negative probabilities) or becoming encrusted with ad hoc hypotheses. In this sense, a rigid theory is one that *uniquely* meets the minimal design specification of the realm at issue. Trivially, no one wants a theory more complicated than it need be. This is a methodological minimalism. Ontological minimalism is the thought that the reality itself is in some sense simple, reflected by the fact that a rigid theory is available that offers a uniquely satisfying explanation of the phenomena.

Chomsky (LM, RR, NH, *On Nature and Language* (ONL), BEA) has often appealed to physical theory in defence of the generative enterprise and MP in particular.[1] This has attracted charges of 'rhetoric' with the implication (sometimes explicit) that linguists are taken in by the delusion that the generative enterprise is somehow at a stage of inquiry comparable to contemporary particle physics (Lappin, et al. 2000a, b, 2001, Postal, 2004; Seuren, 2004; Pinker and Jackendoff, 2005). A few remarks are in order.

No one believes that the generative enterprise is anywhere near the success enjoyed by the physics of Galileo, still less current research on a unified field theory (what Weinberg has in mind when speaking of 'rigidity'). The point of the analogies is to indicate that our best science is in search of a kind of minimalism by continually asking why are things the way they are as opposed to any other way, the idea being that such questions cease when one hits a form of necessity or rigidity. Now, the fact that linguistics is not at the stage where we may sensibly hope for a 'final theory' does not mean that the same approach should not be followed. That was Kant's message as regards the unity of nature, and a similar thought has animated physics post-Galileo long before anyone had a clue about unified field theory. Resistance to this methodology appears to arise from the method-ological dualism discussed in Chapter 1. The advice appears to be that one should wallow in data and never dare to make a general hypoth-esis that simplifies phenomena and deepens explanation in one area for fear that it will be refuted by data elsewhere. Explanation is OK for the physicist, but the linguist should be blinded by data. Associated with this dualism is an empiricism that values data coverage over explanation. The problem here is threefold.

First, every theory faces anomalies and there is no algorithm for what to do with them; only the further development of inquiry will tell one if the data are refuting or can be accounted for by some principle required elsewhere (e.g. Einstein's 'Cosmological Constant' of general relativity is now surplus to requirement (it can be set to 0) because the universe is not in a steady state). Second, a deep (mini-mal) explanation in one area may serve as a paradigm, even if it looks not to hold in general. This is what Chomsky ('Derivation by Phase' (DbP), p. 2) means by the 'therapeutic value' of MP. For example, Lappin, et al. (2000a) and Pinker and Jackendoff (2005) suggest that many linguists jumped the GB ship even though MP offered no explanation of the bulk of data covered by GB models. Let us assume that this is true. It does not follow that the desertion was irrational (or rat-like). An explanation of a given class of constructions can show that what one previously thought of as explanation was merely description or stipulation. As we shall see, if certain phenomena become explicable by allowing *move* to apply before a complete structure is built, then that signals that levels are an artefact of the theory. However, if levels go, then so go most of the GB principles, which are defined over levels. Of course, one has a choice, but it is not irrational to favour one kind of explanation (a minimal one) at the temporary expense of data, especially if the old explanations do not favourably compare. Third and correlatively, one cannot say a priori what is to count as explanation or falsification. In the spirit of these remarks, let me quote a leading physicist, Leonard Susskind (2005, p. 194):

Good scientific methodology is not an abstract set of rules dictated by philosophers. It is conditioned by, and determined by, the science itself and the scientists who create the science. What may have constituted scientific proof for a particle physicist of the 1960's – namely the detection of an isolated particle – is inappropriate for a modern quark physicist who can never hope to remove and isolate a quark. Let's not put the cart before the horse. Science is the horse that pulls the cart of philosophy. (cf., NW, p. 112)

This is a fine statement of methodological naturalism. As linguistics has developed, the standard of explanation has shifted as have the resources one may call upon. Our criterion of what counts as language changes to follow the contours of what counts as a good explanation. This is as it should be.

Following these lines of thought, Chomsky (M1, p. 96) offers a 'strong minimalist thesis':

(SMT) Language is an optimal solution to legibility conditions

The thesis is that 'a system that satisfies a very narrow subset of empirical conditions – those it must satisfy to be usable to all – turns out to satisfy all empirical conditions' (ibid., p. 96). So, a theory that optimally satisfies our (virtual) conceptual necessities (i.e. is generative of an unbounded range of interpretable/legible expressions from lexical items) turns out to be empirically adequate in regard to the problems of language acquisition, neurological realization, language change, evolution, contribution to parsing etc. The interest of this thesis turns on the fact that it looks to be false. This can seem strange, but the reasoning is perfectly rational. We should want the simplest theory we can get. Viewed ontologically, this means that we expect reality itself to be simple, just as Galileo expected reality to conform to precise geometrical reasoning. On the face of it, however, reality is a mess, but rather than simply cataloguing the mess, we seek the strictest principles in order to explain the mess as deviation, much as friction explains deviation from strict mechanical principles. As Kant also taught in the third *Critique*, the beauty in science is where we find a unity underlying apparent heterogeneity, as if reality is designed to be understood in the simplest possible way.

Now, of course, reality might inform us that it just is messy, but that possibility does not stymie optimality theses. As Chomsky (MI, p. 98) explicitly notes, optimal theses have a heuristic value. Even if it turns out that an optimal solution is unavailable, we should have arrived at a much better theory by the attempt to find optimality. The point here is analogous to Kant's appeal to the *regulative* nature of a design perspective. If we do not begin with a conception of under-lying simple unity and are not continually animated to find it realized in nature, then why should we pursue inquiry into nature at all? It would appear as if we might as well arbitrarily stop at a stage of inquiry satisfied with a catalogue of relations of sameness and difference.

We mentioned above that the ultimate goal of MP is to explain why the language faculty is the way it is. How does this goal relate to SMT? Chomsky ('Beyond explanatory adequacy' (BEA), TFLD) appeals to the idea of *principled explanation*. On the face of it, there are three factors in language design (TFLD, p. 6):

(TF)   (i)   A species uniform genetic endowment
       (ii) Experience leading to variation
       (iii) Principles not specific to the language faculty

A principled explanation will appeal to these three factors alone. The important factor is the last one. Linguistic explanation appears to require a whole host of principles and operations that are specific to language. These preclude a principled explanation for they are posited simply to accommodate the data but do not give way to any more fundamental explanation. If, however, SMT is correct, the language faculty optimally answers to interface conditions. First, the interface conditions are not language specific, on reasonable assump-tions, although this is an empirical question. Second, we expect an optimal computational map to expressions to be of a kind that is not sensitive to the fact that it has expressions as its range as opposed to another kind of information. In other words, the computational procedure is constitutive of the language faculty, not because it is linguistic in some essential respect, but because it is integrating distinct autonomous systems. We get a language system because of the kind of information that is integrated in expressions, but no part of the system has to be linguistic in a more primitive sense. Chomsky writes:

> Each linguistic expression generated by the I-language includes instructions for performance systems in which the I-language is embedded. It is only by virtue of its integration into such performance systems that this brain state qualifies as a language (NH, p. 27).

The language computation could/might have been utilized for locomotion or navigation in a differently organized mind/brain. If all this is on the right lines, then a theory that meets SMT will be consistent with (TF), and so we should then be in a position to explain the design of the faculty in a principled way by appeal to non-linguistic factors alone.

The discussion has been abstract so far; let us put some flesh on the bones.

3 THE STRONG MINIMALIST THESIS

As I said, SMT appears to be false. For Chomsky (MI, p. 113), SMT involves four major predictions.

(SMP) (i) The only significant levels are the interface levels.
      (ii) The *Interpretability Condition*: LIs [lexical items] have no features other than those interpreted at the interface, properties of sound and meaning.
      (iii) The *Inclusiveness Condition*: No new features are introduced by C_{HL} [the computational procedure of human language].
      (iv) Relations that enter into C_{HL} are either imposed by legibility conditions or fall out in some natural way from the computational process.

If we reflect on the work surveyed in Chapter 7, we find that each of these predictions are contradicted. (i) is in disagreement with the existence of D-structure and S-structure. (ii) is in disagreement with Case and agreement features on verbal heads. (iii) is in disagreement with traces. (iv) appears to be refuted by phrase structure itself, which looks to have no natural explanation or interface rationale, and movement/displacement. If SMT is our measure of perfection, then the language faculty looks far from perfect. On the other hand, if the facts are anywhere not as they seem, and we manage to show that explanation and theoretical simplicity is improved by moving towards SMT, then this gives us encouragement to think that SMT might be at least approximately true. This is the course Chomsky and others are currently following. To give a taste of this research, let us consider the above disagreements (in the following I shall follow the outline of *The Minimalist Program*, a collection of Chomsky's collected papers from 1995).

3.1 Merge

According to post-*Aspects* theories, phrase structure is determined by the X-bar schema. This is a vast improvement on the rule-based old phrase structure component. Nevertheless, X-bar looks like a stipulation. It captures the required generalizations but in a way that does not flow from any fundamental principle. In relation to SMT, the X-bar schema is not a natural feature of computation. Worse, it contains redundancy. Every projection constitutes three tiers: a lexical level (X_0), an intermediary level (X') and a maximal level (XP). Now, the benefit of this is that intermediate levels can form constituents, such as the I' of a sentence minus its subject, whose inclusion produces the IP. However, the intermediary levels are also often redundant, in, for example, a noun *Bill* projecting to a maximal NP to form the SPEC subject of an IP. The intermediary level there is wholly redundant.

Towards replacing X-bar theory, Chomsky's considers what is the simplest operation of combination. The obvious answer is set formation as found in the branch of mathematics called set theory. On the face of it, however, set theory is ill-suited as a basis for phrase structure. First, set formation is indifferent to the number or nature of the elements involved. If phrase structure were set formation, we would expect any combination of elements to be well-formed structures, including the empty set and singletons. Second, sets are indifferent to order; they are essentially symmetrical, that is, $\{x, y\}$ = $\{y, x\}$. Phrase structure, on the other hand, is asymmetrical because for each combination of lexical items, one of them projects to be the head. It is not the case that [$_{VP}$ love Bill] = [$_{VP}$ Bill love]. Let us consider each of these problems in turn.

It is true that sets are indifferent to their elements, but that is precisely what we want, if SMT is true. The problem is to preclude garbage and mere appeals to simplicity do not tell us how to do that. We can, however, consider set formation to be the simplest operation not in itself but relative to interface conditions. Think of primitive set formation as an infinite family of operations. The zeroth operation forms a set of no members (the empty set), the first operation forms the singletons (sets with one member), the second operation forms couples (sets with two members) and so on up to the first transfinite bound. Now, all of these operations are as simple as each other, but they are not equally simple relative to interface conditions. The first two operations lead to absurdity, for the result of either operation is uninterpretable at the interface. The second operation produces interpretable results, for we know that we require at least binary branching. The question now is, do we need more than an operation that couples items? If the answer is 'yes', then we have departed from the simplest possible case, for we know that we need at least binary branching without ternary branching. We appear, however, not to require any operation other than the second one, for by the X-bar schema itself, all branching is binary. The simplest operation relative to interface conditions, then, would be the second option, and this appears, in fact, to suffice. Chomsky calls such an operation *merge*. The operation is recursive: merge targets two objects, the objects themselves can be either lexical items or the results of previous operations of merge. This captures the discrete infinity of phrase structure. (Merge also allows for a resuscitation of generalized transformations, where merge applies to two products of merge, as in the merge of a complex subject with a predicate.)

So, although merge is the simplest operation possible, it still produces any combination of lexical items. The resolution to this is to be found in the fact that lexical items assign θ-roles and subcategorize (these are now often refereed to as s-selection and c-selection, respectively; hereon, I shall speak about 'selection', context permitting). Merge itself, then, is indifferent, but the lexical items impose conditions upon each other to which the interfaces are sensitive. Headedness is determined by c-selection: the head is the item that selects that with which it is merged. In order to distinguish the head, Chomsky proposes that it serves like a label for any merge. Formally, $\{Y, Z\} = \{X \{Y, Z\}\}$, where X is the head contained (properly or improperly) in the object Y or Z. Thus, we have the VP [love [love Bill]], where *love* is the head. It is important to bear in mind here that merge remains indifferent; it is the lexical items that impose head relations and not merge itself.

Merge also avoids the redundancy embodied in X-bar theory. Recall that intermediate levels of projection are often vacuous, a mere result of the architecture of the theory. Chomsky proposes a relational analysis of the bar projections:

(RP) (i) X_0 = a lexical item
      (ii) XP = a merged object that does not project
      (iii) X' = a merged object that is neither X_0 nor XP

On this analysis, there will be no vacuous X' projections, for such projections are not the result of merge. The analysis also avoids the need to stipulate the position of SPECs, COMPs and adjuncts relative to the head. All of them will drop out as XPs (maximal projections) determined by the selection features of the head.

Linearity remains a contentious topic, and space precludes a proper discussion of the issue. Let the following suffice. We do not actually want phrase structure to have an inherent order to it, for grammatical relations appear to be essentially hierarchical, to do with domination, not order. The problem is to figure out how to map from the hierarchical structure of syntax to the linear order demanded of PF. There are fascinating proposals about how this might be achieved.[2] The crucial point is simply that the lack of inherent order in merge is not an argument against merge being the combinatorial operation of the faculty; it is quite the opposite: SMT rules against inherent order as this is a variation determined by experience.[3]

3.2 Eliminating levels

According to SMT, the syntax is the optimal (simplest) computational operation that meets interface conditions. Let us agree that merge is the operation. The existence of any levels of representation other than interface ones is thus a departure from SMT, for a level is where certain conditions apply that are then carried through the derivation, but only interface conditions now exist, per SMT. Chomsky expresses this thought by saying that D-structure and S-structure are theory internal posits; they are not sanctioned by the conditions the faculty must meet to be useable at all. (Chomsky's arguments against S-structure are quite complicated and bear on issues we have not much discussed, such as Case and binding; let us, then, just focus on D-structure.)

Of course, the mere fact that SMT does not sanction D-structure is no argument against the level. If, however, we find reasons to be suspicious of D-structure, then that would give us a reason to think that SMT is on the right lines, for the thesis does not sanction non-interface levels. Thus, we would have a reason to think that SMT might be true in general.

D-structure is defined as the level where (i) lexical insertion into an X-bar schema occurs and (ii) grammatical function matches the position of θ-assignment. Merge, as our single combinatorial principle, already casts doubt on D-structure. Merge is a step by step operation that builds structures. It would appear to be an arbitrary stipulation to say that every merged structure reaching a certain level of complexity (where, say, every θ-role is assigned) is a D-structure. For example, if we have the structure [$_{VP}$ love Bill], then, by merge alone, the THEME role of *Bill* can be assigned before the AGENT of *love* is merged to the VP. There is, in other words, no good reason to stipulate that operations must apply or conditions be met only after a structure of a certain complexity has been built, if those operations and conditions can be met earlier, as soon as the relevant items are merged. We might, indeed, expect an optimal system to perform necessary operations as soon as possible.

Chomsky appealed to an empirical case to support this abstract reason. Consider so-called 'tough constructions', which we have now met many times:

(1)   Bill is easy/tough/hard to catch

As we have seen from previous discussions, such constructions are problematic in that, in this example, *Bill* is the understood object of *catch* (the THEME), with the sentence saying how easy/tough/hard it is for one to catch *Bill*. Thus, *Bill* should appear as the object of *catch* at D-structure. This, in fact, as we have seen, was an argument Chomsky himself made in support of D-structure. The problem, however, is to account for the movement of *Bill* from its apparent D-structure position. On the face of it, there appears to be no sound reason for the movement (Case is ruled out as a reason, for *Bill* can receive accusative Case in its putative original position; again, if Case assignment can happen early, then it should). Chomsky's (LGB) solution was to propose a covert operator that moves into a position scoping over the infinite IP:

(2)   [Bill is [easy [OP$_i$ [PRO to catch t$_i$]]]]

Here, [easy [OP$_i$ [PRO to catch t$_i$]]] forms a complex predicate from which *Bill* acquires its role. This seems to be on the right lines, but now the conditions on D-structure are out of step. *Bill* can acquire its role only after the movement of OP, that is, after the formation of the complex predicate. So, either *Bill* is inserted at D-structure and lacks a role, or the item is inserted after the formation of D-structure. Either way, the insertion into D-structure position does not match the position of θ-assignment.

Chomsky proposed that tough constructions might mark an exception, with late (post-D-structure) lexical insertion creating a position for θ-assignment. Even if we could tolerate such an ugly exception, the problem is not resolved. Consider:

(3)   a. Bill's brother is easy to catch
      b. Bill being easy to outrun is easy to catch

(3)a tells us that the exception would have to accommodate not just lexical items but complex phrases, such as *Bill's brother*, which do not occur in the lexicon. Worse, as (3)b demonstrates, the subjects of tough predicates can themselves contain tough predicates, so now it appears that some tough constructions can enter into θ-assignment before others, making a mockery of the exception.

The natural solution Chomsky (MP) adopts is to dispense with D-structure as a level where lexical insertion matches θ-assignment position. With no level where the two relevant conditions apply, operations of both merge and movement can be interleaved, with θ-assignment occurring wherever it is determined. The analysis offered in (2) is now available; the movement of OP can occur before the merge of *Bill*, which, when merged, acquires its θ-role. I should say that the relation between *Bill* and OP is problematic by other minimalist principles (*inclusiveness*). Still, we appear to have good reason for thinking that D-structure is unformulatable; its defining conditions are in conflict in a way that does not arise under a merge model where merge and move can interleave.

3.3 Movement as copy

The Inclusiveness Condition (Chomsky, MP and MI) says that the computation cannot add new information, that is, the information that makes up the expressions legible at the interfaces is already contained in the lexical items selected for merge. In TFLD, Chomsky refers to this idea as a 'no tampering principle'. It follows straightforwardly from SMT. First, by SMT, the computation should be the simplest combinatorial operation that builds structures that meet the interface conditions; if the computation can tamper with the structures, providing new information, then the computation is in some sense non-natural or designed for language, that is, it guarantees legibility independent of the interfaces. Another way of making the same point is that a tampering computation would operate as if it were able to 'look ahead' to the interface conditions, again, making the computation language specific. Second, merge, an independently sanctioned operation, is non-tampering.

The condition rules out a host of previous technology, including traces, indexes and intermediate projections. We have already seen that merge does away with the independently unwanted projections, establishing mutual support between inclusiveness and merge. The fate of indexes is more controversial. Indexes are widely used in the GB model to indicate relations of construal between pronouns and their antecedents, PRO and its controllers, chains of traces, and operators and their variables (see the above case of tough constructions). Space precludes discussion of the virtues of the various index-free theories on the market that might accommodate the phenomena. I shall focus on the fate of traces, as that is perhaps the most interesting case. It is worth pausing, though, to reflect on just why indexes should be suspicious.

An n-tuple of indexes marks a joint or disjoint construal between two or more items. What establishes this relation for any given structure? It cannot, in general, be inherent properties of the constituent lexical items, for they can stand in a myriad of other relations to other lexical items or to none at all (reflexives are an exception, as we shall see). A noun like *Bill*, for example, does not need to be co-indexed with a lower pronoun; likewise, a pronoun can occur as the only noun in a structure. The same holds for PRO (traces apparently do require indexes, but we shall deal with them separately). The only other option for establishing the desired relations is the structural relations between the items, but if such relations determine the relations of construal (joint or disjoint), then the indexes look to be redundant.

Let us consider some cases.

(4) a. [Bill$_i$ thinks [Sam$_j$ likes himself$_{*i/j}$]]
     b. [[Every philosopher]$_i$ thinks [he$_{i/j}$ is a genius]]
     c. [She$_i$ believed [Mary$_{*i/j}$ to be her$_{i/k}$ friend]]

(4)a exhibits so-called Principle A: *Reflexives must be bound by a local antecedent* (for our purposes, let 'local' mean 'within the same clause'). In this case, however, we know from the morphology of the reflexive that it requires an antecedent, and if the antecedent must be local, then *Bill* is ruled out. The indexes are redundant. (4)b exhibits so-called Principle B: *Pronouns cannot be bound by a local antecedent.* Here we have an ambiguity, where the pronoun *he* serves either as a variable-like item, with the structure meaning, [Every philosopher x thinks x is a genius], or as a free term, which picks up its referent from the context: [Every philosophy x thinks y [= Kant, Descartes, . . .] is a genius]. Again, the indexation is redundant. The structural principle obviates a local construal, and so leaves the pronoun to be bound or not by a higher NP; the indexation merely repeats this information. (4)c exhibits both Principle B and Principle C: *A Referential term (e.g. a proper name) cannot be bound.* Thus, *Mary* cannot be bound by the higher pronoun, but the genitive *her* can be. Again, the indexation merely records this structural information. On the face of it, then, knowledge of the kind of item involved and its structural position suffices to determine what relations of construal it *can* stand in; that is, the syntax determines a restricted space of options, but it does not determine particular construals, save for by obviation. Of course, we can index a particular construal for the purposes of disambiguation or simple clarity, but in such cases the indexation looks merely notational, for lexical and structural constraints only determine necessary construals – the limit of obviation. On this basis, it appears as if disambiguation, as in (4)b, is simply not part of the syntax, for the ambiguity is neither lexical nor structural. There is no a priori reason to insist that all ambiguity is caught in the syntax, especially when the only mechanism available is to parachute in indexes that have no essential role other than disambiguation. I do not here pretend to have decided the complexities of binding; rather, I have presented some of the reasoning behind the search for index-free theories. Indexes look like a descriptive device rather than an explanation; the explanation comes from lexical features and the structural relations that obviate certain construals.[4]

Unlike indexation, trace theory appears to be essential to the structure of syntax, θ-assignment and movement. Trace theory, however, clearly contravenes inclusiveness. Traces are not lexical items, but items the computation deposits in the launch site of movements: a derivation involving traces is a tampering derivation. Chomsky (MP, MI) proposes an alternative that, in essence, predates trace theory, although there are differences. Instead of movement leaving a trace, we can say that movement is a *copying* operation, where the moved item is copied higher in the structure, creating a pair (more generally, a chain) of the same item. For example,

(5) a. Bill seems <Bill> to be happy
     b. Who does Mary love <who>?
     c. France was defeated <France>

(Here, <*x*> marks the merged copy.) On the face of it, this is a simpler operation, as it does not involve move+trace but only copy. This was not evident in the early framework, which adopted a copy theory, for the map to surface structure necessitated a deletion of the copy (copy+delete). It thus appeared as if trace theory were an advance. If, however, the map goes to covert LF, then delete cannot apply without making the structure illegible at the interface; that is what the projection principle is meant to guard against. Of course, only one copy (the highest) is spelt-out (i.e. has a phonological register); there are good ideas on how PF can select the highest copy. Whatever the best story might be here, trace theory is not at an advantage, for traces amount to a stipulation that the positions are not spelt-out. We should like an explanation as to why not. The demand for linearization at PF looks a likely contender.

With copies in place, we can gain even greater economy. Chomsky (BEA, TFLD) proposes that we can understand movement as just another case of merge. *External merge* introduces a lexical item into a structure. *Internal merge* merges an item already in a structure into a higher position. Copy theory, in other words, allows us to eliminate *Move* α in favour of an independently required operation. In fact, on reflection, one can see that merge and copy really play the same role. We can think of external merge as copying an item from the lexicon and internal merge as copying an item within a structure. In a real sense, then, we should *expect* internal merge, for if we already have merge, then we require a reason to bar internal merge; on the face of it, such a bar would be a violation of SMT.[5] Further, if we adopt a label-free bare phrase structure model (see above), then projection is just another species of copying. In short, the replacement of trace theory with copy theory produces a net loss of technology, rather than a substitution of technology, without apparent loss of empirical coverage. Again, this offers support to SMT.

There are also empirical reasons to favour copying. Consider:

(5) a. Mary wondered which picture of himself Bill bought
     b. Bill liked himself, as did Sam
     c. *Mary liked herself, as did Bill

By Principle A, *himself* in (5)a must be bound by an antecedent in its clause, but there is no such antecedent: *Bill* is outside of the clause. On the GB model, this kind of case is accounted for by the covert computation to LF being able to reconstruct the phrase *which picture of himself* in the object position of *buy*. This is very ugly, for the phrase starts at D-structure in the object position, moves to SPEC CP at S-structure and then is reconstructed at LF in its original position, so that Principle A can hold at S-structure and LF. If we take the higher phrase to be a copy, then reconstruction is not required, for there remains a copy in the object position. Similar reasoning applies to the case of ellipsis. (5)b is interpreted as claiming that Sam likes himself, not Bill. The elided material, therefore, cannot be a trace whose interpretation is inherited from the higher antecedent. The elided material, however, must be of the same form as the higher item, for one cannot impose an interpretation on elliptical material; the construal is determined by visible material. This is what makes (5)c unacceptable; otherwise, it could mean that Mary and Bill respectively like themselves. The natural answer to the problem is to take the elided VP to be an externally merged copy of the visible VP, the copies differing in their interpretation due to their taking distinct subjects.

As with the case of binding, I am not suggesting here that the copy theory immediately solves all problems with reconstruction and ellipsis; indeed, the interpretation of copies raises a host of intriguing problems. My present point is merely that copy theory is an improvement on trace theory, both theoretically and empirically. Furthermore, since copy theory is in line with inclusiveness, the theory supports SMT.

3.4 Movement and uninterpretable features

Recall that, according to SMT, the language faculty consist in an optimal map from lexical items to expressions, where the latter meet the legibility conditions of external systems of 'sound' (processes that exploit phonological information) and 'meaning' (processes that exploit information relevant to thought and intention). A priori, the optimal solution would be one where lexical items directly map onto the interfaces. Assuming, then, that the interfaces require structures to be built, the next best option is one where structures are directly mapped to the interfaces. This option, however, is ruled out by the chief phenomenon that the generative enterprise tackles: the mismatch between apparent form and semantically significant form, which calls for transformations (or movement/displacement or copying). Why should there be displacement? As suggested above, this might be the wrong question to ask. If displacement is simply internal merge, then we should expect displacement within an optimal system that has merge, if the operation leads to interface legibility. We shall see how this plays out.

A second apparent imperfection is uninterpretable features of lexical items. Assume a principle of *Full Interpretation* (Chomsky, KoL, MP):

(FI) Structures legible at the interfaces only contain features that are legible at the interfaces.

(FI) is in line with SMT: if the syntactic derivation is driven optimally to meet interface conditions, then those conditions must discriminate what is legible to them and what is not. After all, if the interfaces were non-discriminatory, then the very idea of legibility conditions would cease to be an explanatory factor in the design of the faculty (e.g. (FI) appears to explain why natural languages do not feature vacuous quantification – *Who does Mary love Bill*). In short, the existence of lexical uninterpretable features is in conflict with the interface demands.

Chomsky (NH, AL) saw these two factors as key imperfections in language, a departure from SMT. More recently, however, Chomsky (e.g. ONL, TFLD, L&M, 'Approaching UG from below' (UGB)) has suggested that the two factors conspire to produce a potentially optimal solution that allows us to understand the semantic interface as being the principal condition on the syntax.

Uninterpretable features include Case on nouns and agreement features on functional heads, such as number agreement on I. The Case of a noun makes no difference whatsoever to its interpretation. Likewise, number agreement is empty as a feature, given that the subject is already marked for number. A further feature is EPP, which is currently controversial. Let us assume it is an *edge* feature of functional heads that attracts phrases to its SPEC, but is uninterpretable (items at the edge are usually interpretable as operators scoping over their lower copies). Now, Chomsky's idea is that merge (internal and external) eliminates uninterpretable features under specific matching conditions. The uninterpretable features remain an imperfection, in a sense, but the syntax acts like a system of antibodies that eliminates the 'virus' from the system. Let us go through a very simple example.

First, assume the following:

(TA) Verbal theta assignment takes place in verbal domains.
(TEN) Tense heads are merged post the formation of verbal domains and carry uninterpretable features.
(COP) All uninterpretable features must be valued (for at most morphological purposes) by a matching of features or by movement/copying.

3.4.1   A Sample derivation

a. Bill sleeps
b. $[_{VP}$ Bill$_{\{+3rd, +sing, -Case\}}$ sleep]
c. $[_{T\{+Pres, \underline{-Per}, \underline{-Num}\}, -EPP\}}$ $[_{VP}$ Bill$_{\{+3rd, +sing, \underline{-Nom}\}}$ sleep]]
d. $[_{TP}$ Bill$_{\{+3rd, +sing, \underline{-Nom}\}}$ $[_{T\{+Pres, \underline{-3rd Per}, \underline{-Sing Num}, \underline{-EPP}\}}$ $[_{VP}$ <Bill$_{\{+3rd, +sing, \underline{-Nom}\}}$> sleep]]]

Key:

+ = interpretable
– = uninterpretable
Num = number
Pres = present tense
—— = valuation of uninterpretable feature
Nom = nominative case
3rd = third person
sing = singular

BY (TA), the verb *sleep* assigns AGENT to *Bill*. Now we need tense, T, which merges with the VP. According to (TEN), however, T carries uninterpretable features, that is, properties which show up in the morphology but which carry no semantic significance. Indeed, *Bill* carries such a feature (Case). Assume that all uninterpretable features enter into the derivation *unvalued*. This makes perfect sense, for such features are determined only in configuration with other items, not inherently, for example, *Bill* has no inherent Case feature. According to (COP), such features must be valued as semantically uninterpretable, if the structure is to be interpretable at the semantic interface (and marked for morphological purposes). If we have a *match* between uninterpretable features on T and interpretable features on *Bill*, we can think of the latter as valuing the former and thus marking them for morphological purposes alone. Thus, the uninterpretable agreement features of person and number on T are valued by such interpretable features (third person, singular) that are part of *Bill* (we can assume here that Case on *Bill* is reflexively eliminated as well, but marked as nominative for morphology, if required, as in *he* rather than *him*). The T head still has its EPP feature. Thus, *Bill* is copied into the SPEC TP position. The final line of the derivation has all uninterpretable features valued or marked for (potential) morphological realization but not for semantic interpretation.

If this picture is on the right lines, then movement/copy is a potentially optimal mechanism (because otherwise required as merge) for sorting between the bundles of features within lexical items so that the respective interfaces can meet with legible features alone. The model also suggests an order of priority between the interfaces. On the face of it, PHON is as important as SEM. Note, though, that (i) semantically interpretable features come valued; they are inherent features of the items; (ii) all copies are semantically interpretable and (iii) copying appears not to be induced for semantic reasons, although it is semantically interpretable. This suggests that the syntax is designed for optimality in relation to the semantic interface and not the phonological interface. First, the derivation does not lose information. Second, the derivation does not tamper with the built structures. Third, the structures are fully interpretable, even post copying. On the sound side, there is radical loss of information and tampering, for only the highest copies are spelt-out (perhaps for linearization). We can also think more broadly about the difference. Language as heard is rife with ambiguity and gaps (those created by restricted spell-out). If the faculty were designed for efficient communication, then we would not expect this. We find, of course, no such problem on the semantic side, which is just what we should expect if language is designed to be optimal at the semantic interface. A further thought is that the faculty is not designed for any particular communicative interface, in that it can exploit speech, if available, but can equally exploit hand gestures in sign languages. The interface to semantics, however, appears to be fixed, invariable. If these thoughts are correct, then the faculty looks not too distant from SMT, as an optimal solution to the demands of the semantic interface while accommodating the extraneous demands of the 'sound' interface in an efficient way.

These are issues that are at the heart of current research and remain controversial. My suggestions, following Chomsky's reasoning, are not intended to be dogmatic but demonstrations of how minimalist thinking can cast new and fruitful light on the issues.

The architecture of the language faculty now looks something like this:

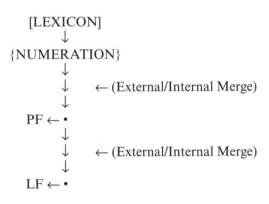

A numeration is a set of lexical items copied from the lexicon that provides an inclusive bound on the material available to the derivation. It is called a numeration because a numerical index indicates how many copies of a particular lexical item can be externally merged. For example, in a construction such as *Mary believes that Sam believes that Chomsky is a linguist*, *believe* and *that* occur twice. They thus must be marked in the numeration as {belive$_2$} and {that$_2$}. The derivation allows no more operations of external merge after each index is reduced to zero.

4 A LEVEL-FREE ARCHITECTURE

In Chomsky's most recent work, he has suggested the possibility of an elimination of all levels, including the interface levels of PF and LF (Chomsky, MI, DbP, BEA, TFLD, L&M, UGB). On this model, the derivation works in *phases*, particular chunks of structure, which are accessed by the interfaces simultaneously (on the most minimal assumption), transferring their information as available rather than procrastinating until the whole structure is built. If this is correct, we may say that the syntax operates according to an 'asap' principle: as soon as an operation can apply, it applies (see the above discussion of tough constructions). Again, this is a 'least effort' principle that cuts the cost of computational load. Chomsky (MI) hypothesizes that phases are CP and *v*P. First, a little explanation of the latter notion is in order.

Since the late 1980s, it has been hypothesized that the verbal domain in which at least two θ-roles are assigned is split, and Chomsky (MP and subsequent work) has adopted the proposal. A phonologically null verbal element *v* selects a VP as its complement. All θ-roles are assigned within the maximal projection of *v*, with its SPEC being the external argument (the AGENT) and other arguments being internal (THEME, BENEFACTIVE etc.). The best example of *v* at work is offered by ditransitives, such as *give*. On the face of it, the double object construction requires ternary branching, but this is in conflict with independent principles of binary branching, binding principles and θ–assignment. The split hypothesis solves the problem:

(6) a. Bill showed the boys themselves [in the mirror]
    b. [$_{TP}$ Bill [$_{vP}$ <Bill> [$_v$ *v*+show [$_{VP}$ the boys [$_{v'}$ <show> themselves]]]]]

c. Bill gave flowers to Mary

d. [$_{TP}$ Bill [$_{vP}$ <Bill> [$_v$ *v*+give [$_{VP}$ flowers [$_{V'}$ <give> to Mary]]]]]

(Incidentally, note that this analysis also casts further doubt on the existence of D-structure, as θ-roles are assigned in the *v* domain *after* the copying of the verbs.) There are a host of theoretical and empirical reasons to adopt the split hypothesis and various ways of implementing it, but, due to the demands of space, let us just take it on trust.

According to Chomsky, then, at a stage of a derivation where a *v*Ps and CPs are completed, the built structures interface with the external systems. Clearly, however, not all the information can be transferred. Consider the above examples. If at *v*P, all the information is accessed, then *Bill* cannot be copied to SPEC TP. Consider, also, long distance *wh*-copying:

(7) [$_{CP}$ Who did Mary say [$_{CP}$ <who> that Bill believes [$_{CP}$ <who> that [$_{vP}$ Sally loves <who>]]]]?

Here we take *who* to be copied through the open SPEC CPs. If a phase was wholly shipped to the interfaces, then *who* would never make it out of *v*P. From (7), however, we can see that the SPEC positions form a kind of escape-hatch; more generally, since heads can also be affected by later operations, it seems that the edge of a phase (SPEC+head) cannot be transferred. What remains? The complement of the head remains, which is no longer affected by later operations, e.g. all uninterpretable features are valued and the phase complement cannot be copied. Chomsky (MI) codifies this reasoning as a *Phase Impenetrability Constraint*:

(PIC) At a phase PH, only the SPEC+head of PH is accessible to later operations; the domain/complement of PH is not so accessible.

This just means that the complement is no longer active within the derivation and so can be accessed by both interfaces. In general, then, at each phase completion, the interfaces access the remainder of the previous phase up to the complement of the currently active phase head. To see this idea in practise, consider the structure in (7).

Its phase history will be as follows, where underlining marks what is transferred at the given phase:

First phase: [$_{vP}$ <who> Sally love [$_{VP}$ <love> <who>]]
Second phase: [$_{CP}$ <who> that [$_{TP}$ [$_{vP}$ <who>Sally love . . .]]]]
Third phase: [$_{vP}$ <who> Bill believe [$_{VP}$ <believe> . . .]]]]]
Fourth phase: [$_{CP}$ <who> that [$_{TP}$ [$_{vP}$ <who> Bill believe . . .]]]]]]]
Fifth phase: [$_{vP}$ <who> Mary say [$_{VP}$ <say> . . .]]]]]]]]]
Sixth phase: [$_{CP}$ Who did [TP Mary [$_{vP}$ <who> <Mary> say . . .]]]]]]]]]]
Seventh phase: [$_{CP}$ Who did . . .]]]]]]]]]]]

Here we see *who* cycling through the phase head SPECS, a copy escaping each transfer until it eventually lands in the topmost SPEC (the seventh phase is just what remains). We now have an architecture along the following lines:

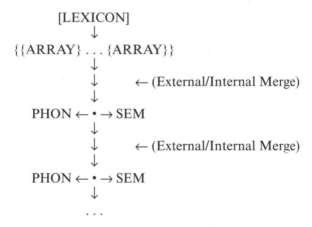

We take the input to a derivation to be a number of phase arrays (a phase head + SPEC and complement) drawn from the lexicon (this allows us to distinguish between copies and distinct lexical items, for copies will be restricted to phases and if the derivation works from phase arrays, then its memory is phase restricted). The derivation exhausts each array.

These issues are presently highly controversial, with many arguments against the very idea of phases and disagreements over the character of phases, if there are any. These debates cannot be broached here.[6] To end the syntax, though, we should pause over a peculiar feature of Chomsky's phase approach.

It is natural to think of syntax as delivering a structure for each sentence, where the structure encodes the proposition expressed. The D-structure of *Aspects* served that end and so did LF. This was the crucial factor in attracting philosophers of language to generative linguistics. It seemed as if linguistics might resolve many of the issues of logical form, for it had long been noticed (at least since Frege and Russell) that semantically significant form departs from apparent form (see Chapter 7). In fact, however, it was never an essential job of generative theory to provide a *level* of structure that encodes propositional logical form. The earliest theories dealt with T-markers, across which were splashed the semantically significant structure. The extended standard theory posited two levels where semantic significant structure occurs. In a sense, the phase derivation model is a return to the early model, where semantic structure occurs throughout a derivational history. The difference is that on the latest model, structure is accessed as soon as the derivation is finished with it. So, while the computation must answer to the interface conditions, if those conditions demand a finished structure corresponding to the size of a proposition, then the computation is reciprocally inefficient, as it carries along structure that cannot affect the computation. Hence, Chomsky's hunch is that we go with an optimally efficient computation. There is possibility of confusion here. Chomsky (MI, DbP, BEA) does point out that phases are *propositional*, that is, they are either full verbal projections (*v*Ps) or clauses (CPs). This gives phases a natural unity at the interfaces. However, the phases are not transferred at the interfaces, only the complements are. Thus, the propositional nature of phases does not mean that the interface accesses propositional sized structures; precisely not, for what is transferred are the complements. Further, the interfaces do not impose the phase structure on the syntax; rather, it so happens that it is only at those particular stages where the complements are complete relative to operations within the syntax; thus, they no longer affect the computation and so can be transferred.

This leaves us with the problem of how propositional structures are built up outside of the syntax. If by proposition is meant the packages of information that underlie human judgements (if not, the notion is just a philosophical abstraction, which may continue to be in good health independent of empirical inquiry), then there is no reason whatsoever to think that such a complex can be pinned on syntax. The complex is clearly a massive interaction effect, of which the syntax contributes just one aspect. The idea of a proposition being linked to a visible sentence form is central to our folk psychology, but that is no good reason for the idea being a constraint on inquiry. As empirical inquiry into mind and language progresses, we are learning to give up many ideas central to our self-conception. Giving up the idea that propositions are tied to syntactic forms is just another step, a step in line with SMT.

NOTES

5   THE REVIEW OF SKINNER

[1]   For example, see Fodor (1983, pp. 4–5): 'what is innately represented should constitute a bona fide object of propositional attitudes; what's innate must be the sort of thing that can be the value of a propositional variable in such schemas as 'x knows (/believes/cognizes) that P' (cf., Fodor, 2000, pp. 10–11.) This constraint goes back to Fodor (1975) and is echoed in Fodor (2000, 2001). See below for Chomsky's rejection of this constraint. Interestingly, Fodor (1981) spells-out 'the right view of what linguistics is about'; he makes no appeal to the propositional attitudes but rests content with the sound observation that a grammar is not merely evidentially constrained by intuition.

[2]   For the refutation, see LSLT, chapter 5. In fact, the falsity of the substitutional model simply follows from the requirement of transformational analysis. For example, (ii) is an autoclitic substitution instance of (i), but only in (i) does the prepositional phrase include the understood agent of the passive verb; in (ii), the prepositional phrase is a pure adjunct.

(i)   The picture was painted by a new artist.
(ii) The picture was painted by a new technique.

See previous chapters.

[3]   Throughout the review, Chomsky does point out that the folk's vernacular is more fine-grained than Skinner's jargon, but this is a comparative judgement that is trivially true.

[4]   In LSLT, Chomsky is perhaps at his most explicit: '[I]f [a new analysis of meaning or significance] is at all adequate, it seems that it will rule out mentalism for what were essentially Bloomfield's reasons, that is, its obscurity and inherent untestability' (ibid., p. 86). Note that here Chomsky is not commending Bloomfield's behaviourism; indeed, later in the same chapter Chomsky makes clear that the evidential basis for the construction of a grammar is primarily speakers' 'intuitions', which provide a basis more robust than any imaginable behavioural test. If some such test were to contradict our most primitive intuitions, then we would properly reject the test (especially see p. 102).

[5]   In more recent work, Chomsky has used 'mentalism' to refer to naturalistic inquiry of cognitive phenomena (brain states and their function): a research programme as legitimate if not as advanced as those of chemistry or biology (e.g. NH, p. 5–6). Again, the use of 'mentalism' here does not imply any a priori commitment to the integrity of folk explanation.

⁶ For Chomsky's characterization of a grammar and/or our *knowledge of language* as being theoretic, see LSLT, pp. 77–8, SS, pp. 49–50, RSVB, pp. 574–8; EML, pp. 528–9/535, AST, pp. 58–9, RL, pp. 15–20, RR, pp. 102–3. See Matthews (1984) for an account of the importance to 'rationalism' of the theoretical vocabulary. The demise of the 'theory' terminology arose from the development of the *principles and parameters* model that views linguistic development not as hypothesis confirmation but more as a physical process of *growth* or parameter setting of a polymorphic system, as is found throughout biology. (Just what parameter setting involves is notoriously obscure, but the thought is that it is mechanistic, notwithstanding the 'theoretical' elaboration it sometimes receives.) The basis of this idea goes back to Lenneberg (1967), who was a major influence on Chomsky's thought (see RL and RR). For recent discussion of the earlier 'theory' conception, see (TFLD, pp. 7–8; PML, pp. x–xi).

⁷ 'Rational achievement' is an expression of Higginbotham's (1991), although I take the sentiment to express the traditional view of generative linguistics. See Collins, 2004.

⁸ In LSLT, p. 119, Chomsky presented *general linguistic theory*, soon to be psychologized as universal grammar, as being a 'philosophy of science', where the science in question was the particular grammars or theories developed for particular languages.

⁹ Especially see (OI) for an explicit elaboration of what 'Cartesian' is meant to cover, although the point is explicit enough in the preface to Chomsky's CL.

¹⁰ It is sometimes suggested that the divergence between competence and performance with garden path sentences and similar constructions supports the idea of linguistic error, as if the normal speaker is in error in not recognizing, for example, *The horse raced past the barn fell,* to be grammatical. This thought is highly dubious. Would we want to say that normal speakers are in error in not recognizing a construction with 20 central embeddings to be grammatical? The attributions of error are, it seems, simply misleading ways of marking the competence/performance distinction. More generally, 'misrepresentation' and 'error' are folksy notions that might well mark out real phenomena, but our explanations are not beholden to the notions, just as we can explain aspects of linguistic judgment without resorting to the idea of a grammatical error (see RE).

¹¹ This follows trivially from the unbounded character of linguistic competence. For example, competent English speakers can recognize or judge that (i)a–b are synonyms and (ii)a–b are not, and that (iii)a–b are acceptable and (iv)a–b are not, even if they have not previously been exposed to the sentences:

(i) a. Bill expected the doctor to examine Mary.
     b. Bill expected Mary to be examined by the doctor.
(ii) a. Bill persuaded the doctor to examine Mary.
     b. Bill persuaded Mary to be examined by the doctor.
(iii) a. Bill expected to examine Mary.
     b. Bill expected to be examined by the doctor.
(iv) a. *Bill persuaded to examine Mary.
     b. *Bill persuaded to be examined by the doctor.

[12] As Fodor (1981) noted, there is no restriction on potentially relevant data. The fact remains, however, that research on syntax via, for example, neuronal and deficit studies is guided by syntactic theory, whose evidential base is preponderantly native speaker/hearer intuitions. Indeed, it is difficult to imagine the situation being otherwise: could neuronal studies persuade us that a given sentence is not ambiguous in the way we imagined it was? See (LSLT, pp. 101–3) for an early discussion of this point.

6 LANGUAGE: INSIDE OR OUTSIDE THE MIND?

[1] Jerry Fodor (2001) takes the 'Martian problem' to be answered by a distinction between a grammar and its internal representation; that is, the objection simply insists on a kind of behaviourism that elides a potential difference in the internal states and what they represent, namely, the extensionally equivalent grammars for us and the Martians (Fodor's argument is foreshadowed in his 'Some notes on what linguistics is about' (1981)). Fodor is right in the sense that the argument is behaviourist in spirit, but it can be defeated without making any appeal to a distinction between internal states and what they represent. By the reasoning of Chapter 5 and the above, a grammar is not represented as an external object, not even a notional one; a grammar, or an I-language, is simply a state of the mind/brain, albeit abstractly described. In this light, the Martian argument does not so much need to be answered as simply diagnosed as a piece of commonsense reasoning about the conditions under which we would say that an organism speaks English. See Collins (2004) for a detailed response to Fodor.

[2] For Chomsky's recent views on the evolution of language, see FL, ELF, TFLD. For opposition, see Pinker (1994), Pinker and Bloom (1990), Jackendoff (2002), Pinker and Jackendoff (2005) and Jackendoff and Pinker (2005). For wider discussion, see Jenkins (2000), Hinzen (2006) and Collins (forthcoming).

8 THE MINIMALIST PROGRAM

[1] For linguists' fascination with physics, see Uriagereka (1998), Jenkins (2000), Martin and Uriagereka (2000), Freidin and Vergnaud (2001), Epstein and Seely (2002, 2006), Boeckx and Piattelli-Palmarini (2005), Boeckx (2006b) and Hinzen (2006).

[2] See Kayne (1994) and Nunes (2004). The basic problem is to specify a design that will read a particular order from a particular hierarchical structure.

[3] Chomsky (BPS) (cf., C. Collins (2002)) has proposed a label-free bare phrase structure, where copied heads serve as labels. The issues here are complex and will be ignored in the following.

[4] See Safir (2004a,b) for a developed theory of binding along these lines. However, also see Baker (2003) for a use of indexes as inherent features of nominals, which is a somewhat different approach from the standard use of indexes.

⁵ Chomsky, however, appeals to a 'Merge over Move' preference. Consider:

  (i) There seems to be someone in the room
  (ii) *There seems someone to be in the room

Following a suggestion in (MP), Chomsky (MI) suggested that the explanation for this difference is that there is a preference for Merge over Move, which means that when the structure is at stage (iii)

(iii) [T to be someone in the room],

the derivation merges *there* from the numeration into SPEC TP rather than move *someone* to that position. So, the derivation leading to (ii) is blocked. Apart from certain empirical problems with this proposal, it appears to lack motivation once we view move as simply internal merge, and so not anymore 'imperfect' or complex as external merge (move does involve Agree in the latest framework, but Agree appears to hold for external merge as well).

⁶ Mention should be made of the 'pure derivational' model of Epstein and Seely (2006), foreshadowed in Epstein, et al. (1998). Epstein and Seely take the MP sanction against levels one stage further and attempt to avoid all conditions on representations (including phases), that is, any condition or operation that appeals to the properties of a built structure. All conditions are to be stated as properties of the derivation (merge). While Chomsky (MP, MI, DbP, SOE) clearly favours derivational conditions over representational ones where available, 'pure derivationalism' faces the problem that any derivation is defined over structures that, by definition, cannot be opaque to representations (this is what Brody (2003) refers to as 'weak representationalism'). Epstein and Seely, however, propose that the interfaces access the computation at each stage of merge. The problem now is that this appears to be a rejection of Full Interpretation: how can a structure containing uninterpretable features be legible at the interface? It is as if the accessed structures are in a kind of limbo waiting for more structure to be built to become legible. I do not see this as a species of pure derivation, for the interfaces still only properly access structure once built in the syntax, at least if Full Interpretation is to be respected.

REFERENCES

Baker, M. (2001), *Atoms of Language*. New York: Basic Books.

Baker, M. (2003), *Lexical Categories: Verbs, Nouns, and Adjectives*. Cambridge: Cambridge University Press.

Barber, A. (ed.) (2003), *Epistemology of Language*. Oxford: Oxford University Press.

Bennett, J. (1976), *Linguistic Behaviour*. Indianapolis: Hackett.

Berwick, R. and Weinberg, A. (1984), *The Grammatical Basis of Linguistic Performance: Language Use and Acquisition*. Cambridge, MA: MIT Press.

Boeckx, C. (2006b), *Linguistic Minimalism: Origins, Concepts, Methods, and Aims*. Cambridge: Cambridge University Press.

Boeckx, C. and Piattelli-Palmarini, M. (2005), 'Language as a natural object – linguistics as a natural science'. *Linguistic Review*, 22, 447–66.

Brandom, R. (1994), *Making It Explicit: Reasoning, Representing, and Discursive Commitment*. Cambridge, MA: Harvard University Press.

Brody, M. (2003), *Towards an Elegant Syntax*. London: Routledge.

Clark, A. (1997), *Being There: Putting Brain, Body and World Together Again*. Cambridge, MA: MIT Press.

Collins, C. (2002), 'Eliminating labels', in S. Epstein and D. Seely (eds.), *Derivation and Explanation in the Minimalist Program*. Oxford: Blackwell, pp. 42–64.

Collins, J. (2003), 'Cowie on the poverty of the stimulus'. *Synthese*, 136, 159–90.

Collins, J. (2004), 'Faculty disputes'. *Mind and Language*, 19, 503–34.

Collins, J. (2006), 'Proxytypes and linguistic nativism'. *Synthese*, 153, 69–104.

Collins, J. (forthcoming), 'Why is language the way it is and not some other way?'. *Croatian Journal of Philosophy*.

Cowie, F. (1999), *What's Within? Nativism Reconsidered*. Oxford: Oxford University Press.

Crain, S. and Pietroski, P. (2001), 'Nature, nurture, and universal grammar'. *Linguistics and Philosophy*, 24, 139–86.

Crain, S. and Thornton, R. (1998), *Investigations in Universal Grammar: A Guide to Experiments in the Acquisition of Syntax and Semantics*. Cambridge, MA: MIT Press.

Davidson, D. (1984), *Inquiries into Truth and Interpretation*. Oxford: Oxford UniversityPress.

Davidson, D. (1990), 'The Structure and Content of Truth'. *Journal of Philosophy*, 87, 279–328.

Davidson, D. (1997), 'Seeing through language', in J. Preston (ed.), *Thought and Language*. Cambridge: Cambridge University Press, pp. 15–27.

Deacon, T. (1997), *The Symbolic Species: The Co-Evolution of Language and the Brain*. New York: Norton.

Dennett, D. (1995), *Darwin's Dangerous Idea: Evolution and the Meanings of Life*. London: Penguin Books.

Devitt, M. (2006), *Ignorance of Language*. Oxford: Oxford University Press.

Devitt, M. and Sterelny, K. (1987), *Language and Reality*. Cambridge, MA: MIT Press.

Dretske, F. (1981), *Knowledge and the Flow of Information*. Cambridge, MA: MIT Press.

Dummett, M. (1978), *Truth and Other Enigmas*. London: Duckworth.

Dummett, M. (1989), 'Language and communication', in A. George (ed.), *Reflections on Chomsky*. Oxford: Blackwell, pp. 192–212.

Dummett, M. (1993), *Origins of Analytical Philosophy*. London: Duckworth.

Einstein, A. (1954), *Ideas and Opinions*. New York: Bonanza Books.

Epstein, S. and Seely, D. (ed.) (2002), 'Introduction: on the quest for explanation', in *Derivation and Explanation in the Minimalist Program*. Oxford: Blackwell, pp. 1–18. Epstein, S. and Seely, D. (2006), *Derivations in Minimalism*. Cambridge: Cambridge University Press.

Epstein, S., Groat, E., Kawashima, R. and Kithara, H. (1998), *A Derivational Approach to Syntactic Relations*. Oxford: Oxford University Press.

Feynman, R. (1965), *The Character of Physical Law*. London: Penguin Books.

Fodor, J. (1968), *Psychological Explanation*. New York: Random House.

Fodor, J. (1975), *The Language of Thought*. Cambridge, MA: Harvard University Press.

Fodor, J. (1981), 'Some notes on what linguistics is about', in N. Block (ed.), *Readings in the Philosophy of Psychology, Vol. 2*. Cambridge, MA: Harvard University Press, pp. 187–216.

Fodor, J. (1983), *The Modularity of Mind*. Cambridge, MA: MIT Press.

Fodor, J. (1987), *Psychosemantics*. Cambridge, MA: MIT Press.

Fodor, J. (2000a), *The Mind Doesn't Work That Way: The Scope and Limits of Computational Psychology*. Cambridge, MA: MIT Press.

Fodor, J. (2000b), 'Doing without *What's Within?*: Fiona Cowie's critique of nativism'. *Mind*, 110, 99–148.

Fodor, J. D. (1995), 'Comprehending sentence structure', in L. Gleitman and M. Liberman (eds), *Language: An Invitation to Cognitive Science* (second edition). Cambridge, MA: MIT Press, pp. 209–46.

Freidin, R. and Vergnaud, J-R. (2001), 'Exquisite connections: some remarks on the evolution of linguistic theory'. *Lingua*, 111, 639–66.

Grodzinsky, Y. (1990), *Theoretical Perspectives on Language Deficits*. Cambridge, MA: MIT Press.

Grodzinsky, Y. and Finkel, L. (1998), 'The neurology of empty categories'. *Journal of Cognitive Neuroscience*, 10, 281–292.

Guasti, M. (2002), *Language Acquisition: The Growth of Grammar*. Cambridge, MA: MIT Press.

Higginbotham, J. (1991), 'Remarks on the metaphysics of linguistics'. *Linguistics and Philosophy*, 14, 555–66.

Hinzen, W. (2006), *Mind Design and Minimal Syntax*. Oxford: Oxford University Press.

Jackendoff, R. (1972), *Semantic Interpretation in Generative Grammar*. Cambridge, MA: MIT Press.

Jackendoff, R. (2002), *Foundations of Language: Brain, Meaning, Grammar, Evolution*. Oxford: Oxford University Press.

Jakendoff, R. and Pinker, S. (2005), 'The nature of the language faculty and its implications for evolution of language (reply to Fitch, Hauser, and Chomsky)'. *Cognition*, 97, 211–25.

Jenkins, L. (2000), *Biolinguistics: Exploring the Biology of Language*. Cambridge: Cambridge University Press.

Kant, I. (1781/87/1998), *Critique of Pure Reason*. Trans. and ed. by P. Guyer and A. W. Wood. Cambridge: Cambridge University Press.

Kant, I. (1790/2000), *Critique of the Power of Judgement*. Trans. by P. Guyer and E. Edwards and ed. by P. Guyer. Cambridge: Cambridge University Press.

Katz, J. (1981), *Language and Other Abstract Objects*. Totowa, NJ: Rowman and Littlefield.

Katz, J. and Postal, P. (1964), *An Integrated Theory of Linguistic Descriptions*. Cambridge, MA: MIT Press.

Katz, J. and Postal, P. (1991), 'Realism vs. conceptualism in linguistics'. *Linguistics and Philosophy*, 14, 515–54.

Kayne, R. (1994), *The Antisymmetry of Syntax*. Cambridge, MA: MIT Press.

Lappin, S., Levine, R. and Johnson, D. (2000a), 'The structure of unscientific revolutions'. *Natural Language and Linguistic Theory*, 18, 665–71.

Lappin, S., Levine, R. and Johnson, D. (2000b), 'The revolution confused: a response to our critics'. *Natural Language and Linguistic Theory*, 18, 873–90.

Lappin, S., Levine, R. and Johnson, D. (2001), 'The revolution maximally confused'. *Natural Language and Linguistic Theory*, 19, 901–19.

Lees, R. (1957), 'Review of *Syntactic Structures*'. *Language*, 33, 375–407.

Lenneberg, E. (1967), *Biological Foundations of Language*. New York: Wiley.

Martin, R. and Uriagereka, J. (2000), 'Some possible foundations for the minimalist Program', in R. Martin, D. Michaels and J. Uriagereka (eds), *Step by Step: Essays on Minimalist Syntax in Honor of Howard Lasnik*. Cambridge, MA: MIT Press, pp. 1–30.

Matthews, R. (1984), 'The plausibility of rationalism'. *Journal of Philosophy*, 81, 492–515.

May, R. (1985), *Logical Form: Its Structure and Derivation*. Cambridge, MA: MIT Press.

McDowell, J. (1978/98), 'On "Reality of the Past"', in J. McDowell (ed.), *Meaning, Knowledge, and Reality*. Cambridge, MA: Harvard University Press, pp. 295–313.

McDowell, J. (1994), *Mind and World*. Cambridge, MA: Harvard University Press.

Millikan, R. G. (1984), *Language, Thought, and Other Biological Categories*. Cambridge, MA: MIT Press.

Millikan, R. G. (2005), *Language: A Biological Model*. Oxford: Clarendon Press.

Nunes, J. (2004), *Linearization of Chains and Sideward Movement*. Cambridge, MA: MIT Press.

Petitto, L-A. (2005), 'How the brain begets language', in J. McGilvray (ed.), *The Cambridge Companion to Chomsky*. Cambridge: Cambridge University Press, pp. 164–80.

Phillips, C. and Lasnik, H. (2003), 'Linguistics and empirical evidence'. *Trends in Cognitive Science*, 7, 60–1.

Pietroski, P. and Crain, S. (2005), 'Innate ideas', in J. McGilvray (ed.), *The Cambridge Companion to Chomsky*. Cambridge: Cambridge University Press, pp. 164–80.

Pinker, S. and Bloom, P. (1990), 'Natural language and natural selection'. *Behavioral and Brain Sciences*, 13, 707–84.

Pinker, S. (1994), *The Language Instinct*. London: Penguin Books.

Pinker, S. and Jackendoff, R. (2005), 'The faculty of language: what's special about it?' *Cognition*, 95, 201–36.

Postal, P. (1964), 'Limitations of phrase structure grammars', in J. Fodor, and J. Katz (eds), *The Structure of Language: Readings in the Philosophy of Language*. Englewood Cliffs, NJ: Prentice-Hall, pp. 137–51.

Postal, P. (2004), *Skeptical Linguistic Essays*. Oxford: Oxford University Press.

Pritchett, B. (1992), *Grammatical Competence and Parsing Performance*. Chicago: Chicago University Press.

Prinz, J. (2002), *Furnishing the Mind*. Cambridge, MA: MIT Press.

Pullum, G. and Scholz, B. (2002), 'Empirical assessment of the stimulus poverty Arguments'. *Linguistic Review*, 19, 9–50.

Putnam, H. (2000), *The Threefold Cord: Mind, Body and World*. New York: Columbia University Press.

Pylyshyn, Z. (1984), *Computation and Cognition: Towards a Foundation for Cognitive Science*. Cambridge, MA: MIT Press.

Quine, W. V. O. (1960), *Word and Object*. Cambridge, MA: MIT Press.

Quine, W. V. O. (1969), 'Linguistics and philosophy', in S. Hook (ed.), *Language and Philosophy*, New York: NYU Press, pp. 95–8.

Quine, W. V. O. (1970), 'Methodological reflections on current linguistics'. *Synthese*, 21, 386–98.

Reichenbach, H. (1951), *The Rise of Scientific Philosophy*. Berkeley: University of California Press.

Rey, G. (1997), *Contemporary Philosophy of Mind: A Contentiously Classical Approach*. Oxford: Blackwell.

Rey, G. (2003a), 'Chomsky, intentionality, and a CRRT', in L. M. Antony and N. Hornstein (eds), *Chomsky and His Critics*. Oxford: Blackwell, pp. 105–39.

Rey, G. (2003b), 'Intentional content and a Chomskian linguistics', in A. Barber (ed.), *The Epistemology of Language*. Oxford: Oxford University Press, pp. 140–86.

Safir, K. (2004a), *The Syntax of (In)dependence*. Cambridge, MA: MIT Press.

Safir, K. (2004b), *The Syntax of Anaphora*. Oxford: Oxford University Press.

Searle, J. (1972), 'Chomsky's revolution in linguistics'. *New York Review of Books*, June 29, 16–24.

Searle, J. (2002), 'End of the revolution'. *New York Review of Books*, February 28, 33.

Seuren, P. (2004), *Chomsky's Minimalism*. Oxford: Oxford University Press.

Soames, S. (1984), 'Linguistics and psychology'. *Linguistics and Philosophy*, 7, 155–79.

Stich, S. (1972), 'Grammars, psychology, and indeterminacy'. *Journal of Philosophy*, 69, 799–818.

Strawson, P. (1970), 'Meaning and truth', in *Logico-Linguistic Papers*. Oxford: Oxford University Press, pp. 131–46.

Susskind, L. (2005), *The Cosmic Landscape: String Theory and the Illusion of Intelligent Design*. New York: Little, Brown and Company.

Turing, A. (1952/2004), 'Can automatic calculating machines be said to think?, in J. Copeland (ed.), *The Essential Turing*. Oxford: Oxford University Press, pp. 494–506 (printed from the transcript of a BBC radio broadcast).

Uriagereka, J. (1998), *Rhyme and Reason: An Introduction to Minimalist Syntax*. Cambridge, MA: MIT Press.

Uriagereka, J. (1999), 'Multiple spell-out', in S. Epstein and N. Hornstein (eds), *Working Minimalism*. Cambridge, MA: MIT Press, pp. 251–82.

Uriagereka, J. (2002), *Derivations: Exploring the Dynamics of Syntax*. London: Routledge.

Weinberg, S. (1993), *Dreams of a Final Theory*. London: Vintage.

Weinberg, S. (2001), *Facing Up: Science and Its Cultural Adversaries*. Cambridge, MA: Harvard University Press.

Weyl, H. (1949), *Philosophy of Mathematics and Natural Science*. Princeton: Princeton University Press.

Wittgenstein, L. (1953), *Philosophical Investigations*. Oxford: Blackwell.

Wright, C. (1989), 'Wittgenstein's rule following considerations and the central project of theoretical linguistics', in A. George (ed.), *Reflections on Chomsky*. Oxford: Blackwell, pp. 233–64.

Yang, C. (2002), *Natural Language and Language Learning*. Oxford: Oxford University Press.

Yang, C. (2006), *The Infinite Gift: How Children Learn and Unlearn the Languages of the World*. New York: Scribner.

INDEX

A

Acquisition 30, 85, 97, 150–2, 192–3
also see 'poverty of stimulus'
Ambiguity 64, 71–2
Autonomy 39ff, 80
Auxiliary verbs 61, 68ff, 73, 108–9

B

Baker, M. 220n4
Behaviourism 29–30, 113–5
Bennett, J. 14
Berkeley, G. 11
Binding 206, 208
Bloomfield, L. 25, 29, 78, 218n4
Brandom, R. 13
Brody, M. 221n6

C

Case 89, 185, 203, 204, 210–11
Church/Turing thesis 49
Clark, A. 154
Communication 14, 135, 137, 212
Competence/performance 13, 94ff, 117–8, 144–5
Contraction 187–8
Copy 205–9
Cowie, F. 15, 100
Creativity 84, 115, 153
Cudworth, R. 96, 125

D

Davidson, D. 13, 137
Deacon, T. 154

D (Deep structure)

Deep structure 160–2, 165–8, 203–5, 216
Dennett, D. 154
Descartes, R. 11, 96, 102, 125, 126, 128
Devitt, M. 15, 100, 137, 139
Discovery procedure 26
Dummett, M. 12–3, 137

E

Ebonics 136
Economy 170
Einstein 196
E–language 131, 139ff
Empiricism vs. rationalism 96ff
Empty categories 186–7
Ergative verbs 173
EPP 210–11
Evaluation/simplicity 37–8, 77–8
Evolution 154–5, 220n2
Euler, L. 11

F

Features 209–12
Finite state machines 53–4, 58
Fodor, J. 114, 125, 127, 134, 218n1, 220n12, n1
Folk psychology 111–2, 119–20
Frege, G. 216
Full interpretation 209, 221n6

G

Galileo, G. 11, 95, 195, 196, 198
Garden path sentences 219n10

General linguistic theory 35–7, 78, 83, 219n8
Generative semantics 160
Grammar
as theory 30–5, 90–2, 121–5, 219n6
descriptive adequacy 86
explanatory adequacy 86
external adequacy 37, 83
internal adequacy 37–8, 83
traditional 87–9

H

Harris, Z. 25, 29, 66
Headedness 171, 174, 202
Higginbotham, J. 219n7
Hockett, C. 29
Humboldt, W. 125
Hume, D. 11, 96

I

I-language 3, 20, 131, 139ff
Immediate constituent analysis 28
Inclusiveness 199, 205, 207
Indexes 205–7
Infinity 32–3
Intuitions 33–4, 37, 145–6

J

Jackendoff, R. 6, 182

K

Kant, I. 11, 77, 125, 196, 198
Katz, J. 6, 127, 143, 148
Katz-Postal hypothesis 159, 180
Kernel 67, 157
Knowledge of language 8–9, 121, 131, 133–4, 142ff, 219n6

L

Lambert, J. 11
Leibniz, G. 11, 96, 102, 125
Lenneberg, E. 126
Level-free architecture 213ff
Lexical insertion 163

Lexicon 78–9, 162ff, 177ff
Linearity 202, 207
Locke, J. 96, 97
Logical form (LF) 183, 188–9, 216

M

Martian consideration 143, 146–8, 220n1
Mathematics, as similar to linguistics 148–50
May, R. 183
Merge 200–2
McDowell, J. 13
Mentalism 120–1
Methodological dualism 25
Minimalist program 157, 160, 191ff
principled explanation 198–99
strong minimalist thesis 197–8, 199–200, 217
Millikan, R. 15
Move-alpha 184
also see Copy

N

Native-American languages 26, 27, 60
Nativism 96ff, 112–3
Naturalism 16–9
Newton, I. 11, 90
Neural networks 111
Normativity 136–7
Numeration 213

P

Passive 185
Phases 213, 214
Phrase structure 55–6, 58, 59ff, 170–6
Plato 96, 102
Polar interrogatives 107ff
Port-Royal 166
Postal, P. 6, 60, 148
Poverty of stimulus 98, 101ff
Principles and parameters 125, 192–3, 219n6

Prinz, J. 15
Propositions 216–7
PRO 187, 205, 206
Projection principle 189
Propositional calculus 47–8, 57
Pure derivation 221n6

Q

Quantifiers 166, 182
Quantifier raising 183, 188–9
Quine, W. 96, 127, 143, 146

R

Recursion 48–9, 77, 85
Reference 177–8
Rey, G. 121, 127
Ross, J. 184
Russell, B. 216

S

Safir, K. 220n4
Schelgel, K. 125
Searle, J. 5, 14
Selection 163–5
Semantics 159–60, 181–4
also see 'Autonomy'
Seuren, P., 5, 160
Spinoza, B. 11
Skinner, B. 29, 111ff
Stich, S. 143, 146
Strawson, P. 14
Strong generative capacity 10, 50–2, 147
Subcategorization 163–5, 173, 178, 201

Surface structure 160–2, 169, 203
Susskind, L. 197
Syntactic Structures 9–11, 22–4, 46ff

T

Theta theory 179–80
Tough constructions 203–5
Trace theory 184–5, 205, 207–9
Transformations 66ff, 157, 170, 184
generalized 157, 160, 201

U

Universal grammar 85, 90, 98, 100–1, 151–2, 184, 192–3
Unaccusative verbs 173
Uriagereka, J. 177

V

Variability of language 134–5
Virtual conceptual necessities 192, 194–5, 197

W

Weak generative capacity 10, 24, 50–2, 133, 147
Weinberg, S. 195, 196
Wittgenstein 139
Wright, C. 14

X

X-bar theory 170ff, 200–1

Y

Yang, C. 105